IS SHYLOCK JEWISH?

EDINBURGH CRITICAL STUDIES IN SHAKESPEARE AND PHILOSOPHY
Series Editor: Kevin Curran

Edinburgh Critical Studies in Shakespeare and Philosophy takes seriously the speculative and world-making properties of Shakespeare's art. Maintaining a broad view of 'philosophy' that accommodates first-order questions of metaphysics, ethics, politics and aesthetics, the series also expands our understanding of philosophy to include the unique kinds of theoretical work carried out by performance and poetry itself. These scholarly monographs will reinvigorate Shakespeare studies by opening new interdisciplinary conversations among scholars, artists and students.

Editorial Board Members
Ewan Fernie, Shakespeare Institute, University of Birmingham
James Kearney, University of California, Santa Barbara
Julia Reinhard Lupton, University of California, Irvine
Madhavi Menon, American University
Simon Palfrey, Oxford University
Tiffany Stern, Oxford University
Henry Turner, Rutgers University
Michael Witmore, The Folger Shakespeare Library
Paul Yachnin, McGill University

Published Titles

Rethinking Shakespeare's Political Philosophy: From Lear to Leviathan
Alex Schulman
Shakespeare in Hindsight: Counterfactual Thinking and Shakespearean Tragedy
Amir Khan
Second Death: Theatricalities of the Soul in Shakespeare's Drama
Donovan Sherman
Shakespeare's Fugitive Politics
Thomas P. Anderson
Is Shylock Jewish?: Citing Scripture and the Moral Agency of Shakespeare's Jews
Sara Coodin
Chaste Value: Economic Crisis, Female Chastity and the Production of Social Difference on Shakespeare's Stage
Katherine Gillen

Forthcoming Titles

Making Publics in Shakespeare's Playhouse
Paul Yachnin
Derrida Reads Shakespeare
Chiara Alfano
The Play and the Thing: A Phenomenology of Shakespearean Theatre
Matthew Wagner
Shakespearean Melancholy: Philosophy, Form, and the Transformation of Comedy
J. F. Bernard
Shakespeare and the Fall of the Roman Republic: Selfhood, Stoicism, and Civil War in Julius Caesar and Antony and Cleopatra
Patrick Gray
Conceiving Desire: Metaphor, Cognition, and Eros in Lyly and Shakespeare
Gillian Knoll

For further information please visit our website at edinburghuniversitypress.com/series/ecsst

IS SHYLOCK JEWISH?

CITING SCRIPTURE AND THE
MORAL AGENCY OF SHAKESPEARE'S JEWS

◆ ◆ ◆

SARA COODIN

EDINBURGH
University Press

Edinburgh University Press is one of the leading university presses in the UK. We publish academic books and journals in our selected subject areas across the humanities and social sciences, combining cutting-edge scholarship with high editorial and production values to produce academic works of lasting importance. For more information visit our website: edinburghuniversitypress.com

© Sara Coodin, 2017

Edinburgh University Press Ltd
The Tun – Holyrood Road, 12(2f) Jackson's Entry, Edinburgh EH8 8PJ

Typeset in 12/15 Adobe Sabon by
IDSUK (DataConnection) Ltd

A CIP record for this book is available from the British Library

ISBN 978 1 4744 1838 6 (hardback)
ISBN 978 1 4744 1839 3 (webready PDF)
ISBN 978 1 4744 1840 9 (epub)
ISBN 978 1 4744 5240 3 (paperback)

The right of Sara Coodin to be identified as the author of this work has been asserted in accordance with the Copyright, Designs and Patents Act 1988, and the Copyright and Related Rights Regulations 2003 (SI No. 2498).

CONTENTS

Preface vii
Acknowledgments ix
Series Editor's Preface xiii

Introduction: Is Shylock Jewish? 1

1. Renaissance England and the Jews 26

2. Parti-Coloured Parables 85

3. Stolen Daughters and Stolen Idols 140

4. Rebellious Daughters on the Yiddish Stage 197

Conclusion 245

Index 249

PREFACE

Romanising non-English printed materials always presents a challenge to those of us who write books in English. Those challenges can become more complex when the task includes transliterating both Hebrew and Yiddish into English. Hebrew and Yiddish share a common script but not a single standard transliteration system for rendering that script into a Roman alphabet. There are multiple transliteration alphabets to choose from for romanising Hebrew. In Yiddish, the standard romanisation scheme is known as the YIVO transliteration alphabet; however, in actuality, the YIVO scheme is often not used, a fact evident when we consider Yiddish words like *chutzpah*, which the YIVO alphabet would transliterate as *khutspe*, an unlikely spelling almost never seen in print or used in library catalogues. The widespread use of non-YIVO transliterations of Yiddish words, titles and names, along with the lack of accord between the transliteration systems used to romanise Hebrew and Yiddish, presents a set of puzzles to English-language researchers and writers who, like me, do not aim to reproduce Hebrew type in their book because their intended audience is primarily English-speaking.

In the present book, I follow the YIVO transliteration alphabet for romanising Yiddish words, titles and names, except in cases of widely used alternative spellings. For example, I use the more common 'Sholem Aleichem' as opposed to the unlikely YIVO rendering of 'Sholem Aleykhem'. For transliterating Hebrew into English, I adhere to the same rule, maintaining commonly used spellings even where they differ from the Library of Congress system whose transliteration guidelines I follow throughout this book. Details of that system can be found in *Hebraica Cataloging* (Washington, DC: Library of Congress, Cataloging Distribution Service, 1987). I also adhere to the conventions of capitalisation common to specific time periods, geographical locations and languages when I cite the titles of written and performed works. For Yiddish titles, that means reproducing the capitalisation of proper names and places along with the first word of a work's title, but not capitalising other title words commonly capitalised in modern English. When citing early modern English titles, I have made every effort to retain the idiosyncratic capitalisations and spellings of the early printed text, including title words.

Unless otherwise noted, the edition of William Shakespeare's *The Merchant of Venice* that I cite from throughout the book is the 1993 Oxford World's Classics, edited by Jay L. Halio. My use of particular English translations of the Hebrew Bible is too lengthy a topic to be explained here, but I discuss the particulars of the editions and translations I use in the endnotes to Chapters 3 and 4.

ACKNOWLEDGMENTS

This book's early life began as a collaborative research project that then turned into a chapter of my doctoral dissertation. These episodes of creative exploration and writing took place under the guidance of my advisor and mentor at McGill University, Michael Bristol. I can confidently say that this project's creative spark would not have ignited without his unwavering intellectual support and keen sense that scriptural citation was an important way into this particular Shakespeare play. I do not know whether Mike was aware that my early background in the study of the Hebrew Bible and its rabbinic commentaries was going to prove as useful as it did, but for that background I have my earliest educators at the Jewish People's and Peretz Schools and Bialik High School to thank. Without the formative education in Hebrew Bible studies and especially the Yiddish language – a true rarity in modern Jewish primary and secondary education – I would quite simply not have the intellectual or moral foundation that proved so vital to this project's development. For that education I also need to thank both of my parents, for whom the Yiddish language has always remained a centrepoint of Jewish identity, culture and creative expression.

Funding for this project began when I was a doctoral student at McGill University. The Fonds de Recherche du

Québec, Societé et Culture (FRQSC) provided generous financial support in the form of a doctoral research grant. The FRQSC also provided funding to the Shakespeare and Performance Research Team Project (SPRiTE) housed at McGill and directed in those days by the terrifically energetic Paul Yachnin. SPRiTE brought together an inter-disciplinary team of researchers and theatre experts that also provided funding for several years' worth of research assistantships during my doctoral studies, as well as affording a venue for the scholars and graduate students involved in the project to share research in progress. During those years I learned an invaluable lesson about the virtues of productive collaboration – namely, that such a thing is possible in the humanities among peers who share a passion for their subject matter and, perhaps most crucially, also a generosity of spirit. As I advance in my own career, I realise with every passing year how rare that kind of collaboration is among colleagues, and I hope that those formative experiences have helped make me a better and more generous collaborator in my own working life.

Funding for the early stages of this book's development was made possible by Junior Faculty grants from the University of Oklahoma's College of Arts and Sciences. OU's summer fellowship programmes for junior faculty made much of the research for this book possible at archival centres such as the Huntington Library and the YIVO Institute for Jewish Research. OU's travel grants also made it possible to present chapters-in-progress at a number of annual conferences, including the Shakespeare Association of America, the Renaissance Society of America, and the Borrowers and Lenders conference on appropriation in the age of global Shakespeare hosted by the University of Georgia. Without a doubt, each of those meetings led to key insights into the structure and intellectual scope of the book, and I am thankful to all of those seminarians, panellists, audience members and panel chairs who were willing to proffer their questions and comments on my work. When I reflect on the immense value of those meetings and their impact on my work, I am made increasingly thankful for those funding opportunities that made it possible to attend conferences and symposia, which continue to be among the most important venues for sharing ideas that lead to publications in the humanities. The Schusterman Centre for Judaic and Israel Studies at the University of Oklahoma has also been a source of support in providing financial help to attend conferences, and through its Judaic Studies Brownbag lecture series, which offers those of us who work in Judaic Studies at OU an opportunity to share our research. I also want to acknowledge the National Endowment for the Humanities and the Folger Shakespeare Library for hosting the 2010 summer Institute Shakespeare: From the Globe to the Global', which provided an invaluable three weeks to exchange ideas with fellow scholars that greatly enhanced my sense of the global dimensions of both Renaissance culture and Shakespearean adaptations.

Two of my recently published essays have served as foundations for parts of the current book. ' "This was a way to thrive": Christian and Jewish Eudaimonism in *The Merchant of Venice*' was published in the 2015 collection *The Renaissance of Emotion*, edited by Richard Meek and Erin Sullivan for Manchester University Press. 'Well-Won Thrift', co-authored by Michael Bristol, appears in the 2015 collection *Shakespeare's World of Words*, edited by Paul Yachnin and published by Bloomsbury Arden Shakespeare, a division of Bloomsbury Publishing. Both publications represent early stages in the long and gradual process of shaping this book, particularly its third chapter that addresses Jewish scriptural exegesis.

Finally, I would like to thank my husband, Kevin Butterfield. As a fellow scholar, Kevin is well aware of how trying and exhilarating the process of writing a book can be, and he managed to support me throughout this process with generosity, kindness and encouragement, particularly through the challenges and trials of moving from my home of Montréal to a part of the United States that continues to feel unfamiliar to me. I am grateful every day for Kevin's compassion and companionship that helped ease my *mal de pays*.

SERIES EDITOR'S PREFACE

Picture Macbeth alone on stage, staring intently into empty space. 'Is this a dagger which I see before me?' he asks, grasping decisively at the air. On one hand, this is a quintessentially theatrical question. At once an object and a vector, the dagger describes the possibility of knowledge ('Is this a dagger') in specifically visual and spatial terms ('which I see before me'). At the same time, Macbeth is posing a quintessentially *philosophical* question, one that assumes knowledge to be both conditional and experiential, and that probes the relationship between certainty and perception as well as intention and action. It is from this shared ground of art and inquiry, of theatre and theory, that this series advances its basic premise: *Shakespeare is philosophical*.

It seems like a simple enough claim. But what does it mean exactly, beyond the parameters of this specific moment in Macbeth? Does it mean that Shakespeare had something we could think of as his own philosophy? Does it mean that he was influenced by particular philosophical schools, texts and thinkers? Does it mean, conversely, that modern philosophers have been influenced by *him*, that Shakespeare's plays and poems have been, and continue to be, resources for philosophical thought and speculation?

The answer is yes all around. These are all useful ways of conceiving a philosophical Shakespeare and all point to lines of inquiry that this series welcomes. But Shakespeare is philosophical in a much more fundamental way as well. Shakespeare is philosophical because the plays and poems actively create new worlds of knowledge and new scenes of ethical encounter. They ask big questions, make bold arguments and develop new vocabularies in order to think what might otherwise be unthinkable. Through both their scenarios and their imagery, the plays and poems engage the qualities of consciousness, the consequences of human action, the phenomenology of motive and attention, the conditions of personhood, and the relationship among different orders of reality and experience. This is writing and dramaturgy, moreover, that consistently experiments with a broad range of conceptual crossings, between love and subjectivity, nature and politics, and temporality and form.

Edinburgh Critical Studies in Shakespeare and Philosophy takes seriously these speculative and world-making dimensions of Shakespeare's work. The series proceeds from a core conviction that art's capacity to think – to formulate, not just reflect, ideas – is what makes it urgent and valuable. Art matters because unlike other human activities it establishes its own frame of reference, reminding us that all acts of creation – biological, political, intellectual and amorous – are grounded in imagination. This is a far cry from business-as-usual in Shakespeare studies. Because historicism remains the methodological gold standard of the field, far more energy has been invested in exploring what Shakespeare once meant than in thinking rigorously about what Shakespeare continues to make possible. In response, Edinburgh Critical Studies in Shakespeare and Philosophy pushes back against the critical orthodoxies of historicism and cultural studies to clear a space for scholarship that confronts aspects of literature that can neither be reduced to nor adequately explained by particular historical contexts.

Shakespeare's creations are not just inheritances of a past culture, frozen artifacts whose original settings must be expertly reconstructed in order to be understood. The plays and poems are also living art, vital thought-worlds that struggle, across time, with foundational questions of metaphysics, ethics, politics and aesthetics. With this orientation in mind, Edinburgh Critical Studies in Shakespeare and Philosophy offers a series of scholarly monographs that will reinvigorate Shakespeare studies by opening new interdisciplinary conversations among scholars, artists and students.

Kevin Curran

INTRODUCTION: IS SHYLOCK JEWISH?

In a 1923 essay titled 'The Background of Shylock', Anglo-Jewish historian Cecil Roth offers the kind of careful forensic reconstruction of Shakespeare's fictional moneylender that one might expect of a scholar of Renaissance Jewry. Roth observes that 'it is not difficult in our present state of knowledge to reconstruct Shylock's actual background and to depict, without leaving much margin for error, those details which Shakespeare relegated to the imagination.'[1] To these ends, Roth begins to narrate Shylock's Venetian existence, positing that he must have been a German Jew or, as they were referred to by their contemporary Italians, the *Nazione Tedesca*, the oldest and most sizeable of the three ethnographically Jewish groups living in Italy at the end of the sixteenth century, and the only group permitted to work in moneylending.[2] Roth praises Shakespeare's verisimilitude, noting that 'Shakespeare's intuition has enabled him to sketch in trivial details with such remarkable fidelity as to render it quite conceivable (as has been conjectured) he knew Italy at first-hand.'[3] Jessica's theft of her father's jewels along with his bags of ducats and the man's livery suit that she uses as a disguise, Roth observes, would have come from bond securities left by Shylock's wealthy Venetian customers who had entered into loan contracts with him.[4] Roth notes that German Jews, unlike their Portuguese and Turkish counterparts, spoke fluent Italian; however, it was unlikely that Shylock would have been granted citizenship in sixteenth-century Venice, whose laws prohibited Jewish citizenship until the late eighteenth century.[5] The location of the synagogue that Shylock mentions as a meeting-place with Tubal in act 3, scene 1 would not have been Venice's renowned Spanish synagogue, which Roth derides as 'at present the show-place of the Venetian ghetto, in which sentimental tourists think of Shylock and of Jessica.'[6] Instead, Roth points to the city's two Ashkenazi synagogues, the *Scuola Grande Tedesca* founded in 1529 and the *Scuola Canton* founded in 1532, where services were held according to German-Jewish tradition. 'It is in one of these that Shylock must have worshipped, and in which, if anywhere, his restless spirit must be sought today.'[7]

The project of locating the historical Shylock, reconstructed with the kind of meticulous detail that Roth summons, is at once a compelling and puzzling exercise. That sentimental tourists seek Shylock out in Venice's Spanish synagogue is as misguided as if they were to attempt to find him according to Roth's prescription in a less tourist-ridden Ashkenazic temple. Shylock is, of course, nowhere to be found in any of these locales; he was no historical person but a fictional agent – a figure without actual eyes, hands, organs or dimensions, as Roth well knew. Yet, the historian's impulse to reconstruct a detailed and accurate past for Shakespeare's fictional Jew has not so much gone away within the last hundred years as it has evolved into new avenues of historicist inquiry.

Within the last century, the imperative to locate Shylock has shifted from detailed, character-focused, Bradleian detective work to the materialist scholarship of the past several decades that reads Shakespearean drama against texts and objects from the early modern past. Scholars of the English Renaissance continue to summon this play in discussions of early modern currency and emerging models of English nationhood, to name only two recent areas of emphasis.[8] Shylock's locale has also shifted over time; scholars today tend to treat sixteenth-century England as the play's more relevant context, far more so than Renaissance Italy. Discussions of *The Merchant of Venice*'s history have also widened considerably beyond Shakespeare's immediate lifetime to include the four hundred years of the play's production and reception history. Both Charles Edelman and Emma Smith have recently published studies examining why and to what ends scholars have presumed that Shakespeare's original performance featured Shylock dressed as a stock comic Jew in a red wig and large hooked nose,[9] a topic that was also the basis of a heated dispute in the *New York Review of Books* between James Shapiro and Stephen Greenblatt.[10]

Smith's work in particular has aptly called attention to the strong ties between historical scholarship on this play and the ideological and ethical investments of those who have undertaken to study it. She has convincingly argued that Victorian critics actively shaped the English past to suit an ideal of Englishness predicated on excluding Jews, an ideal whose implications I discuss in Chapter 1 of this book.[11] Cecil Roth's essay on Shylock can be usefully contextualised by considering the long-standing imbrication of historical scholarship with ideals of Englishness, ideals in which Jews were often portrayed as reviled outsiders. The notion of a sympathetically painted Shylock, or of Shakespeare, apotheosis of English literary greatness, as potentially sympathetic to Jews, is one that many critics and audiences over the long history of the play have found deeply threatening. Through a forensic reconstruction of Shylock's life, Roth seizes an opportunity to flesh out the existence of a living, breathing sixteenth-century Jew. There is a deliberately humanising imperative to his reconstruction of that life, not in the naive sense of mistaking Shylock for an actual living person, or even in the sense that L. C. Knights disparages when scholars give serious consideration to fictional characters' experiences off the page.[12] In fleshing out Shylock's life, Roth reflects the degree to which he sees in him the routine details of a human being, affording Shylock an ordinary dignity that quietly cuts against vicious and dehumanising stereotypes. Those stereotypes and Roth's response to them are briefly and poignantly referenced in the essay's final lines, where he writes:

> Professionally, he [i.e. Shylock] was a moneylender, his activities being regulated by the terms of the periodical *condotte* of his 'nation', renewed every ten years. Incidentally, he sometimes came into possession of a variety of second-hand wares, as well as precious stones: though traffic in them was not his main activity. As, according to legend, Pope remarked, with reference to Macklin's production, in the most execrable couplet in English literature: 'This is the Jew / That Shakespeare drew.'[13]

The 'execrable' couplet to which Roth refers is the one widely attributed to the English poet Alexander Pope who is reputed to have uttered it about Charles Macklin's 1741 performance. In that performance, Macklin refashioned Shakespeare's Jew as an arch predator in a far more vicious and, to Pope's mind, more credible mould than the buffoonish comic portrayal that had been in vogue during the early part of the eighteenth century.[14] This new, cruelly villainous Shylock, according to Pope, was the true Jew, one that he found convincingly Shakespearean. The first line of the couplet, 'This is the Jew', is intended to reflect not only Shakespeare's Jew but all Jews. It is to this vision and the critical tradition that has followed in its footsteps that Roth, with a single conclusive adjective, proclaims his disgust.

Cecil Roth's citation of Pope's infamous remark acknowledges a bitter truth about *The Merchant of Venice*: Shylock is a figure closely bound up not only with the fictionalised landscape of anti-Semitism on the page but also with its lived history off of it. *The Merchant of Venice* has furnished notable turns of anti-Semitic phrase, foremost among them the term 'Shylock' which has come to describe a cut-throat type of Jewish profiteer. This play and its Jewish moneylender's tendency to bleed messily off the page into historical actuality is something that Roth also reflects on in his essay:

> That Shylock was a sheer figment of Shakespeare's imagination, there has never been any doubt. Yet this figment has acquired an objective reality more vital than that of most creatures of flesh and blood. His actions are still a byword, his name is a reproach, and his unfortunate co-religionists actually taxed sometimes with his reputed misdeeds.[15]

Jews remain inextricably if unwittingly bound to Shakespeare's fictional moneylender because of the ways in which he and Jessica have helped construct Jewishness in the popular imagination. In looking at Shylock and being confronted with turns of phrase from the play which, like Shylock himself, have become bywords in vernacular speech, modern Jews glimpse a reflection of their ethnographic identity through the distortive lens of interpolated stereotypes that have played a significant role in shaping cultural perceptions of Jews over time.

Growing up in the cosmopolitan city of Montréal, Québec, I spent the first seventeen years of my life attending a Jewish day-school where my closest and most routine interactions were with other Jews. As a teenager, part of that experience involved contending with the perceived necessity of dating and, ultimately, marrying Jewish boys, a requirement not entirely promoted by my own parents, but not entirely not-promoted by them either. One of the things that came with dating Jewish boys in those days was a discourse of attractiveness and desirability that centred on whether or not a girl 'looked' Jewish. The more Jewish you looked the less obviously desirable you were in the eyes of many of the Jewish men I encountered. I can remember being on a double-date with a close friend, a girl whom everyone agreed did not 'look' Jewish in ways that I supposedly did, and I recall being told by my date that he wasn't convinced I was Jewish when he first met me because, although I looked the part, I didn't 'seem' or 'act' or 'talk' like a Jewish girl. Conversely, he asserted, my friend who did not 'look' Jewish at all was unmistakably 'Jewish-sounding', in his opinion, and he would therefore never have considered dating her.

Even as I struggled to contend with the sting of his comments, it was clear to me in the moment that my date thought that he was offering me a compliment. Apparently my manner of speech and comportment compensated for my 'Jewish looks'. The compliment, of course, was an extraordinarily bitter pill to have to swallow. The 'happy' ending that this young man attempted to script for me that evening prescribed that certain Jewish women could overcome the physiological signs of Jewishness because of their demeanour and manner of speech, even where most, sadly, could not. It took many years and several advanced degrees before I saw that the exchange in Shakespeare's *The Merchant of Venice* in which Jessica asserts that 'though I am a daughter to his [Shylock's] blood, / I am not to his manners' (2.3.18–19) formed an integral part of the evaluative judgment and self-understanding of that young man, four hundred years after Shakespeare scripted those lines.

The Merchant of Venice can certainly be read as a digest of anti-Semitic rhetoric that registers a dizzying number of historically situated ideas about Jews and Jewishness. But more than merely serving as a catalogue of Elizabethan anti-Semitisms, *Merchant* also animates what, for me, was an uncomfortably poignant moral and emotional experience of being Jewish in a world marked by invidious anti-Semitic stereotypes, ones also absorbed and rehearsed by Jews themselves. Having attended a Jewish day-school where I studied Jewish history, the Hebrew Bible, Hebrew and Yiddish languages, and Jewish traditions through all of elementary and high school, I also had the opportunity to experience first-hand the great richness of Jewish culture and theology that had virtually no relationship to those stereotypes. For me, one of *Merchant*'s lingering questions has centred on whether Shakespeare's play includes any of the richness that informed that dimension of my first-personal experience of Judaism. What new meanings might be made available if we considered Shylock and Jessica as Jewish characters in a way that sourced Jewishness not only through interpolated ethnic stereotypes, but via distinctively Jewish traditions and practices? Does Shakespeare's play conjure this type of Jew – what I sometimes find myself thinking of as a *real* Jew – in this play?

'Jew' is of course the primary term used to designate Shylock in *The Merchant of Venice*, a term that appears fifty-five times in the text of this play, over fifty more times than in any other Shakespeare play.[16] *Merchant* makes readily available a roster of invidious epithets that are ascribed to Jews and Jewishness, including Antonio's description of Shylock as a 'devil [who] cites Scripture for his purpose', through which he denigrates Shylock as an immoral businessman and slanders all Jews as vicious predators who twist and deform Christian morality. It is easy enough to see the world of this play and its Jewish moneylender through such taunts, or to extrapolate from them the anti-Semitic designs of its author. There are a dispiriting number of slanderous voices in this play that attempt to frame Shylock as a villainous antagonist and cast his daughter as potentially redeemable only insofar as she is able to expunge the taint of her Jewish lineage. However, Shakespeare's plays and the dramatic medium in which he chose to write are, by contrast, insistently multivocal. Shylock is spoken of very poorly by Antonio, Portia, Bassanio, and even his own daughter, Jessica; but he also speaks for himself, particularly when he remarks on the exploits of his biblical ancestor, Jacob.

It is among the play's greatest and most difficult moral challenges to listen carefully to Shylock in such moments, surrounded as he is by detractors. In his discussion of *Lear*, Stanley Cavell describes such attentiveness as 'acknowledgment',[17] and it entails a willingness to get close enough that Shylock begins to come into view through the moral compass of his own intentions and motivations and not just those of his persecutors. Antonio would have us read – and dismiss – Shylock as an immoral usurer. But Shylock's own perspective and his argument about 'what Jacob does' is substantially more sophisticated than Antonio would have us believe.

Some of the most widely anthologised essays on this play have read Shylock as a cipher through which *The Merchant of Venice* works out a Christian moral message.[18] Mercy triumphs over hard-hearted literalism, and so concludes the play when Shylock is defeated in the courtroom and forced to become a Christian. Most scholars today no longer feel much inclined to read the play this simplistically or allegorically; however, echoes of the allegorical approach that insists that there is no Jew in Shakespeare's play, not in the sense that I found myself wondering about, have persisted into present-day scholarship. James Shapiro's influential recent study of *The Merchant of Venice* has explored in detail the place that Jewishness held in the early modern imagination, examining Shylock as a cipher for a vast amalgam of Elizabethan anti-Semitic stereotypes that circulated in early modern England that included blood-libel legends and the fear of circumcision and castration by Jews.[19] Other scholars have examined Jews and Jewishness in the play as placeholders for things that have little to do with religion or ethnography – for example, contemporary ideas about immigrants, or the circulation of social energies in Renaissance England.[20] In this book, I endeavour to reorient the conversation yet again. While the long-standing view of Shylock as an allegorical Jew or product of the Elizabethan anti-Semitic imagination or placeholder for something other than Jews and Jewishness may be entrenched in *Merchant*'s critical history, that perspective and way into this play locates the sources of Shylock's identity anywhere and everywhere but the Jewish tradition.

In this book, I consider the moral agency of Shylock and his daughter Jessica by inquiring into the habits of mind evidenced by their words and actions in the play, some of which, I argue, reflect recognisably Jewish patterns. In the chapters that follow, I discuss how Shylock's and Jessica's use of biblical language and allusion afford key insights into the ideals that motivate them, ideals that are importantly underwritten by the Jewish identity that the play assigns to them. However, unlike accounts of Shylock's Jewishness that reduce Jewish ethnography to a series of invidious stereotypes, this book offers a very different account of what it means to consider Shylock and Jessica as Jews, and sources their identity from the Judaic tradition's distinctive way of reading and interpreting biblical stories.

Interactions between Christians and Jews in *The Merchant of Venice* are threaded through with language that is overwhelmingly scriptural. When Shylock discusses the terms of his loan with Antonio in act 1, scene 3, he does it by appealing to the biblical figure of Jacob and a parable from Genesis 30 to describe how he understands the act of lending money. That biblical story becomes a medium through which he coordinates his relationship with Antonio and understands the moral scope of his profession, arguing that 'thrift is blessing if men steal it not' by appealing to 'what Jacob did' (1.3.74) when he bred Laban's livestock (1.3.87). The Hebrew Bible furnishes a key discourse through which disputes are framed, bonds are established, and rivalries are structured throughout this play, foremost among these the contest over who has the authority to interpret a shared set of authoritative writings. In act 1, scene 3, Antonio claims that it is the unique prerogative of Christians to cite from the Bible. He maligns Shylock for attempting to use a scriptural parable to explicate his lending practices.

> Mark you this, Bassanio,
> The devil can cite Scripture for his purpose.
> An evil soul producing holy witness
> Is like a villain with a smiling cheek,
> A goodly apple rotten at the heart.
>
> (1.3.94–8)

In such moments, *The Merchant of Venice* not only raises questions about who has the authority to cite scriptural precedent; it also poses a more fundamental question about whose Scripture is being cited when Jews and Christians invoke these episodes. For Jews, narratives like the one that Shylock discusses are not from the Christian 'Old Testament'; they form part of the Torah, a source of moral intelligibility that allows individuals to align present-day decisions with authoritative scripts. Traditionally, biblical exegesis has offered a way to locate meaningful orientation in a space of moral questions for Jews,[21] whether working out the terms of a loan contract or reflecting on the perils of religious intermarriage. The practice of aligning these stories with the exigencies of daily life is known as *midrash*, a style of biblical exegesis that originates in rabbinic commentary, and provides a way to engage authoritative texts along with a vast interpretive tradition that is continually re-reading them in relation to new first-personal practical circumstances. In the chapters that follow, I argue that the practice of midrash furnishes a meaningful Jewish framework through which he understands the moral implications of his own lending practices.

Is Shylock Jewish? Scriptural Citation and the Moral Agency of Shakespeare's Jews takes up the long and rich tradition surrounding a series of Hebrew biblical stories centred on the life of Jacob, spanning chapters 12–50 of the Book of Genesis, that are invoked repeatedly in the text of Shakespeare's play by Jewish characters. Episodes such as Jacob stealing his brother's birthright, the parable of the parti-coloured lambs, and the abduction of Dinah appear at key moments of moral deliberation for both Shylock and Jessica in *The Merchant of Venice*, These stories address practical ethical questions about commercial relationships among kin, means–end morality, and religious intermarriage. *Is Shylock Jewish?* examines their Jewish interpretive legacy and considers how that legacy helps make sense of the moral universe within which *Merchant*'s Jewish characters commit to courses of action, understand their place in the worlds they inhabit, and reflect on the significance of their predicaments. Central to that discussion is the claim that biblical interpretation figures a kind of ethical deliberation that is foundational to Shylock and Jessica's moral agency as characters. Such deliberations are inseparable from what Aristotle recognised as the constituents of human *ethos*, those practices that constitute a moral life. Like Cecil Roth's effort to bring the routine details of Shakespeare's Jewish moneylenders to the fore of the discussion of Shylock's character, *Is Shylock Jewish?* treats the parsing of those intentional and emotional states as part of the requirements of ethical readership when it comes to this play.

A great deal of *Merchant* criticism has already attended to the Christian theological implications of its numerous scriptural references, with the effect of generating an overwhelmingly Christian set of meanings for the play. However, virtually no scholarship has discussed the Judaic interpretive tradition. This book turns to the play's vast network of Hebrew biblical citations, and argues that it is through dialogues with Scripture that *The Merchant of Venice* generates an authentic Jewish presence. Dialogues with Scripture represent vital sites of moral orientation for *Merchant*'s Jewish characters, and by studying them we can more fully account for the presence of 'real' Jews in *The Merchant of Venice* that resist reductive stereotyping. Jewish writers have also refashioned the play by expanding its scriptural inter-texts. The final chapter of this book explores the ways in which *Merchant*'s biblical inter-texts have been developed by nineteenth- and twentieth-century Jewish writers, who expanded them in order to pose probing, sometimes unsettling questions about the nature of Jewish identity and the future of traditional ways of life in the modern diaspora.

In focusing on biblical inter-texts, this book might appear to be following in the tradition of nineteenth- and early twentieth-century criticism that studied the particulars of biblical references in the play in order to determine Shakespeare's position on specific theological issues. In fact, this book articulates a very different claim, one that is entirely uninterested in Shakespeare's confessional status or the theological 'message' of the play, but takes a pointed interest in Shylock's and Jessica's moral agency as Jews. *Is Shylock Jewish?* considers the ways in which biblical stories' Judaic interpretive legacies have figured in the long historical life of this play, and maintains that there is immense interpretive and ethical merit to considering Jewish modes of reading in a play that is itself explicitly focused on scriptural hermeneutics.

What new meanings are made available by considering *Merchant*'s biblical inter-texts as stories with long and complex interpretive histories that include Jewish voices? This question serves as a prompt for both the historical work I undertake in this book, which seeks to understand the range of meanings attributed to Jews and their sacred writings in early modern England, as well as the ethical work that positions the interpretation of Shakespeare's writing as an undertaking inseparable from where we as readers stand in the present and the concerns that animate our reading practices today. It is far from incidental to the aims and parameters of this book that I am a Jewish scholar whose formative training in the study of the Torah and its Hebrew commentaries compels my curiosity about the presence or absence of patterns of Jewish moral thought in Shakespeare's Jewish play. I also approach this play as someone who sees myself reflected in its Jewish characters. I have always been puzzled by the insistence that such questions – first-personal Jewish questions – are illegitimate when we ask them of Shakespeare's Jewish play, or what point there could be to denying the relevancy of who we are when we read and interpret his work. Such standards instead proclaim a discipline's exclusionary assumptions about who it imagines is legitimately authorised to ask questions about canonical works of literature, and whose assumptions and background knowledge are thought to really matter or merit being brought to the study of Shakespeare.

The type of presentist approach to that I am outlining here shares common ground with the recent call by Peter Erickson and Kim F. Hall to rethink the parameters and aims of Shakespeare scholarship in order to better align it with the imperatives of social justice work and critical race studies.[22] Present-day concerns are crucial not only to formulating meaningful and full responses to what Michael Bristol terms 'the maximum of semantic precision with the maximum of verbal play' that Shakespeare's works make available to readers;[23] those same concerns are also essential to helping cultivate a scholarly community around the study of Shakespeare's works that accurately reflects the diversity and vitality of his present-day interpreters.

The central question that motivates this book – is Shylock Jewish? – is unavoidably first-personal for those of us who identify or have been identified by others as Jewish, or for anyone living in the long shadow cast by racial and ethnic prejudice. That legacy, crystallised by Shakespearean turns of phrase found in plays such as *Merchant* and *Othello*, remains deeply interwoven with lived experience and historical memory for many of Shakespeare's present-day readers. Where claims to interpret Shakespeare based on present-day first-personal concerns are sometimes disparagingly designated as 'presentist', another label for that kind of readership might simply be 'ethical', a term that in the Classical tradition implies the presence of the whole person, the composite totality of their intellectual and emotional resources, and a lifelong commitment to the pursuit of an objectively meaningful ideal.

One of the things this book does not attempt to do is take up the discourse of political philosophy to explore questions of political membership for Jews or Christians, a turn that makes *Is Shylock Jewish?* very different in its focus and methodology from Julia Reinhard Lupton's recent monograph *Citizen-Saints*.[24] Instead, *Is Shylock Jewish?* focuses on identifying those practical moral questions that Shylock and Jessica evoke in the play, questions that Antonio, along with many scholars, have occluded or read past. In *Citizen-Saints*, Lupton identifies threshold-scenarios in *The Merchant of Venice* as key moments of deliberation about political belonging and the overlapping claims made on citizen-members, and she engages twentieth-century political thought throughout the book to respond to the questions of membership that she locates in Shakespeare's plays. My interest in threshold-scenarios in *The Merchant of Venice* also focuses on questions of belonging, particularly in relation to Jessica's character; however, unlike Lupton's book, my study focuses intensively on Jewish ethical scripts that attempt to make sense of the play's liminal scenarios where individuals, like Jessica, are positioned at the outer perimeters of their communities. My discussion of Jewish ethical scripts and Jessica's character argues for the importance of biblical women as vitally important figures through which questions of belonging and membership were being negotiated within both Jewish and Christian traditions. Even where responses to those scripts reflect trenchant doubts about authoritative stories' capacity to chart relevant courses of action in the present, biblical narratives continued to remain a backbone within even secular Jewish American writing well into the twenty-first century, as I discuss in the final chapter of the book.

In addressing the Judaic legacy associated with scripturalism in *The Merchant of Venice*, *Is Shylock Jewish?* ranges over a considerable span of time, from Renaissance English responses to Hebrew biblical source-materials to modern adaptations of the play by Jewish writers that deepened *Merchant*'s biblical inter-texts. This book's extensive scope builds upon the kind of critical work undertaken by Daniel B. Schwartz in his award-winning recent book *The First Modern Jew: Spinoza and the History of an Image*.[25] Schwartz's monograph offers a rich and wonderfully comprehensive discussion of the ways that an early modern Jewish figure has given rise to culturally significant conversations about Jewish identity over the long term, a concern shared by the present book when it comes to Shylock and Jessica's legacies. His book, along with Lupton's, reflects a commendable willingness to step outside a strict historicist paradigm in responding to ethical questions posed by historically situated texts and figures, a willingness that is also shared by the present study.

Because Shakespeare was a writer with a virtually boundless curiosity about social languages, whose work reflects a sustained interest in the expressive potential of biblical words, themes, and figures, his use of the Bible as inter-text and source-text is evidenced throughout his dramatic *oeuvre*, a fact that Hannibal Hamlin's recently published *The Bible in Shakespeare* makes abundantly clear.[26] Ken Jackson's *Shakespeare and Abraham* demonstrates the immense interpretive potential of even singular, terse Hebrew biblical scenes such as the binding of Isaac for a wide range of Shakespeare's plays.[27] Unlike Jackson's book, which studies a range of plays but only one biblical verse, this book studies a single play and a range of biblical chapters that comprise the Genesis Jacob cycle of stories. In the pages that follow, I consider how Shakespeare tests the expressive potential and interpretive richness of scriptural language, dramatising the ways in which diverse approaches to reading biblical scripts suggest at differing, often incompatible ways of life, practical habits, and belief-systems – in effect, the practical foundations of human ethics.

Like Emma Smith's essay 'Was Shylock Jewish?', this book also questions the way the scholarly tradition has actively and selectively shaped evidence to create a 'desired historical narrative' that positions Shylock as a figure devoid of moral agency, signalling a caricature of Jewishness rather than an authentic Jewish presence.[28] Those arguments have often relied on flawed assertions about the Elizabethan English past that posit it as a place wholly inimical to Jews and impervious to Jewish influence. To that end, early sections of this book discuss why it is important to re-examine the sixteenth-century English context and contemporary attitudes towards Judaic culture, language and learning. Studies by historian Anthony Grafton and classicist Stephen Burnett have convincingly argued that Christians' engagement with Jewishness, Hebrew, and Jews in the early modern period was complex, profound, and highly generative.[29]

Recent scholarship on trade, eastern imports and antiquity has also begun to flesh out English culture's preoccupation with exotic and Classical imports in the sixteenth century.[30] Among those imports were Hebrew texts, which were highly valued as exotic antiquities. The English proclivity for importing these materials raises important new questions about the reception of Hebrew and Judaic culture in light of England's increasingly global sensibility in this period. How did the fascination with Hebraic texts and exotic peoples condition English attitudes towards Jews and their culture and language? *Is Shylock Jewish?* is positioned to contribute productively to this emerging conversation by considering the question of a Jewish presence in early modern England through the period's complex, highly ambivalent responses to the Hebrew language and Jews. By offering an account of the complexity of early modern attitudes and perceptions, I suggest that Shakespeare had a great many contemporary cultural resources from which to draw in constructing a Jew who cited Scripture with something other than a Christian moral framework in mind. In discussing early modern perceptions of Jews, Judaic culture, and Hebrew, I argue that the multi-vocality of Hebrew biblical narratives was something to which Shakespeare's own culture was sensitively attuned, far more so than we tend to recognise in the twenty-first century, and far more than has been addressed in scholarship that labels *The Merchant of Venice* a Christian play.

Chapter 1 of this book begins by discussing the highly convincing recent account provided by Emma Smith of how Victorian-era discussions of *The Merchant of Venice*'s original historical context became heavily bound up with ideals of Englishness from which Jews were pervasively excluded. How and why did those ideals succeed in occluding the ambivalence and even praise that accompanied early modern English encounters with Judaic culture, theology, and language? In Chapter 1, I examine how English Renaissance humanists, biblical scholars, and reformers encountered and wrote about Jews, Judaic culture, and the Hebrew language in the sixteenth century. Sixteenth-century English Hebraists relied upon direct contact with Jewish scholars and converts in continental Europe, contact that contributed to a far more dimensional appreciation of Judaic culture and theology as well as Jews themselves. I discuss how that kind of contact, which was shaped by an emerging fascination with non-English cultures and their goods, contributed to a growing cosmopolitanism in English culture in which foreign influences were being brought closer to English readers in increasingly unmediated ways.

Following Chapter 1's discussion of historical context and the interpretive history of Shakespeare's play, Chapter 2 turns to the text of *The Merchant of Venice* and reads it as a multi-vocal work that sustains both Christian and Jewish readings of shared sacred texts, along with distinctively Christian and Jewish approaches to moral quandaries. I demonstrate how the play's multi-vocality is evidenced during moments of scriptural citation such as the discussion of the parable of the parti-coloured lambs in act 1, scene 3. Chapter 1 then engages in a comparative reading of Christian and Jewish interpretive traditions' key insights on Shylock's biblical parable, and considers how the meaning of the scene and the wider play is transformed when these episodes are read through rabbinical or, alternately, patristic accounts. By looking to the Judaic tradition and the seminal commentaries of Rashi, Nahmanides and Maimonides, I consider Shylock as an interlocutor who speaks with a serious investment in Judaic modes of reading, as serious as Antonio's evident investment in a Christian typological account of that same scriptural story. In looking to the rabbinic tradition's interpretive legacy on these episodes, this chapter considers the midrashic potential of Shylock's biblical citation in which he claims the moral authority of the biblical Jacob as a strategy to legitimise the work that he does and valorise his 'well-won thrift',

Thus far I have said a great deal about Shylock as a prototypical Jewish reader of Scripture in the play, but relatively little about his daughter Jessica. Jessica's plotline in fact draws in equally profound and complex ways from the cycle of biblical stories that chronicle the life of Jacob in chapters 12–50 of Genesis. The most definitive of these inter-texts is the story of Dinah from Genesis 34, from which Shakespeare derives Jessica's seduction by a non-Jewish man, her subsequent religious conversion, as well as the ensuing vengeance of her bereaved male kin.

Chapters 3 and 4 both focus on Jessica's storyline and the development of her character through biblical narratives. Chapter 3 discusses two key inter-texts from the Genesis Jacob cycle whose plot features and moral predicaments are mirrored in *The Merchant of Venice* – the abduction of Dinah, and Rachel who steals her father's idols before departing from his home. Chapter 3 outlines these stories' importance to Shakespeare's characterisation of Jessica as a liminal figure neither willing to remain defined by her Jewish parentage nor able to fully integrate as a Christian. Turning to Genesis 34, I address a long-standing question among rabbinical exegetes: Dinah's consent in her sexual liaison with a non-Jewish man, a question that I consider in relation to Jessica's conversion and marriage. Where the concept of consent offers a way of understanding religious membership as a form of moral answerability in the Judaic tradition, moral answerability itself was seen, particularly in a Renaissance English context and particularly for women, as the product of sound moral instruction. The story of Rachel stealing her father's idols from Genesis 31, polarising for Christian and Jewish exegetes alike, becomes for Renaissance English writers a story about the merits and limits of moral education for women. By examining the episode featuring Rachel's theft of her father's idols and its importance to

Renaissance English moral instruction literature for women, I discuss Jessica's position in *Merchant* as a figure who signals both the promises and limitations of what moral education can accomplish.

Chapter 4 addresses modern adaptations of *The Merchant of Venice* by Yiddish-language writers. Nineteenth- and twentieth-century adaptations of *The Merchant of Venice* into Yiddish draw extensively and overtly on the biblical stories of Rachel and Dinah as they develop and expand Jessica's character. Through a study of two Yiddish-language adaptations of *Merchant*, the 1898 novella *Der koyfmann fun Venedig* by Meir Freid and Maurice Schwartz's 1947 play *Shayloks tochter*, this chapter considers how Jessica's story and the biblical inter-texts that underwrite it have continued to galvanise discussions about what it means to be Jewish, dramatising the changing concerns of Jewish life in the modern era. For many Jewish playwrights, Jessica comes to embody the pressing challenges of modernity, the threat of religious intermarriage, and women's emerging roles in the workforce, which includes a history of social activism. Chapter 4's discussion of Yiddish adaptations of *Merchant* brings an important chapter of *The Merchant of Venice*'s history into view that has too long been excluded from Shakespeare studies, and looks at Yiddish adaptations through an innovative lens that emphasises the ongoing importance of biblical citation and interpretation to Jewish literary expression in the twentieth century.

Notes

1. Cecil Roth, 'The Background of Shylock', *Review of English Studies*, 9: 34 (April 1933): 148–56 (149–50).
2. The two other communities of Jews living in Italy were refugees from Spain and Portugal (the 'Ponentines') and those who came from Turkey ('Levantines'). Roth stresses that all

three groups received very different treatment and maintained separate institutions and synagogues in Venice. Levantine and Ponentine Jews were professionally restricted to commercial activities and were not permitted to work as moneylenders. Roth, 'Background', 150–2.
3. Roth, 'Background', 151.
4. Roth notes that wealthy Venetians with palaces on the Grand Canal were notorious for collecting extravagant jewels, so much so that sumptuary laws were enacted to limit how much they could wear at one time. Roth, 'Background', 151.
5. Roth, 'Background', 152.
6. Roth, 'Background', 155.
7. Ibid.
8. For a recent discussion of the play's economic aspects, see Linda Woodbridge (ed.), *Money and the Age of Shakespeare* (New York: Palgrave Macmillan, 2003) and Lars Engle, '"Thrift is Blessing": Exchange and Explanation in *The Merchant of Venice*', *Shakespeare Quarterly*, 37 (Spring 1986): 20–37, as well as Engle's essay 'Money and Moral Luck in *The Merchant of Venice*', *Shakespearean Pragmatism: Market of His Time* (Chicago: Chicago University Press, 1993): 77–106. See also Richard Posner, 'Law and Commerce in *The Merchant of Venice*', in Bradin Cormack, Martha C. Nussbaum and Richard Strier (eds), *Shakespeare and the Law: A Conversation Among Disciplines and Professions* (Chicago: University of Chicago Press, 2013): 147–55; and David Landreth, 'Dismembering the Ducat in *The Merchant of Venice*', in *The Face of Mammon: The Matter of Money in English Renaissance Literature* (Oxford: Oxford University Press, 2012): 150–83. On notions of national identity in *The Merchant of Venice*, see Laura Tosi and Shaul Bassi (eds), *Visions of Venice in Shakespeare* (Farnham: Ashgate, 2011), and Margaret Tudeau-Clayton, 'The "Trueborn Englishman": *Richard II*, *The Merchant of Venice*, and the (Future) History of the English', Willy Maley and Margaret Tudeau-Clayton (eds), *This England, That Shakespeare: New Angles on Englishness and the Bard* (Farnham: Ashgate, 2010): 63–85.

9. Charles Edelman, 'Which Is the Jew That Shakespeare Knew? Shylock on the Elizabethan Stage', *Shakespeare Survey*, 52 (1999): 99–106; Emma Smith, 'Was Shylock Jewish?' *Shakespeare Quarterly*, 64: 2 (Summer 2013): 188–219.
10. Stephen Greenblatt, 'Shakespeare & Shylock', *New York Review of Books* (30 September 2010). James Shapiro, reply by Stephen Greenblatt, 'Shylock in Red?' *New York Review of Books* (14 October 2010). James Shapiro, reply by Stephen Greenblatt, 'Shylock on Stage and Page', *New York Review of Books* (9 December 2010).
11. Smith, 'Was Shylock Jewish?'
12. Roth's opening sentence makes precisely this point: 'That Shylock was a sheer figment of Shakespeare's imagination, there has never been any doubt.' Roth, 'Background', 148. For the argument that musing about the background of fictional characters is a critical misstep, see the famous essay by L. C. Knights, 'How Many Children Had Lady Macbeth? An Essay in the Theory and Practice of Shakespeare Criticism' (1933), in *Explorations: Essays in Criticism Mainly on the Literature of the Seventeenth Century* (New York: New York University Press, 1964): 15–54.
13. Roth, 'Background', 360.
14. The popular 1701 adaptation of the play was by George Granville, entitled *The Jew of Venice*, which reframed Shylock's role as that of a laughably burlesque clown. Pope's comment, though apocryphal, is often read as a response to Macklin having finally restored Shylock to his rightful likeness as a vicious villain.
15. Roth, 'Background', 148. Roth's essay also appears in reprinted and edited form in the collection William Baker and Brian Vickers (eds), *Shakespeare and the Critical Tradition: The Merchant of Venice* (New York: Continuum, 2005). Baker and Vickers choose to omit the opening section of Roth's essay in their reprinted version, and along with it these extremely significant lines. They paraphrase the omitted material, which also contains Roth's speculations about the etymology of Shylock's name, with the heading 'Roth

16. *Two Gentlemen of Verona* is the only play that features the word 'Jew' more than once (the term appears only twice in that play).
17. Stanley Cavell, *Disowning Knowledge in Seven Plays of Shakespeare* (Cambridge: Cambridge University Press, 2003).
18. This has been the perspective of influential critics like Barbara Lewalski, whose argument on allegory in the *Merchant of Venice* patently takes Antonio at his word and reads not only Shylock but also Jewishness as an allegory for what she terms 'thrift' and 'niggardly prudence'. For Lewalski, *Merchant*'s Jewish 'thrift' and 'prudence' serve as counter-points to Christian selflessness and self-sacrificial 'venturing'. Barbara K. Lewalski, 'Biblical Allusion and Allegory in *The Merchant of Venice*', *Shakespeare Quarterly*, 13: 3 (1962): 329–30.
19. James Shapiro, *Shakespeare and the Jews* (New York: Columbia University Press, 1996).
20. Smith concludes 'Was Shylock Jewish?' by citing immigration and the problems of multicultural urban coexistence as among the most relevant topics referenced through the play's term 'Jew' (219). Smith is particularly adamant in maintaining that the semantic potential of the term 'Jew' exceeds the category of Jewishness. On *The Merchant of Venice* as a play that dramatises the circulation of social energies in early modern England, see especially John Drakakis, 'Historical Difference and Venetian Patriarchy', *The Merchant of Venice*, ed. and intro. Martin Coyle (New York: St. Martin's Press, 1998): 181–213, especially 186.
21. I rely here on Charles Taylor's very useful discussion of identity as an orientation in a space of moral questions, *Sources of the Self: The Making of Modern Identity* (Cambridge, MA: Harvard University Press, 1992).
22. Peter Erickson and Kim F. Hall, '"A New Scholarly Song": Re-reading Early Modern Race', *Shakespeare Quarterly*, 67: 1 (2016): 1–13.

23. Michael Bristol, 'Macbeth the Philosopher: Rethinking Context', *New Literary History*, 42: 4 (Autumn 2011): 651.
24. Julia Reinhard Lupton, *Citizen-Saints: Shakespeare and Political Theology* (Chicago: University of Chicago Press, 2014).
25. Daniel B. Schwartz, *The First Modern Jew: Spinoza and the History of an Image* (Princeton: Princeton University Press, 2012).
26. Hannibal Hamlin, *The Bible in Shakespeare* (Oxford: Oxford University Press, 2013).
27. Ken Jackson, *Shakespeare and Abraham* (Notre Dame: University of Notre Dame Press, 2015)
28. Smith, 'Was Shylock Jewish?' 199.
29. Anthony Grafton, 'Christian Hebraism and the Rediscovery of Hellenistic Judaism', in Richard I. Cohen, Adam Shear, and Elchanan Reiner (eds), *Jewish Culture in Early Modern Europe: Essays in Honor of David B. Ruderman* (Pittsburgh: University of Pittsburgh Press, 2014): 169–80; with Joanna Weinberg, *'I Have Always Loved the Holy Tongue': Isaac Casaubon, the Jews, and a Forgotten Chapter in Renaissance Scholarship* (Cambridge, MA: Belknap Press of Harvard University Press, 2011). Stephen Burnett, *Christian Hebraism in the Reformation Era (1500–1660: Authors, Books, and the Transmission of Jewish Learning*, vol. 19, Library of the Written Words (Leiden and Boston: Brill, 2012).
30. A selection of recent monographs includes: Miriam Jacobson, *Barbarous Antiquity: Reorienting the Past in the Poetry of Early Modern England* (Philadelphia: University of Pennsylvania Press, 2014), which addresses how non-English words reshaped Renaissance poetry; Ania Loomba, *Shakespeare, Race, and Colonialism* (Oxford: Oxford University Press, 2002), which discusses Non-Western cultures on the Renaissance stage, as does Emily Bartels, *Speaking of the Moor: From Alcazar to Othello* (Philadelphia: University of Pennsylvania Press, 2008); Lisa Jardine and Jerry Brotton, *Global Interests: Renaissance Art Between East and West* (Ithaca: Cornell University Press, 2000), which discusses the global resonances of Renaissance artworks; and Alison Games, *The Web of Empire: English*

Cosmopolitans in an Age of Expansion (Oxford: Oxford University Press, 2009), which addresses the role of travel, cosmopolitanism and global trade in the fortunes of sixteenth-century England. See also Peter Burke, *Languages and Communities in Early Modern Europe* (Cambridge: Cambridge University Press, 2004), and Paula Blank, *Broken English: Language and the Politics of Dialect in Early Modern England* (London: Routledge, 1996).

CHAPTER 1

RENAISSANCE ENGLAND AND THE JEWS

How many Jews were living in London during the time that Shakespeare wrote *The Merchant of Venice*? Historically, the question of 'how many' has often functioned as a stand-in for far less polite assertions about English identity and the imaginative space Jews have occupied within it. Rather than eliciting statements of historical fact, questions about a Jewish presence in Renaissance England instead tend to occasion assertions about who does and does not belong to a desired vision of English culture. In the opening pages of *Shakespeare and the Jews*, James Shapiro remarks that such questions are 'poor but necessary substitutes for what is really being fought over: the nature of Englishness itself and who has the right to stake a claim in it.'[1]

Historical claims about the composition of the Renaissance English population have long been bound up with a desire to fashion an account of a 'pure' English past free from any vestiges of Jewishness. It was during the Victorian era that a particularly influential narrative took shape that cast Elizabethan England as an era wholly inured to Jewish influence. This same period also saw a robust revival of *The Merchant of Venice* on the London stage when Henry Irving pioneered his performance of a moving and sympathetic Shylock at the Lyceum theatre in 1879. Irving's humanising interpretation of

Shylock's role ran for over 250 performances in its first year alone in England, and managed to garner effusive acclaim while sparking lively debates about its historical accuracy.[2] Irving's interpretation of Shylock galvanised renewed interest in the historical question of Elizabethan attitudes towards Jews. Contemporary debates over Irving's performance emphasized the point that the authentic Elizabethan Shakespeare was thoroughly devoid of any native sympathy for Jews. Ultimately, those debates helped legitimise the fiction of an English past free from affinity for Jews.[3] In 1879, a reviewer for the *Spectator* called attention to Irving's sympathetic portrayal of Shylock as a novel interpretation, one that differed significantly from Shakespeare's original characterization. 'The complex image which Mr. Irving presented to a crowd more or less impressed with notions of their own concerning the Jew whom Shakespeare drew, was entirely novel and unexpected; for here is a man whom none can despise, who can raise emotions both of pity and fear, and make us Christians thrill with a retrospective sense of shame.'[4]

The reviewer's description of Irving's stirring performance calls attention to just how sharply Irving's interpretation of the role deviated from contemporary audiences' understanding of 'the Jew that Shakespeare drew'. Despite audiences coming to the performance with 'notions of their own' about Shylock's character, the reviewer praises their capacity to register the moral sentiment of shame that Shakespeare's original audience would, he implies, have been incapable of feeling in response to a Jew. With this single economical sentence, a hard line is drawn between Irving's humanising modern performance and a very different early modern Shylock, creating a picture of the English past that excluded any vestige of sympathy for Jews and thereby also excluded their problematic presence from England's Golden Age. In her recent article, 'Was Shylock Jewish?' Emma Smith describes this account of English history as a speciously constructed yet enormously influential fiction.[5]

The conviction that England's cultural heritage was free from any native Jewish elements may have been pervasive in certain circles in the Victorian era, but it was not universally shared. Among the most trenchant critique to appear in print was that of Jewish journalist and historian Lucien Wolf, the co-founder of the Jewish Historical Society of England. Wolf's central aim was to actively promote the involvement of Jews throughout English history. Much of the work of the JHSE in its early decades under Wolf consisted of revisiting and re-theorising evidence of Jewish involvement in England's past with a particular emphasis on the early modern period preceding the readmission of the Jews in 1656. His work focused on the shift from Catholicism to Protestantism in Renaissance England, a shift that he reasoned was a crucial ingredient that helped constitute England's enduring national character.

Rather than aiming to provide a merely revised history of English Jewry as a narrow subset of English history, the JHSE under Wolf had more ambitious aims. Wolf and his colleagues endeavoured to provide an account of Jews in England that regarded their presence as central to a defining era. In Wolf's view, England's readmission of the Jews represented a moment of convergence between Christianity and Judaism that was initiated by Protestants' renewed turn to the Hebrew Bible during the Reformation.[6] In his 1893 address to the newly founded organisation, Wolf spoke to those contemporary English historians whose work effaced Jews from English history by omitting their stories from view. He argued for the importance of revisiting evidence of Judeo-Christian encounters in early modern England.

> If the movement of the Jews towards England had behind it a long chain of important historic causes, the reciprocal movement of the English people to welcome them to their shores was also the outcome of a series of events

which neither the English nor the Anglo-Jewish historian can afford to ignore. From this point of view, in fact, a very large part of English history may be said to belong to Jewish history.[7]

The model of English insular purity that Wolf's scholarship attempted to dislodge has proven to be influential, enduring, and pernicious. Janet Adelman calls attention to its persistence in the introduction to *Blood Relations,* in an anecdote, where she describes being told by a colleague at Berkeley that 'Jews shouldn't be allowed to teach Renaissance literature because Renaissance literature was Christian literature.'[8] Adelman's brilliant 2008 in-depth study of *The Merchant of Venice* is itself a trenchant refutation of such notions. In the years since it was published, scholars have further challenged insularist assumptions about England and Englishness in studies of cosmopolitanism and global exchange in the sixteenth century, which saw the flourishing of international trade and the prodigious import of foreign goods into England, including foreign words. In the more specialised domain of early modern Hebraic studies, historian Anthony Grafton's work has discussed how Jewish texts and the Hebrew language formed as integral a part of English Classicism in the Renaissance as Greek and Latin studies.[9] Classicist Stephen Burnett's recent monograph on Christian Hebraism offers a conclusive and detailed analysis of the creation and transmission of printed Hebraica during the Reformation era, where Hebrew texts became a veritable obsession in the wake of the Protestant return to original biblical writings.[10] Political theorist Eric Nelson's work is perhaps the most evident bearer of Lucien Wolf's imprint; Nelson argues that Hebraic and Talmudic modes of reasoning influenced seventeenth-century English politics as well as the American founding.[11] In the wake of such scholarship, the question has become not if but in what ways a Jewish presence was constituted in early modern England.

The question of 'how' rather than 'if' is one that this chapter addresses in the context of sixteenth-century England, a period that experienced an unprecedented growth in international trade and the import of foreign texts, commercial goods, animals, plants, and words, including Hebrew words.[12] Like Burnett's and Grafton's work, this chapter maintains that Hebrew biblical writings and the Hebrew language itself were vital sites of contact between Christians and Jews, and vital to the Christian generation of ideas about Jews and Jewishness over the course of the roughly 100-year period between the ascendancy of Henry VIII and the final decade of Elizabeth I's reign, shortly after Shakespeare wrote *The Merchant of Venice*.

Shakespeare's Jew is a figure who evokes the misery of a reviled ethnic minority. Shylock refers to his particular misery, 'the badge of all our tribe' as 'suff'rance' (1.3.107), a word that in its sixteenth-century usage denoted both pain and forbearance. However, what Shylock bears is more than just the subjective pain of what he suffers at the hands of Antonio and the Venetian justice system in *The Merchant of Venice*. He is also a bearer of antiquity, a member of an ancient tribe whose texts formed a vitally important part of early Protestant attempts at doctrinal self-definition throughout Europe. Protestants' insistent return to Judaic texts during the sixteenth century occasioned many typological readings of Hebrew Scripture, readings echoed throughout Shakespeare's comedy. However, typological reading was only one facet of the sixteenth-century return to Hebrew biblical texts. Hebrew texts and the 'Hebrews' who remained linked with them in the early modern imagination were also collaborators, tutors, and objects of anthropological curiosity and admiration. Rather than rehearsing fictions of English Renaissance purity that draw sharp dichotomies between ideals of Englishness and Jewishness, or attempting to add to recent accounts that dissect those fictions' internal logic, as James Shapiro undertakes in *Shakespeare and the Jews* and Emma Smith accomplishes in 'Was Shylock Jewish?', this chapter instead emphasises encounters and exchanges between Jews and theologians, monarchs, and translators in the sixteenth century. Early modern Englishmen recognised in Jews and their language an ancient provenance and endurance over time – precisely the forbearance and 'suff'rance' that Shylock cites. That same enduring quality that formed the basis for Jews' imperviousness to cultural assimilation in the minds of sixteenth-century Christian Hebraists also made Jews and Jewish converts vital as tutors to Christians in this period. Jewish scholars' facility with the Hebrew language and knowledge of oral and written Judaic law were highly sought-after by Renaissance Christian Hebraists.

Proficiency in Classical languages, including Hebrew, was a vital commodity in Renaissance England. When England under the direction of Henry VIII became consumed with importing and implementing humanist models of learning, the English also became invested in one of late Renaissance humanism's defining features: multilingualism.[13] The ability to communicate in multiple languages was a key skill enabling transnational exchanges during an era when the English became increasingly immersed in global commercial and cultural networks. Warren Boutcher points towards the writer John Florio as an example of the broader involvement that English writers had in transnational discursivity in the second half of the sixteenth century, describing how many of the period's humanist translators worked not only from original Classical Greek and Latin texts but also utilised French, Spanish, and other vernacular translations of Classical works as they produced new English editions. Boutcher argues that Classical and vernacular

European linguistic fluency in this period signalled an aspiration to converse as well as compete on an international stage, a priority evidenced in the ambassadorial and emissary roles occupied by so many sixteenth-century humanist translators. In this period of England's history, the mastery of languages had strategic practical importance, allowing writers and scholars to position themselves as viable participants on a global stage in a way that attempted to make up for England's insularity and relatively belated cultural advances compared to European neighbour-states like Italy and Spain.

Where does Hebrew fit into the global, competitive humanism of the sixteenth century? Although Hebrew was a far less pragmatic medium of communication than European vernacular languages or even Classical ones like Latin, Hebrew was nevertheless central to the theological landscape of the sixteenth century and English aspirations in particular. Between 1501 and 1660, approximately two thousand Christian Hebrew texts were printed across Europe.[14] Christian printings of the Hebrew Bible and biblical commentaries more than doubled in the period between 1561 and 1660, and sixteen polyglot bibles were produced during this same period, ranging from the relatively simple to the monumental London Polyglot of 1657 that contained nine different language texts on every folio page.[15] The proliferation of printed Hebraica was a direct result of Protestants' renewed interest in studying the Hebrew Bible and its rabbinic commentaries. For reform-minded theologians, returning to the original text of the Pentateuch was key to subverting Rome's authority and fashioning a new spiritual practice modelled on the Apostolic Church. Throughout the sixteenth century, both the Hebrew Bible and the Greek New Testament were being avidly studied in their original languages and translated anew across Europe in efforts to produce more accurate translations that could serve as alternatives to Jerome's Latin Vulgate. The Protestant doctrine of *sola scriptura*, or justification through Scripture alone, meant that the original texts of the Pentateuch and New Testament acquired a pivotal theological importance. Within the atmosphere of religious conflict that spanned Reformation-era Europe, sixteenth-century Christian Hebraists had pressing reasons to return to original texts, and in so doing they began to closely examine and in some cases re-examine their theological forbears. Because Judaic texts represented an increasingly important touchstone where vital spiritual questions were being actively deliberated and worked through, Judaism was therefore, as Frank Manuel claims, 'a living presence in the west even when there were no Jews'.[16]

As the aims of English humanism and Classicism in the sixteenth century became increasingly cosmopolitan, Hebrew enjoyed a unique significance because of its reputation as the primordial linguistic source from which Greek, Latin, and all European languages were imagined to derive. The study of Hebrew in sixteenth-century Europe was marked by a concern for the etymological roots of languages like English and French as well as the ontological roots of human language itself. The English scholar and Hebraist Robert Wakefield (d.1537/8) described Hebrew as the only pre-Babelian language, 'pure and whole' and uniquely uncorrupted over time.[17] He maintained that Hebrew was not only divinely sanctioned but was also the *lingua franca* of the divine, the very linguistic medium through which God conversed with Moses and in which he inscribed Mosaic law.[18] Wakefield writes:

> Although other languages are described as cultured, felicitous and expressive, this one surpasses them all, because to it have been entrusted the truly refined and sacred words

of God ... For *Jehovah*, the God of Gods, did not speak in Greek, the language in which Plato wrote, as Tullius mistakenly supposed he would, but in Hebrew, the language of Moses.[19]

Like Wakefield, many Renaissance Christian Hebraists were motivated by a desire to lay claim to Hebrew's ancient provenance. That provenance became a significant and highly sought-after source of authority for Protestants, who attempted to substantiate their own theological innovations via Hebrew scriptural precedents. However, Hebrew's antique legacy also proved problematic for Christian theologians because that legacy necessarily led back to Jews, the language's original speakers.

The reality of Christian dependence upon living Jews is reflected in the financial imperative driving *The Merchant of Venice*'s bond plot. The present-day financial ventures of Venice's Christians are only made possible through Jewish financial backing in *Merchant*, an arrangement that also characterised medieval-era relations between Christian nations and their Jewish populations across Europe. In *The Merchant of Venice*, Shylock proposes that Tubal, 'a Hebrew of my tribe' (1.3.54), will furnish him with the three thousand ducats for Antonio's loan. Shylock's use of the word 'Hebrew' here serves as a marker of Tubal's Jewish ethnic identity; however, it also recalls the alternate meaning of 'Hebrew' in the period as language. In the case of both the Hebrews' financial assets sought out by Antonio and Bassanio in the play, and the Hebrew language that Christian Hebraists sought to master in the sixteenth century, the acquisition of key, desired commodities lay through contact with living 'Hebrews' or Jews. That dependence made it impossible for Renaissance Christian Hebraists to relegate Jews to the ancient past as dead relics. Although the provenance of their language and, as I discuss shortly, their material constitutions were venerated for their ancient pedigree, Jews were also an insistently present reality for Renaissance Christian Hebraists.

Hebrew's double-meaning in this period, signalling both language and ethnology, recalls the difficulty of erasing Jews from their language. That difficulty persisted for Christian Hebraists despite ongoing attempts to disavow Hebrew's connection to the Jewish people. Although Hebrew was described as a language that could exist independently of Jews – capable of being taught, learned, and mastered in ways that restored it to its original purity, which some Hebraists claimed had been corrupted by Jews over time[20] – the study of Hebrew in this period also reflected the impossibility of effectively detaching Hebrew from its Judaic origins.

The contradictions inherent in the notion of a Hebrew language without Jews became strikingly apparent for sixteenth-century Christian Hebraists who were highly dependent on 'Hebrews', that is Jewish scholars or recent converts, to teach them the language, a predicament that was nearly universal in this period across Europe.

In addition to these logistical dynamics, there were other ways in which the Hebrew language and its Jewish provenance remained strongly linked in the minds of Renaissance Christians in ways that problematised any neat separation of Hebrew from Jews. In *The Merchant of Venice*'s only other reference to the term 'Hebrew', Antonio jokes to Bassanio that the unusually generous terms of Shylock's loan indicate that '[t]he Hebrew will turn Christian; he grows kind' (1.3.175). Antonio's joke hinges on the impossibility of a Jew actually 'turning' Christian, or becoming kin with non-Jews. The notion that Jews were incapable of erasing their origins acquires particular poignancy in the play through Jessica's conversion and marriage plot. Launcelot Gobbo, Gratiano, and even Lorenzo, Jessica's fiancé, each remind Jessica that her conversion from Jew to Christian is no *fait accompli*, a fact further emphasised through the play's failure to stage her conversion. She is referred to at various points as Lorenzo's 'infidel' (3.2.216) and as 'stranger' (3.2.235), described as 'issue to a faithless Jew' (2.4.37) and told that her only salvation lies in the hope that 'you are not the Jew's daughter' (3.5.10).

Janet Adelman's illuminating discussion of these scenes argues that *Merchant*'s recurrent emphasis on Jessica's Jewish paternity and obsessive return to her Jewishness as an inescapable problem (one that is continually being rehearsed by the very Christians who facilitate her absconsion) serves as a reminder that within the play's economy of religious difference, Jessica can never in fact 'turn' Christian because of the perception that she, like her father, has Jewish 'blood'.[21]

Adelman's account of proto-racialised attempts to distinguish Christians from Jews in *The Merchant of Venice* develops the exclusionary implications of Jews as a distinct people, implications that were available to Shakespeare's sixteenth-century English audience and reinforced by the scriptural bond imagined to exist between Christians and Jews. In *Blood Relations*, Adelman discusses how Jews signified 'strangers within' Elizabethan England, perpetually unwanted others with which Elizabethans could never entirely dispense due to their ongoing reliance on a shared set of sacred writings and shared biblical ancestry.[22] When Antonio pronounces to Bassanio, 'The Hebrew [i.e. Shylock] will turn Christian; he grows kind,' he simultaneously asserts the impossibility of a Jew ever becoming properly Christian while suggesting at the looming threat of him doing just that. One way he might succeed in accomplishing this, according to Antonio's equation, is by exhibiting moral kindness, a path to which Jessica adheres as a means of distinguishing herself from her father, as when she pronounces 'But though I am a daughter to his blood / I am not to his manners' (2.3.18–19). The other interpretive possibility suggested by Antonio's line is that Shylock grows 'kind' in the sense of becoming kin with Antonio. In fact, Shylock recalls the source of their ancient kinship throughout this scene when he references Hebrew biblical episodes to sort out the details of the bond, citing the stories of Jacob and Esau and Jacob and Laban, who were often discussed as figures for Jewish and Christian nations in early modern writing.

What the play manages to reinforce through its emphasis on distinctions of blood is the desire to have Jews remain perpetually unassimilable into genteel Venetian Christian life; however, in so doing, it implicitly recalls the lingering problem of ongoing kinship and the proximity between Christians and Jews, sourced in the very biblical texts that Christians were attempting to appropriate. Jews were marked as both ineradicable perpetual aliens and also irrevocably close cousins reminding Christians of their secondary, belated status relative to their Jewish forbears.[23]

Adelman has discussed this aspect of the play with remarkable clarity and insight in *Blood Relations*, addressing how and why those contradictions recur in *Merchant*'s plot and language. However, it is important to also register how early modern English writers expressed other types of responses to Jewish difference, including admiration and praise. As inextricable as Jews were from the complex picture of Christian self-understanding in the Renaissance, so were admiration and condemnation tightly imbricated in many of the period's responses to Jews. In the 1594 English translation of the Spaniard Juan Huarte's text 'The Examination of Mens Wits', Jews are cited for their remarkable resilience over time and ability to progress through history with their characteristic strengths and proclivities intact.[24] Huarte ponders the question of Jewish constancy over time by wondering how a people can retain their defining features despite a long history predicated upon geographical and climatological displacements. How can Jewish people remain constant in their dispositions, Huarte asks, after 'drinking divers waters, and from not using all of them one kind of food?'[25] Huarte's interest in the constitution of Jewishness is explored materially and geohumorally: he wants to know how Jews have been able to migrate from region to region without being significantly altered by each new environment, and he seeks to determine which locale's characteristics were responsible for their unique traits. His inquiry adopts the language of Galenic humoral psychology to discuss the intricacies of the Jewish diet (including the possibility that manna may have contributed to their constancy over time), the air quality of the desert during their wanderings in the Sinai, and 'what meat they did eat, what water they dranke, and of what temperature the aire was where they trauailed'.[26]

The fact that Jews were regarded as impervious to the effects of local ecosystems and as foreigners not subject to the influence of their neighbours is, of course, wrong from a strictly factual perspective, but these assumptions nevertheless carry important implications for our understanding of English cultural response to Jews and their writings in the sixteenth century. Even amid efforts to assimilate Hebrew biblical works and the Hebrew language, English encounters with living 'Hebrews' continued to evoke ways in which Jews and their language proved resistant to cultural assimilation. The English travel writer Thomas Coryat figures this as a characteristic form of Jewish 'unruliness', which he describes in his observations of a Venetian synagogue whose religious services were full of 'an exceeding loud yaling, undecent roaring, and as it were a beastly bellowing of it forth'.[27] Where difference was understood to be a persistent feature of Jewish identity, that difference could sometimes be a mark of distinction, as it is in Huarte's account. Coryat also notes that the Venetian Jews he encountered were 'most elegant and sweet-featured persons', in contrast to the pervasive stereotypes that described Jews as 'sometimes a weather beaten warp-faced fellow, sometimes a phreneticke and a lunaticke person, sometimes one discontented'.²⁸ Jews were both eminently frustrating to Christians who pressed for their mass conversion, as Coryat does when he writes about his encounters with them in *Coryats Crudities*, but they are often too a source of fascination, as they are in Huarte's account, precisely because of their stubborn refusal to be readily influenced.

Due to their reputation for enduring extensive hardships and geographical displacements over thousands of years, Jews and their Hebrew language also signalled a complex relationship to time for early modern Christians. In the early modern imagination, Jews signalled a resistance to what Jonathan Gil Harris terms the 'temporality of supersession,' in which the present is prioritised to the exclusion of other temporalities, especially the past.²⁹ Jews were renowned for their antique pedigree; their culture, language, and learning was invested with a value imagined to have been accrued since the dawn of creation. This antiquity was uniquely compelling to Protestants in particular, who longed for the validation and authority that came from those ancient origins, and who sought to pre-empt the established authority of the Roman Catholic Church by returning to the early apostolic church to generate a providential vision of a reformed Christian future.

The Hebrew language also functioned as a sign of Jews' cultural and ethnological antiquity, connecting them with the first man and the Garden of Eden. Hebrew's appearance in England indicated the persistence of the various strata of the past whose traces remained visible in the present.³⁰ Harris's discussion of Renaissance 'untimeliness' argues that Renaissance English culture was deeply invested not in the 'temporality of supersession' wherein objects' and spaces' pasts were subjected to erasure by newer, present-day innovations. Rather, he claims, texts like John Stow's

1598 *Survey of London* mapped the polychronous nature of the city. The Hebrew inscriptions that Stow discovers on Ludgate's crumbling city wall and then transcribes into his survey, first in Hebrew, then in Latin translation, and finally in English, are reflective of a sensibility that was sharply attuned to the juxtaposition of multiple temporalities and complex interplay between them. Hebrew is particularly evocative of those multiple layers because of its reputation as a primary ur-language, but in Stow's account it is also explicitly connected to the social and political history of London whose Jewish quarter is revealed in the traces of Hebrew writing that Stowe transcribes.[31] Stow writes of that history:

> I reade that in the year 1215. the 6 of king *Iohn*, the Barons entering the City by *Ealdgate*, first tooke assurance of the Citizens, then brake into the Jewes houses, searched their coffers to fill their owne purses, and after with great diligence repaired the walles and gates of the Citie, with stones taken from the Jewes broken houses.[32]

The Hebrew inscription narrates the overlaid, disassembled past of London's long-absent Jews, an absence that Stow makes present once again through his narration of their history and successive translations of the inscription. Rendering the inscriptions into Latin and then English rehearses the progressive stratifications and transformations accrued over multiple time periods, like the stones from the Jews' homes that were re-purposed and turned into city walls.

Rather than marking something that needed to be erased, the ancient pedigree accorded to Jews and to Hebrew in this period constituted a mark of distinction and complexity that the English had a desire to excavate and preserve. The recent emphasis in early modern scholarship on anti-Semitic slander and invidious cultural stereotypes that circulated about Renaissance Jews describing them as well poisoners and ritual murderers in fact only reflects a partial sense of how Jews and Judaic culture, language, and theology were being encountered, evaluated and made present within English culture in the early modern period.[33] A fuller account of their significance must include the integrity ascribed to them in texts like Huarte's *Examination of Mens Wits*, and the trans-temporal dimensionality that followed from their ancient pedigree, a pedigree that made the study of Hebrew particularly alluring to Christians in this period, and also linked that pursuit to the history and experience of living Jews.

There were also important practical exigencies tied to the sixteenth-century study of Hebrew that contributed to a newly dimensional understanding of Jewish culture and appreciation for the humanity of Jews among Renaissance Christians. In late medieval Europe, staged theological disputations between Christians and Jews had the aim of humiliating Jews on their own Scriptural terrain, the Hebrew Bible.[34] Renaissance encounters with Jews that centred on the Hebrew Bible tended to reflect new prerogatives and dynamics that included collaboration. One of the key prompts for those shifts was practical need. Larger numbers of Christians, mostly Protestants but also Catholics, were interested in learning Hebrew in the sixteenth century, driven by the imperative to study the Hebrew Bible in its original language. Christian scholars depended on the efforts of Jewish tutors and recent converts to instruct them.[35] These educational relationships and the close study of Jewish traditions, theology, and culture undertaken by the era's foremost Christian scholars had the effect of generating increased familiarity, even intimacy with Jews. Although that familiarity could still form the basis for incisive persecution, it often generated a sense of respect for Jewish scholarship and even fraternity with Jewish people and the world of Jewish learning.

The Hebraist Robert Wakefield exemplifies both a typically condemning posture as well as the complicating contradictions that attended Christian Hebraists' relationships with Jews and their language and theology in the sixteenth century. In his 1524 text *Oratio de laudibus et utilitate trium linguarum*, Wakefield argues that the study of Hebrew affords an opportunity for Christians to better equip themselves for theological disputation with Jews. Wakefield articulates the familiar medieval claim that studying the Bible in Hebrew allowed Christians to position themselves to distinct advantage relative to Jews in order to better dispute Jewish interpretive claims. The idea was to do this with a more complete knowledge of the original text of the Hebrew Bible and its hermeneutic implications.[36] The underlying belief that Jews fundamentally misunderstood their own Scripture, a belief evidently shared by Antonio in act 1, scene 3 of *The Merchant of Venice* when he pronounces that Shylock has misread the parable of the particoloured lambs, also underwrites contemporary discussions of Hebrew as a fundamentally universal language of Christian truth from which Jews were imagined to be excluded.[37]

It was by necessity that English theologians sought out the assistance of Jewish tutors; however, those encounters often generated a sense of closeness and even sympathy with Jews and their world of theological scholarship. In the *Oratio*, Wakefield lavishes praise on the Jewish grammarians who hosted him abroad and assisted his Hebrew studies, and throughout his treatise he extols medieval Jewish theologians and their exegetical and grammatical expertise, naming the eleventh-century Torah commentator Rashi as a particularly praiseworthy authority.[38] Indeed, one of the striking features of Wakefield's text is its continual and unwaveringly positive referencing of rabbinical authorities as well as its ample use of Hebrew expressions, aphorisms and turns of phrase. At various points the *Oratio* becomes a veritable showcase of Hebraic learning highlighting the excellence of Hebraic materials as well as Wakefield's own grasp of them.[39]

Accounts such as Wakefield's illustrate how Judeo-Christian encounters often succeeded in generating complex, ambivalent attitudes towards Jews, attitudes that on the one hand reflected medieval tropes of conversion-through-acquaintance while on the other signalled a far more dimensional appreciation of Jews and their theological and exegetical legacy. The Protestant desire to plumb Judaic texts succeeded in not only opening up new paths of reformed worship for Christians; it also brought Jews to life in three dimensions in ways that challenged many of the textual stereotypes penned during the medieval period.

The roots of Renaissance Christian Hebraism in England are primarily located abroad in Continental Europe, where the Christian study of Hebraic texts first began in Italy under Petrarch.[40] In Petrarch's view, biblical writings were first and foremost poetic works to be treated in much the same ways as other works of poetry, approached philologically and through questions of stylistic integrity and beauty. Increasingly over the course of the fifteenth century, other humanist scholars began turning to Jerome's Latin Vulgate with questions about its lack of stylistic appeal and its inaccuracies. Questions about the Vulgate were framed through the kinds of intensely language-focused queries that humanists applied to other texts and the same focused philological inquiries into the ways in which the texts of the Bible had been edited, translated, and copied.

While the seeds of initial interest in Hebrew germinated early in the fifteenth century in Italy out of a desire to convert Jews by first learning their sacred language, the central impetus to study Hebrew soon acquired independent scholarly motivation in the fifteenth and sixteenth centuries. Giannozzo Manetti (1396–1459), ambassador at Florence and secretary to Pope Nicholas V in Rome, was among the first of the humanists to learn Hebrew. With the help of Jewish scholars, Manetti began to study the Hebrew Bible in the mid-fifteenth century. He intended to offer a new translation that differed from the Latin Vulgate, and his efforts culminated in the creation of the first printed multiple-language psalter that enabled readers to compare different versions of the text. In the copy of the psalter that Manetti presented to the king of Naples, he provided a new translation of the Hebrew beside a pair of translations attributed to Jerome. One drew directly from the Hebrew and one was based on the Greek Septuagint. This formal innovation of facing dual-language bible editions proved enormously influential to subsequent humanist scholarship and new translations of the Bible undertaken by humanists.

England's belated embrace of humanist curricula and methods in the mid-sixteenth century meant that it was in a position to benefit greatly from the precedents set by Continental humanists. Innovative academic curricula and educational reforms such as those brought to the trilingual humanist college at Louvain, which was largely inspired by Erasmus' ideas, served as important models for English scholars interested in bringing humanist learning to English universities. Among the most important of these Continental models for the English was Francisco Jiménez de Cisneros's (1436–1517) curriculum at the University of Alcalá. Jiménez revised the theological programme at Alcalá with a view towards training a new generation of Spanish clerics versed in the original languages of the Bible, including Hebrew. His efforts culminated in the assembly and publication of the much-imitated Complutensian Polyglot Bible, the first of its kind to draw substantively on Manetti's prototype and offer side-by-side versions of text in a single volume. The Complutensian Bible managed to negotiate sensitive theological terrain deftly by steering clear of blaming Jerome for the Vulgate's many errors – a great priority for the Catholic Jiménez – while also offering readers access to multiple versions of the text that provided alternatives to the Vulgate translation. The six-volume bible, printed between 1514 and 1517 and published in 1522, also included the works of three converted Jews who prepared sections of the Hebrew text: Pablo Coronel, Alfonso de Toledo, and Alfonso de Zamora. Zamora, a Jewish convert who had been educated in Northern Spain, was appointed by Jiménez to serve as the first professor of Hebrew at Alcalá in 1508.

Jiménez's Continental example set several precedents that influenced theologians and scholars across Continental Europe and in England for the next hundred years, including the appeal to original biblical sources as a way of undercutting Jerome's Catholic Latin translation, enlisting the assistance of Jewish exegetes to help read and interpret the text, and producing polyglot bibles that undertook to improve upon and supplant the Complutensian Bible through the addition of more foreign language texts.[41]

During the early decades of the sixteenth century in England, humanist scholars looked to European Hebrew studies for an opportunity to implement domestic educational reforms within English universities. In reality, few sixteenth-century English scholars possessed linguistic proficiency in Hebrew, even among those Hebraists who, like Robert Wakefield, argued for implementing Hebrew education at Cambridge and Oxford. Wakefield's own story is a testament to English Hebraist ambitions being outweighed by a lack of domestic expertise in the early decades of the sixteenth century. Although he was appointed the first professor of divinity at St John's College, Cambridge in 1524, Wakefield spent the years preceding his appointment abroad acquiring the requisite proficiency in Hebrew and Arabic. Educated at the Dutch trilingual humanist college at Louvain where he acquired an MA degree, Wakefield lectured at Louvain in 1519 before returning to England and to Cambridge for several years after which he again went abroad, taking up a Hebrew lectureship at Tübingen in 1522 as successor to Europe's pre-eminent Christian Hebraist Johannes Reuchlin.[42]

English Hebraists such as Wakefield formed part of a small international European community of Classical and Oriental language scholars during the early 1600s, a community that numbered as few as seventy-three men.[43] Oxford's Corpus Christi College was founded on the aspiration of providing a trilingual education in Greek, Latin, and Hebrew modelled on Continental European universities such as Louvain and Alcalá, but the curriculum at Oxford did not actually include much Hebrew instruction, nor did Oxford have in its collections many Hebrew books until midway through the sixteenth century.[44]

The situation at Cambridge underwent a dramatic change when John Fisher (1469–1535), Bishop of Rochester, was awarded the chancellorship in 1504.[45] Fisher was a cleric noted for his intellectualism and love of learning; he patronised leading Continental scholars such as Erasmus, who stood at the forefront of Classical and Hebraic studies. Fisher was an admirer and personal friend of Erasmus, whose newly published, immensely popular edition of the New Testament provided readers with the Greek text alongside a newly revised text of the Vulgate.[46] Under Fisher's directorship Erasmus was appointed the first teacher of Greek at Cambridge in 1511 and resided there until 1514, coinciding with Fisher's presidency. Like Erasmus, Fisher was convinced of the necessity of studying biblical texts in their original languages; his personal collection included a Hebrew Bible by the famed Venetian printer Daniel Bomberg as well as Pagninus' Hebrew lexicon, which he later bequeathed to the university.[47]

It was Fisher who acted as the main agent of humanist curriculum reform at Cambridge. Early in the 1510s he succeeded first and foremost because he was a well-connected and effective fund-raiser for his cause. He secured the patronage of Henry VII's mother Lady Margaret Beaufort whose funds eventually furnished the endowment for St John's College. Although there was considerable dispute over Lady Margaret's endowment in the months immediately preceding the

Renaissance England and the Jews

College's founding with both her servants and the king vying to obtain portions of it for themselves, Fisher eventually succeeded in obtaining most of the money (though Henry took a large share for himself) and applied it to St John's, which opened in April of 1511. Fisher drew up its statutes, which established an important place for the study of Hebrew and Greek and attempted to implement a programme of immersion study. The statutes even went so far as to specify that all students must converse in Hebrew, Greek, or Latin at all times except during their private hours spent in their rooms or during feast days.[48]

John Fisher's plans to develop Hebrew scholarship at Cambridge aimed at cultivating a comprehensive trilingual Classics programme on English soil, and he managed in the early days of St John's' founding to secure funds from the king to create lectureships in Greek and Hebrew and eventually establish the permanent professorship in Hebrew first occupied by Robert Wakefield. The new model of higher learning that included Latin, Greek, and Hebrew enjoyed powerful though by no means universal support from individuals at court and within ecclesiastical circles during Henry VIII's reign, most notably from Henry himself.

The king's embrace of Hebrew and Greek is exemplified in a 1545 commemorative medal celebrating Henry's declaration as head of the Church, inscribed with Latin on the obverse and Greek and Hebrew on the reverse, detailing proclamations of the king's glory (see Figures 1.1 and 1.2). The Latin inscription on the face of the coin reads as follows:

> HENRICVS . OCTA . ANGLIÆ . FRANCI . ET . HIB . REX .
> FIDEI . DEFENSOR . ET . IN . TERR . ECCLE . ANGLI .
> ET . HIBE . SVB . CHRIST . CAPVT . SVPREMVM.
>
> (Henry VIII, King of England, France, and Ireland, defender of the faith, and under Christ the supreme head on earth of the Church of England and Ireland.)

Figure 1.1 Gold portrait medal, obverse, featuring bust of Henry VIII, 1545. © The Trustees of the British Museum.

Figure 1.2 Gold portrait medal, reverse, featuring Greek and Hebrew script, 1545. © The Trustees of the British Museum

The medal was struck as a commemoration of Henry's sovereignty over the state as well as the Church of England, a fact formally proclaimed by Parliament in January of 1535.⁴⁹ This medal was followed by a similar one commissioned by Edward VI following the same trilingual model.⁵⁰

The king's Supremacy medal and its trilingual inscriptions highlight several key aspects of Christian Hebraism under Henry VIII, most importantly the looming figure of Henry himself who served as the single most significant agent driving England's embrace of Hebrew studies in this early period. The institutional embrace of Hebrew studies was a direct function of Henry's own wilful programming and his political aspirations. Under his rule, English universities increasingly began to regard Hebrew as a third Classical language to be studied alongside Greek and Latin, despite ongoing anxieties about its judaising influence. It was during this same period that England saw an increasing turn towards the study of original texts. This turn was especially significant to the study of the Bible in England, an enterprise bound up with the king's own efforts to re-shape England's religious landscape.

The study of Hebrew and the solicitation of rabbinical opinion on matters of biblical interpretation during Henry VIII's reign were closely bound up with Henry's own political, religious, and intellectual ambitions and, most importantly, with his divorce. John Fisher's life and its abrupt end at the sharp blade of an executioner's axe in 1535 attests to the complex role and place of Hebrew within English Reformation-era politics. In a cruelly ironic twist, Fisher, the man directly responsible for implementing the curriculum that first made Hebrew studies a reality in England, ultimately fell out of favour with the king over the Great Matter of his divorce. Fisher refused to abate his support for Catherine of Aragon and remained among her primary intellectual advocates throughout her trial. He paid dearly for his refusal to sanction Henry's divorce or recognise the king's self-appointment as head of the Church. In June of 1535 he was sentenced to death and beheaded, a punishment that spared him only the grislier forms of execution typically reserved for heretics.

Robert Wakefield's relationship to the king's divorce also attests to the volatile connection between politics and Hebrew studies under Henry. Following the 1528 publication of his *Paraphrasis in Librum Koheleth*, a paraphrase of the Hebrew text of Ecclesiastes, Wakefield was introduced to the king in the belief that his Hebrew skills might prove valuable to Henry's efforts to secure a divorce from Catherine. It was during this period that Wakefield provided Hebrew instruction to Ann Boleyn's uncle James Boleyn as well as to Reginald Pole, the Archbishop of York. However, during the period of his initial residency at Cambridge, Wakefield had sided with Fisher and against the king's divorce. He was to eventually part with Fisher over it. As two of an extremely rarefied group of English scholars proficient in Hebrew, both Wakefield and Fisher butted heads over the use and interpretation of Hebrew Scripture throughout the 1520s. By 1530, Wakefield had moved from Cambridge under Fisher to a new position at Oxford, where he utilised his knowledge of Hebrew and Hebraic Scriptures to try to help the king build a justification for his divorce founded in Mosaic law.

Henry's turn to Mosaic law to establish grounds for divorcing Catherine of Aragon formed an early and important part of his strategy for disposing of her in the interests of marrying Ann Boleyn. One extant 1527 manuscript work by Wakefield attests to Henry's early use of Hebrew Scripture as part of his official campaign to secure a divorce.[51] Throughout Henry's reign, the study of Jewish theology was prompted by a driving need to bypass Rome's authority as well as the authority of the Latin Vulgate by engaging directly with the original Hebrew Bible and its exegetical commentaries. Rabbinic scholars and their skills were still very much required for these kinds of efforts in the sixteenth century. Explanations of Hebrew Bible passages and discussions of Mosaic law in the sixteenth century were almost always furnished by Jews or recent converts; it was not until the seventeenth century that Christian theologians had the proficiency to independently study the text of the Hebrew Bible without Jewish assistance.

England's solicitation of collaborative assistance from Jews during the early sixteenth century was spearheaded by Henry's turn to rabbinical opinion in the Great Matter. In 1529 Henry solicited the opinions of academics across Europe in an attempt to formulate a convincing case for authorising his divorce. However, the Pope stood by Mosaic law to defend the integrity of Catherine's marriage to Henry. When none of the initial opinions Henry procured managed to convince the Pope to change his position, Henry solicited further evidence from six Jewish authorities, among them Mark Raphael, a converted Venetian Jew and Hebraist.[52] In 1530 Henry sent for Raphael, who reached England in January of 1531 despite an attempt by the Spanish ambassador Chapuys to sabotage his trip. Raphael's initial deliberation, as reported by Chapuys, advanced the unlikely suggestion of polygamous marriage as a solution to Henry's problems, stating that Jewish law made a provision for husbands to take on supplemental wives when a first wife fails to produce a male heir. The Spanish ambassador's account of that deliberation explains:

> [T]he Queen's marriage ought not to be disputed, but nevertheless ... the King may and can very well take another wife conjointly with his first ... Although the King's marriage with the widow of his brother was a true and legitimate act, yet he does not style himself properly husband of the Queen, inasmuch as, according to Jewish law, the posterity issue from such union is ascribed to the first husband;

and, as it would be unreasonable that, in order to preserve the name and race of the deceased, the survivor should be prevented from having posterity of his own, the law allows him to take another wife.[53]

Unhappily surprised by this first verdict, Henry urged Raphael to return to Mosaic law to find another means of resolving his predicament. Raphael's second verdict provided a resolution more satisfactory to the king; it seized on the issue of a man's intention to fortify his family line, an intention that could be lawfully satisfied by marrying a brother's widow and producing offspring. Raphael reasoned that in the absence of such an intention, no offspring would be produced. Catherine's failure to produce viable male heirs with Henry proved a lack of requisite intention, and the marriage was thereby subject to dissolution. According to Chapuys' report, Raphael reasoned that:

> It is allowable for a man to take to wife the widow of his brother, provided he do it out of his own desire and will, and with the direct intention of procuring descent to his brother's line. Without such marked intention, the marriage is forbidden by divine law. God said so by the mouth of Moses, and cast his malediction on all those who married without such an intention, for if they did so marry, no generation could spring forth from them, and if any, it could not last long. And as the male children begot by the King in the Queen had not lived long, the King must have married his brother's widow without the above express intention, and consequently his marriage is illegitimate and invalid.[54]

Raphael's opinion was included in a collection of deliberations handed over to Parliament. The king was allegedly so pleased with Raphael's service that he bestowed considerable favour on him in the years following. Raphael accompanied Henry on his journey to France in 1532, where state records indicate a series of payments – 'expenses' and 'rewards' – to him, including a 1532 document indicating that 'Mr. Mark Raphael of Venice' was granted a licence by the crown to import 600 tons of Gascon wine and Toulouse wood.[55]

Henry VIII's collaboration with Jewish exegetes on the issue of his divorce was a strategic move calculated to bypass Rome's authority and locate alternate precedents for divorce or annulment in Mosaic law. His appeal to Hebrew Scripture also evidenced a self-conscious embrace of a humanist ideal, reflecting the king's self-styled image as a wise and powerful philosopher-king who solicited advice from a variety of noble traditions. In this aspect, Henry's turn towards Judaic exegetes represented a nod towards a cosmopolitan humanism in the tradition of other great humanist monarchs, notably Lorenzo de Medici.[56]

The trial proceedings surrounding Henry's divorce and his solicitation of a variety of learned opinions, including Judaic ones, offered opportunities for Henry to construct the appearance of a judicious, philosophically minded leader who carefully weighed a series of arguments before creating policy. Henry's preferred rhetorical form, the philosophical inquiry into a general question, was a format that diffused the potential for direct or personal blame of any of the king's particular actions by de-emphasising his personal stake in decisions while emphasising the triumph of abstract virtues such as justice, wisdom, and prudence. The trials surrounding the king's divorce evidenced just this strategy. Henry cited as cause for the proceedings against Catherine his concern for the state's well-being, concerns that he described as plagues upon his conscience that pressed against his strong personal affections for Catherine.[57]

That same model of strong humanist leadership concentrated in the hands of a judicious monarch also facilitated state-sponsored immersion into Hebrew language studies and the solicitation of rabbinical opinion concerning the king's divorce during the early decades of the sixteenth century. As Fisher's and Wakefield's cases attest, in very direct ways the careers of humanist scholars in England were dependent on having the right kinds of political affiliations and loyalties to the king. Wakefield's move from Cambridge and an affiliation with the soon-to-be-executed Fisher to Oxford where he quickly rescinded his former allegiances and supported the king's divorce proved to be politically rewarding for Wakefield, whose salary at Cambridge had amounted to 100s. in 1528. At Oxford the following year he was paid in excess of £6.

Humanist scholarship and the ambitions of powerful heads of state definitively shaped the course of Hebrew studies across Europe in the first half of the sixteenth century. The 1563 Council of Trent, which brought a decisive split between Roman Catholicism and Protestant dissenters, afforded the crucial impetus for vast numbers of Protestants and also, to a certain degree, Catholics to turn to the study of Hebrew texts with fresh urgency. In the decades that followed, Protestant universities in cities such as Paris became centres for Christian Hebraist instruction, scholarship, and book publication. Burnett explains that

> for the first time in the history of the church a large community of Christian readers came into being who needed Hebrew books of many kinds in order to pursue their interests and tasks. A new class of Christian Hebrew authors, most of them Christians from birth, but some Jewish converts, worked mightily to create the texts needed for these readers to do so.[58]

Although the religious turmoil and rapid succession of monarchs that followed after the death of Henry VIII created a tenuous theological climate in England, Hebrew studies remained a strong and relatively stable academic curriculum offered at Cambridge and Oxford through the sixteenth and seventeenth centuries, particularly in comparison with other European universities.[59]

Hebrew Studies under Henry VIII reflected a sustained effort to engage with the original text of the Hebrew Bible, enabling the king and those who secured his sponsorship to actualise Henry's political aspirations and fashion his public persona as a powerful monarch in the tradition of a Florentine humanist prince. Henry's 1545 Supremacy Medal also referenced an Italian model through the medium of the portrait medal itself, which was intended to resemble an antique coin. Like a coin, the image of the figure's head functioned as a stamp of authority and power.[60] Hugely popular in Italy, portrait medals circulated rapidly across Europe and constituted highly desirable and collectable elite luxury goods in the fifteenth and sixteenth centuries. These medals also held important cultural value in the Ottoman Empire, and as Lisa Jardine and Jerry Brotton discuss, these objects' Eastern provenance was bound up with some of the most important prototypes of the form in fifteenth-century Italy.[61] Henry VIII's Supremacy Medal denotes English aspirations of mastery over the Classical past while recalling England's immersion into an increasingly global political scene, invoked in the words of the medal's inscription and through its inclusion of Greek and Hebrew.

Under Elizabeth I, England's engagement with exogamous cultures and their wares became increasingly significant to English success. Englishness in this period was increasingly being constructed via commodities, words, and prototypes that originated far from English shores, including poetic forms as quintessential as the sonnet, whose origins Roland Greene has traced to Persian and Arab literary cultures.[62] With the growth of international trade through the expansion of existing trading companies and the formation of England's first joint-stock companies, imports were flooding English markets with foreign goods to an even greater degree than before in the later decades of the sixteenth century.

Prized imports such as tulips and horses were still explicitly designated by their foreign names – Turkish in the case of tulips and Arabian for horses.[63]

In the book trade, Hebrew became an important ingredient in the marketing of biblical writings to the English reading public. New translations of the Bible increasingly began to appear with the amended claim of having been newly rendered in consultation with original Greek and Hebrew texts. Hebrew became part of the selling of antiquity to England's reading public through a growing number of Hebrew language indexes, dictionaries, and biblical commentaries containing transliterated Hebrew words and even Hebrew type that had been imported from printers in Italy.

The pages of translated texts served as important threshold sites for encounters with imported ideas, words, and writers, particularly in prefaces that introduced Classical works to English readers and patrons. Sixteenth-century prefaces to Classical works in English valorised the cultural power and sophistication that was imagined to accrue from close contact with non-English poetic voices. In prefaces and epistles, authors cautioned readers and aristocratic patrons against resisting foreign books, urging them to embrace non-English texts as fortifying tonics. Thomas Wilson's 1570 English translation of *Three Orations of Demosthenes* imagines such texts inspiring the kind of cultural flourishing experienced in Italy and France in previous centuries. Wilson advocates a cosmopolitan embrace of diverse cultural goods, advising English readers to seek 'excellencye' wherever it may reside.

> And who can ever come to any such excellencye that doth not acquaynte himselfe first wyth the best, yea and seeketh to followe the chiefest that have traveyled in those thinges, the perfection whereof hee wysheth to get. So did Plato in tyme traveyle from Greece into Aegypt; Aristotell from Stagira in Macedonie, to Athens in Greece to hear

his Maister Plato; and Cicero from Rome to Athens; and Anacharsis that barbarous Scythian to talke with Solon the wyse law maker of Athens, seeking every one of them the best abrode, when they could not have them at home.[64]

Travel is central to the Classical exemplars that Wilson cites. The pursuit of virtue and education, he declares, obeys neither geographical nor temporal restrictions; it represents an international, transgenerational undertaking. Wilson appeals to English audiences to seek out the finest models and sources available regardless of location, while strongly implying that such examples are to be found 'abrode' rather than domestically.

The sixteenth-century imperative to encounter and then import non-English texts into England remained bound up with the sixteenth-century trope of embarrassment over English cultural backwardness and the impoverished state of the English language, which John Clapham described in his 1589 translation of Plutarch as a 'poore Englishe weed', and William Barker designated a 'grosse tongue ... a rude and barren tonge' in his preface to his 1589 English edition of Xenophon.[65] English prefaces often insisted that foreign goods should be embraced because valuable intellectual commodities were necessarily located outside of England and needed to be imported in order for the English people, along with the English language, to reap the benefits. The embrace of foreign texts was sometimes framed as a plea for cultural toleration of foreigners, as when Philemon Holland's epistle to Queen Elizabeth in his 1600 edition of Livy's *Roman Historie* impels her to 'vouchsafe also of your accustomed clemencie shewed to aliens', and

> reach forth your gracious hand to T. Livius who, having arrived long since & converted as a mere stranger to this your lland, & now for love thereof learned in some sort

the language, humbly craveth your majesties favour, to be ranged with other free denizens of that kind: so long to live under your princely protection, as he shalle duly keepe his own allegeance, and acquaint your lieges subjects with religious devotion after his manner, with wisdome, policy, virtue, vallor, loyalty, and not otherwise.[66]

Holland describes Livy's text as the personification of the author's spirit that has wandered from country to country spreading wisdom and currently desires to settle among the English. England would be enriched by embracing the itinerant Livy's work, figured in Holland's account as a well-travelled refugee who 'hath made a voyage by Florence into the same Fraunce and Spaine: and has passed as far as into Arabia one way & Almaine another.'[67] Welcoming Livy's work into England means acquiring the expertise of the many places he and his text have 'traveled' and been translated into vernacular languages. The implication is that it is now England's turn, and in hosting Livy's globally itinerant text, England is positioned to reap the benefits of its cosmopolitan expertise and the wisdom of its worldly wanderings through Italy, France, Germany, and Arabia.

Holland implicitly casts England's reception of Livy's work as a belated one, but that belatedness constitutes a distinct advantage precisely because it positions the English to reap the accrued wisdom and expertise of Livy's long westward migration. By importing such a well-travelled text, Holland suggests that there is no need to go abroad, since England can import Classical voices and derive practical, even strategic value from these texts' long 'travels' through other nations and time periods. England is prepared, Holland asserts, and well-positioned to benefit by importing the intellectual and cultural riches of Classical voices to its shores. Holland incites his readers, 'let it now appeare that this nation of ours (like to reape as great fruit and benefit by his acquaintance as any other) is readie also to receive and embrace him as friendly as the rest.'[68] Texts such as Livy's *Roman Historie* were being imported and translated in ways that reflected a sustained awareness on the part of English translators that their contents would map meaningfully onto present-day English actualities; in fact, this was likely the case with Holland's own translation and its design to influence Elizabeth I in her foreign policy towards Philip of Spain.[69]

Arthur Golding's 1567 translation of Ovid's *Metamorphoses* offers another example of 'Englishing' that celebrates the global turn by encouraging close contact with exotic Classical voices. Golding's lengthy preface to Ovid's poem expresses a clear moralising imperative that showcases Golding's Calvinist convictions and his reservations about translating a pagan poetic work for English audiences. However, Golding's reservations about Ovid's poem are also mediated by a clear desire to encounter and highlight the poem in all of its exoticism and strangeness. In his preface Golding reasons that such works, like Horace's honey-coated pill, are most alluring when cloaked in not only a sweet but an exotic facade. He writes:

> Even so a playne and naked tale or storie simply told
> (Although the matter be in deede of valewe more than gold)
> Makes not the hearer so atteint to print it in his hart,
> As when the thing is well declared, with pleasant termes and art.
> All which the Poets knew right well: and for the greater grace,
> As Persian kings did never go abrode with open face,
> But with some lawne or silken skarf, for reverence of theyr state.[70]

Golding compares the exterior that conceals the poem's inner meaning with a silken scarf worn by a Persian king. Without the artful packaging, the poem is plain, ineffectual, and its contents fail to penetrate or become 'printed into' the English 'hart'. The example Golding cites of Persian kings who cover their faces with silk scarves is intended to figure the affecting rhetorical packaging that conceals the inner meaning of the poem. Golding's imagery calls on foreignness to signal a particular kind of allure, one that Golding associates with the luxury, sensuousness, and exoticism of the East, figured as a foreign monarch swathed in an expensive imported textile. Golding's chosen example insists upon the exoticism and value of Ovid's rhetorical vestments, while also insisting that this very feature affords the poem with its capacity to impress or 'print' itself upon English readers. The description commingles the familiar and the strange, proximity and alienation, suggesting that in Englishing Ovid's poem, Golding brings something distinctly strange closer to the hearts of English readers and does so, rather fittingly, through the medium of literary dissemination: the printing press.

The Englishing of foreign poetic, historical, and philosophical texts was often driven by admiration for these works' exoticism, admiration that in Golding's preface remains surprisingly intact alongside his typological re-readings of *The Metamorphoses*.[71] Together with the Christian hermeneutic that he introduces into the preface, Golding also prioritises the liveliness and exoticism of Ovid's poem. In Golding's view, the author's 'purpose' is to 'paint and set before our eyes / The lyvely Image of the thoughts that in our stomackes ryse. / Eche vice and vertue seems to speake and argue to our face, / With such perswasions as they have theyr doings to embrace.'[72]

Ovid's poetic representations are so vivid that Golding foresees a danger to incautious readers who fail to perceive what he identifies as their essentially Christian moral contents. He is careful to excuse Ovid's poem of any blame, instead pointing towards bad readership as the source of the problem.

> And if a wicked persone seeme his vices to exalt,
> Esteeme not him that wrate the woorke in such defaultes
>   to halt.

> But rather with an upryght eye consyder well thy thought:
> See if corrupted nature have the like within thee wrought.
> Marke what affection dooth perswade in every kind of matter.
> Judge if that even in heinous crymes thy fancy doo not flatter.[73]

Instead of casting suspicion on the poem, Golding points towards incautious, ill-minded readers as the source of trouble. Without apologising for the vividness of Ovid's imagery, Golding emphasises a clear goal in his preface: creating dimensional, colourful, sensually and emotionally exciting 'lyvely images'. Encounters with exotic and stimulating poetry, Golding asserts, move readers in manifestly profound, even visceral ways – ways that 'make our stomackes ryse'.

Golding's digestion image offers a richly physiological rendering of his ideal type of readership, one in which audiences engage in the active processing of potentially dangerous, exogamous materials as they read. Golding's readers are, as Joseph Wallace aptly observes, 'exercising an active, selective principle of interpretation' as they make their way through the poem.[74] That activity is not without inherent risks: Golding cautions readers about the dangers of being devoured by the poem's allurements. However, Golding's central site of culpability remains his readers, whose fortitude he calls on to withstand encounters with exotic poetic nourishment; he incites them to 'digest' Ovid without becoming digested themselves.

The discourse of digestion as a model for encountering exogamous 'others' is also one that theologian John Calvin appealed to in the sixteenth century, asserting in the *Institutes of the Christian Religion* that 'bodily meate, when it findeth a stomach possessed wt evill humors, being it selfe also thereby made euil and corrupted doth rather hurt than nourish.'[75] For Calvin, the individual's stomach represents the determining feature, not the food; a bad stomach can cause even perfectly good food to produce sickness.[76] The maxim printed on the title page of Golding's 1567 translation of Ovid rehearses this same idea through the French 'honi soit qui mal y pense' – shame befalls whomever thinks bad thoughts.[77] Like the Calvinist treatises Golding spent years of his life translating, Golding's 1567 preface to *The Metamorphoses* encourages readers to encounter difference, and locates tremendous value in those encounters, all the while emphasising individuals' responsibility to process those encounters judiciously.

English translators' praise of Classical texts' strange 'otherness' suggests that the operative goal in importing exotic goods was not to defuse exoticism; rather, exoticism formed an important part of these texts' commercial and cultural value. Alison Games has convincingly argued that England's dramatic turnaround success in the sixteenth century was forged through its engagement with distant cultures and its ability to learn and innovate based on those encounters, particularly by Englishmen whose commercial fortunes depended on global travel.[78] 'Far from home, dispersed around the world wherever opportunity might lurk, the English learned foreign languages, visited synagogues and mosques, befriended Asian and European traders, pursued sexual and romantic relationships with indigenous women, fathered children and sometimes shipped them home to England, and sought to understand the cultural mores of an alien land.'[79] England's emergence in the seventeenth century as a 'kingdom on the rise', Games argues, can be traced to the influence of foreign cultures, languages, and people on English travellers, who then brought those influences back into England, where they translated those experiences into new strategies for global commercial and cultural enterprise.[80]

Rather than adhering to the traditional anglocentric narrative of cultural authority that position England as the force whose influence radiated outward, imposing itself onto non-English cultures, Games's study instead theorises that global influences, 'places and people far from Europe defined how the English experienced the world and the empire that emerged in their wake.'[81] England's engagement with Hebrew reflected similar patterns of adaptive reorientation by the end of the sixteenth century. A text written by a relatively obscure and little-studied Elizabethan inventor named Simon Sturtevant (1570–1624?) offers a compelling and illustrative example. Sturtevant died following a decade spent in prison after failing to make good on a patent, a predicament that landed him in serious financial trouble. He was the author of several published and unpublished works on an impressively wide range of subjects, each of which promised a newly invented device that his text attempted to describe and market to wealthy patrons, including Elizabeth I and James I. Sturtevant's list of inventions included a mysterious medicinal cure called a 'Tugro',[82] a contraption known as the 'Merva' that promised to revolutionise warfare,[83] a metallurgical invention for working iron using pit-coal rather than charcoal,[84] a book of eloquently composed one-line *sententiae* drawn from the works of Virgil,[85] and Greek and Latin lexicons,[86] all of which he hoped would provide an avenue towards royal patronage, financial stability and, in the case of his final work on medicinal cures, an avenue out of prison and an audience with King James I.[87]

One of Sturtevant's texts – a short work of only thirty-two pages published in 1602 – was devoted to Semitic language instruction. The text's full title is *Dibre Adam, or Adams Hebrew dictionarie: a rare and new invention for the speedie atteyning, and perfect reteyning, of the Hebrew, Chaldee, and Syriack. Where (by the distinct motion of 66 characters) al the Dictionarie words of the Language of Canaan are truly represented, and cleerly written*. In it Sturtevant promises to deliver a method for learning Hebrew along with two other ancient languages, Syriac and Aramaic, via a new invention that offered quick results. Like his other publications that advertised but did not offer explicit details about the actual workings of his inventions, Sturtevant's *Dibre Adam* promotes a new and, by his own insistence, highly original method for Hebrew language instruction. His method consists of a series of shortcuts that involved learning the 'roots' of key word-groups along with basic principles of Hebrew grammar as an alternative to the approach favoured by many Hebraists, who published long alphabetical dictionaries.

Sturtevant introduces *Dibre Adam* by lauding the Hebrew language, which he cites as the original dialect spoken by Adam and Eve in the Garden of Eden. By acquiring fluency in Hebrew, Sturtevant claims, readers could position themselves to learn the original, true names given to each of God's creatures. Using wonderfully figurative language, he explains:

> At this time Gods new Neophyte, fresh-man, of greater understanding than standing, in the florishing Universitie of Eden, had a shrewd, though glorious lesson imposed upon him, by his master, [Jehovah], rector of the round rouling Globe: for to ten thousand severall things, that is to say, to all those creatures, and all their severall actions with their divers qualities, he must give tenne thousand differing names, and presently be able to recount them again, and to teach them to all his children, *Hic labor hoc opus est.*[88]

Sturtevant's invention has cachet because it enables readers to learn in the same 'Universitie of Eden' attended by the biblical Adam. In its creative refashioning of the biblical story, Sturtevant's text promises to deliver the original language that brings readers back to Adam and Eve's prelapsarian origins. The experience being marketed is one of authenticity, authority, and purity, and the dictionary proffered by Sturtevant – the one that he claims was developed by Adam himself – is advertised as the most ancient, primordial, and valuable kind of immersive education.

Sturtevant's Hebrew dictionary is no mere dry scholarly pursuit; his version of Hebrew studies – condensed, ingeniously simplified, and distilled to the rare essentials – evidences an inventive approach to the commodification and packaging of the language. Inventiveness, resourcefulness, human intelligence, and ingenuity – these are the skills that Sturtevant also locates in the biblical Adam's act of assigning names to a newly created universe of objects. The act of learning the rightful names of things, he explains, represents humankind's due inheritance: *Hic labor hoc opus est*; this effort is necessary.

Not only is it necessary; Sturtevant is also clear that mastery of the world, figured as God's mastery over 'the round rouling Globe', consists of a linguistic kind of dominion. Along with Adam, contemporary man must exert the requisite effort. The particular virtues that Sturtevant attempts to celebrate – effort and ingenuity – are ones that intersect with stereotypically English Protestant merits, particularly those used to distinguish English Protestants from their 'lazy' Catholic counterparts in the late sixteenth century.[89] It is notable that the industriousness Sturtevant describes in Adam is a characteristic not of post-lapsarian labour, but rather of Adam's disposition before he fell into temptation. Apparently there is no rest or complacency for the good English Protestant or his hardworking biblical ancestor. By regaining Adam's linguistic aptitude and imitating his labours – ones that Sturtevant claims are altogether second nature to humans – present-day people stand to regain Adam's original purity through the very same diligence exhibited by Adam in naming all of God's creatures.

In addition to its biblical valences, Sturtevant casts the experience of learning Hebrew as an immersion in a vast marketplace, one that facilitates entry into a richer consumer experience. He describes his dictionary and the Hebrew language as a shopper's delight teeming with wares:

> Dibre is as a storehouse or haberdashers shop, it laith open to the view all kinde of wares and commodities: now although thou canst not see all his riches and goods, yet take up none, handle none, contemplate upon none so much, as that which thou hast neede of: that buy I say and that make thy owne.[90]

Although his final piece of advice recommends tempering brash acquisitiveness and instead purchasing the one truly valuable good – his dictionary – Sturtevant sells his Hebrew guide by yoking it to the fulfilment of consumerist fantasies and the promise of making the great storehouse of merchant's goods the reader's own. Sturtevant links that fulfilment to the exercise of skill and effort, which he positions as the rightful and natural inheritance of English readers who can take up Adam's own skills, even where the language might appear difficult to learn.

Sturtevant's *Dibre Adam* has been read as an example of the English appropriation of Hebrew that was imagined by early seventeenth-century Englishmen to be eminently detachable from Jews and to have been providentially transferred to Christians.[91] However, Sturtevant's dictionary also models a cosmopolitan, outwardly focused approach to the strangeness of an exotic language – one whose Hebrew letters are foregrounded above its English title in Sturtevant's text – that also recalls Alison Games's key insights in *Web of Empire*. In Games's account, the belatedness of Renaissance English success – what amounts to England's shortcomings – drove the kinds of venturesome cultural encounters that, Games argues, succeeded in generating new patterns of thought and a kind of practical troubleshooting based on having observed exotic cultures first-hand. The history play's revival on the English stage in the final decades of the sixteenth-century developed the idea that England could see itself as well-situated to learn from the successes and failures of its predecessors, and adopt as well as adapt the virtues and successes modelled by non-English nations and cultures to distinctly English ends. That tendency in the 1590s to emphasise an outward focus on matters of innovation and invention is certainly present in Sturtevant's *Dibre Adam*, a text that leans heavily on a foreign predecessor: the 1587 Hebrew Bible of Elias Hutter (1553–1605). Hutter, a sixteenth-century German Hebraist who held a professorship in Hebrew Studies at Leipzig, supervised the production of several polyglot bibles as well as a pedagogical edition of the Hebrew Bible in 1587 that was intended to make the original Hebrew more accessible to students. Titled with the Hebrew words 'Derekh Ha-Kodesh' and the Latin 'Biblia Sacra', Hutter's bible innovated in part through typography in the famous 'open and closed' typeface that he developed in which he printed the inflectional part of Hebrew words in hollow letters and the root words in heavily inked black type that enabled students to easily and readily distinguish the different components of Hebrew words.

Hutter's other graphic didactic innovation in *Derekh Ha-Kodesh* consists of a series of tables illustrating Hebrew roots and various grammatical permutations of them laid out in a way designed to simplify the learning of the language and offer a condensed method of instruction that bypassed the need to study lengthy Hebrew vocabulary lists. Sitting atop the indexes is an illustration of a three-dimensional cube that William Sherman describes as a mix between a Rubik's Cube and a slide rule,[92] with a single Hebrew letter inscribed on each of three pieces (see Figure 1.3). One of the corner pieces is itself divided into a miniature cube, producing a *mise-en-abyme* within the illustration.[93] A second figure resembling a cross divided

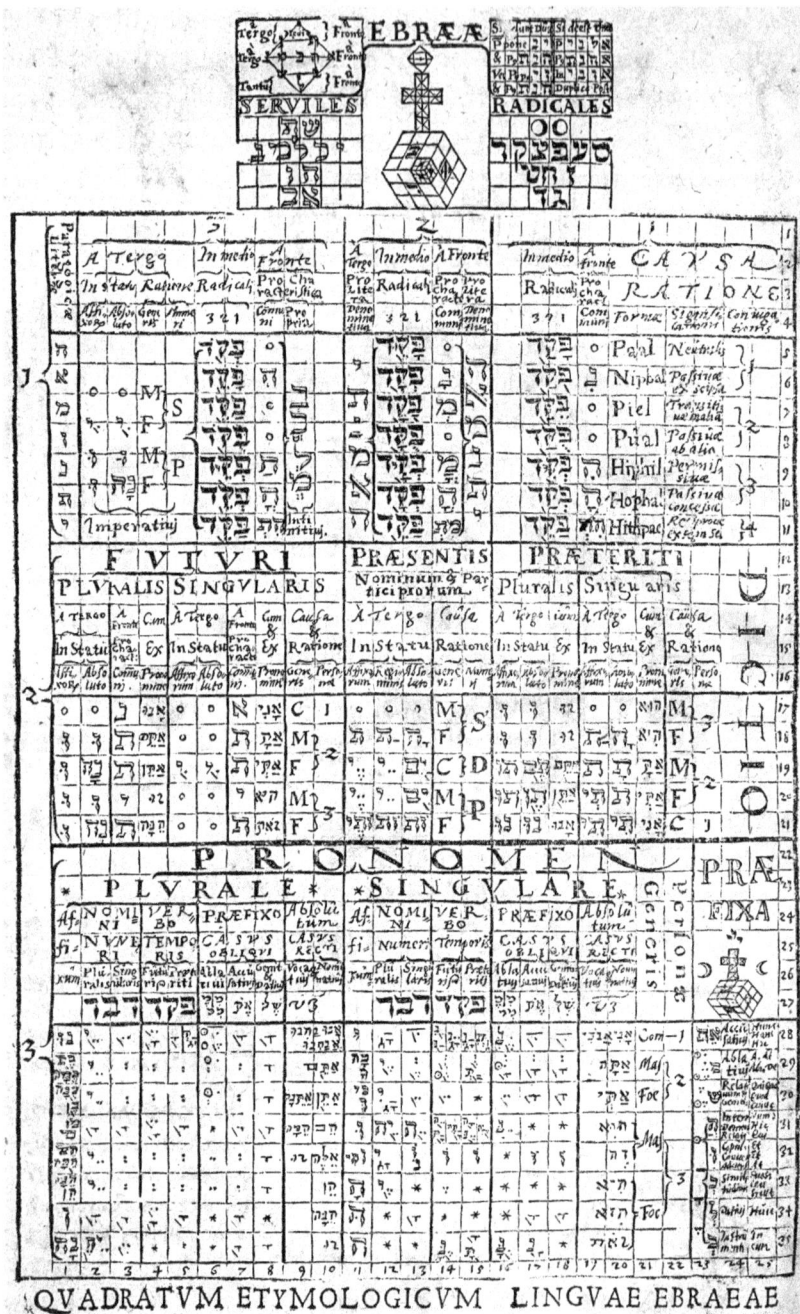

Figure 1.3 Grammar table from Elias Hutter, *Derekh Ha-Kodesh (Biblia Sacra)*, 1587. The Huntington Library, San Marino, California.

into six squares is positioned above the cube, with each square bisected by three lines, resulting in six parts per square. The cross structure appears to model an unfolded version of Hutter's device, with the bisecting lines serving as fold-marks or space divisions where letters would be placed. Tables to the left and right of the illustrations suggest at potential ways in which those spaces might be filled. By all appearances, Hutter's images are a visual rendering of his didactic strategy outlined in the tables below, which is intended to simplify, condense, and organise the study of the Hebrew language for interested students and offer a blueprint for how a manoeuvrable physical device would assist those studies.

Hutter's grammatical tables and Hebrew cube are, in all likelihood, the prototype that inspired Sturtevant's *Dibre Adam*. Sturtevant mentions Hutter and his cube by name, and lengthily discusses the distinctness of his own invention in contrast to Hutter's. He disavows having seen Hutter's Bible, citing a minister, William Blewet, as his witness that he never laid eyes on Hutter's text or its device until very recently, well after the 'eureka' moment of discovering his own unique and original method for mastering Hebrew. He further explains that when Blewet first mentioned the existence of the cube, he subsequently tried to obtain a copy of Hutter's Bible from London, but was unable to procure it.[94]

We may never know just how closely Sturtevant's invented device resembled Hutter's Hebrew cube, since no mechanical prototypes have survived, if any ever existed; Sturtevant is deliberately opaque in his description of the item he tries to market, thereby offering an enticement to potential sponsors who might have been inclined to invest in order to learn more. This strategy, the same one that Sturtevant deploys in all of his promotional writing, was a known way for inventors to guard their secrets while attempting to secure an opportunity to pitch to important patrons, at which point the mystery would be revealed.⁹⁵ However, I think it likely that Sturtevant appropriated significant aspects of Hutter's device and attempted to pass them off as his own in *Dibre Adam*. His protestations reflect a desire to distinguish his invention from Hutter's while loudly attesting to their uncomfortably close mutual resemblance. Sturtevant's willingness to borrow the prototypes developed by other dictionary-writers was already established by the time he published *Dibre Adam* in 1602. Sturtevant's 1597 Greek and Latin lexicons were both largely composed of translations from other European reference books. Sherman, whose study of Sturtevant's career is the only detailed extant treatment of his work and its historical context, explains that Sturtevant's epistle to the reader in the Latin lexicon

> acknowledged that 'I haue sequestered out [of] some Dictionaries and Nomenclators, certaine principall words' (sig.A3v), and the very title of the *Anglo-Latinus Nomenclator* announced that its wordlist was mostly extracted from the 1580 *Lexicon graeco-latinum* of Johannes Scapula (itself full of unacknowledged borrowings from Henri Estienne's great *Thesaurus graecae linguae* of 1572, which filled more than 4,000 folio pages).⁹⁶

Sturtevant's appropriation of Hutter's method, including its overt borrowing from non-English sources that are then overlaid with Sturtevant's own native innovations, can be productively read through the model of English cultural change for which Alison Games argues.⁹⁷ Games attributes England's eventual rise to imperial dominance to key developments in global commerce in the period between 1560 and 1660. Central to English success, Games argues, were individuals who 'circulated the globe in multiple ventures ... Their interest in the world beyond England's shores turned many travellers into cosmopolitans, men who were often able to encounter those unlike themselves with enthusiasm and curiosity.'⁹⁸ This type of venturing entailed bringing the fruits of far-flung international travel back to England and learning from the experiences accrued through encounters with foreign people, places, and practices. Rather than imagining imported texts, including Classical and Hebraic ones, as objects whose cultural strangeness was being erased as they were being 'Englished', Games's work on cosmopolitanism and early modern travel points towards ways in which England's emerging national identity and its strength resided in engagement with other cultures and the ability to learn and innovate based on those encounters. Although Sturtevant's dictionary reflects a desire to appropriate the language of the Jews, his appropriation of Hutter's text also reflects the equally pervasive English pattern of transnational exchange based on England's implication in a web of international relationships and its receptivity to exotic influences.

Like the *mise-en-abyme* in the upper segment of Hutter's Hebrew cube, Simon Sturtevant's Hebrew dictionary reflects a set of recursive textual ancestors that, in *Dibre Adam*'s discussion of the Hebrew language, are imagined to extend all the way back to the time of Adam and the very dawn of time itself. Sturtevant's dictionary, with its heavily borrowed content, offers a suggestive view into a way of thinking about cultural appropriation in the sixteenth century that moves beyond the model of appropriation-as-erasure, and takes into account Elizabethan England's enormous appetite for global imports, exoticism, and the provenance of the antiquities that the English avidly collected, read, and attempted to digest. Although Jews and their texts have often been excluded from that discussion, there is compelling evidence suggesting that they should not be, and that the Hebrew language, Hebrew biblical writings, and Jews themselves carried complex, ambivalent meaning in Renaissance England in ways that merit more sustained discussion.

Was Shakespeare among those who felt intrigued by the ambivalent associations attributed to Jews and the complex and ancient provenance that they and their language evoked in the early modern world? *The Merchant of Venice* in fact keenly explores the kinds of appropriative tendencies that underwrote typological treatments of Hebraic scripture. The chapter that follows calls attention to the multi-vocality of biblical texts. Rather than presuming that Shakespeare merely rehearses the same invidious practices and attitudes towards Jews adopted by characters such as Antonio, this chapter has instead offered a historical account of the far more complex questions and associations surrounding Jews and in sixteenth-century English culture. In the following chapter, I turn to Shakespeare's *The Merchant of Venice* and examine textual evidence for that same complexity and multi-vocality in Shylock's words.

Notes

1. James Shapiro, *Shakespeare and the Jews* (New York: Columbia University Press, 1996): 4. The less polite questions are ones that Shapiro himself addresses in *Shakespeare and the Jews*, which asks how a particular vision of Jews and Jewishness gripped the English imagination in the sixteenth and seventeenth centuries in the absence of significant numbers of Jews there. See p. 1 where Shapiro writes, 'This book is concerned with what Shakespeare and his contemporaries thought about Jews.'
2. For accounts of Irving's performance as Shylock, see James C. Bulman, *Shakespeare in Performance: 'The Merchant of Venice'* (Manchester: Manchester University Press, 1991): 28; and also Linda Rosmovitz, *Shakespeare and the Politics of Culture in Late Victorian England* (Baltimore: Johns Hopkins University Press, 1998).
3. Emma Smith makes this point in, 'Was Shylock Jewish?' *Shakespeare Quarterly*, 64: 2 (Summer 2013): 188–219.

Smith cites evidence from Irving himself, who based his particular interpretation of Shylock on observations of a Jewish man he met while sailing in the Mediterranean. Irving's claim was that Shylock's role itself had no inherent indignity to it, but had been misinterpreted in centuries' worth of maligning performances. See Smith 189–90 for a more detailed discussion of Irving's claims.

4. *Spectator*, 8 November 1879, 1408, cited in Smith 190. See Smith, 'Was Shylock Jewish?', 190–1 for a fuller discussion of Irving's critical reviews that describe Irving's performance as a deviation from the historical Shylock. Smith also cites the work of Linda Rozmovits, who discusses how many of the objections to Irving's performance that couched themselves in historical arguments reflected a trenchant anxiety that Shakespeare may have in fact written this play with the intention of inciting sympathy and toleration for Jews (Rozmovits, *Shakespeare and the Politics of Culture*, 79). Smith also cites Jonathan Freedman's *The Temple of Culture: Assimilation and Anti-Semitism in Literary Anglo-America* (Oxford: Oxford University Press, 2000), which discusses the centrality of Jews to the construction of elite British culture during the Victorian era.

5. See Smith, 'Was Shylock Jewish?', 92ff. where she discusses the importance of two forms of evidence emphasised by Victorian historians: the trial of Roderigo Lopez and the visual characteristics of the early-modern stage Jew. On the first point, Smith discusses how nineteenth-century historians tended to link *The Merchant of Venice* and the trial of Elizabeth I's Jewish court physician Roderigo Lopez, discussing the play as a response to the 1594 trial and execution of Lopez. Smith demonstrates that there is little conclusive evidence establishing that Jewishness played a role in Lopez's trial or conviction (see Smith, 'Was Shylock Jewish?', 192–5). On the issue of Shylock as an Elizabethan comic villain with the supposedly ubiquitous visual trappings of the stage Jew (red hair and a large hooked nose), see Smith, 'Was Shylock Jewish?', 196–201 where she discusses how and why

that evidence was the product of 'purposeful interventions' by Victorian scholars 'actively shaping the evidence to produce their desired historical narrative' (Smith, 'Was Shylock Jewish?', 199).

6. See Lucien Wolf, 'A Plea For Anglo-Jewish History: Inaugural Address Delivered at the First Meeting of the Society, November 11th, 1893', *Transactions (Jewish Historical Society of England)*, 1 (1893–4): 1–7; and 'Origins of the Jewish Historical Society of England', *Transactions (Jewish Historical Society of England)*, 7 (1911–14): 206–21.

7. Wolf, 'A Plea', 4.

8. Janet Adelman, *Blood Relations: Christian and Jew in The Merchant of Venice* (Chicago: University of Chicago Press, 2008) 1.

9. Anthony Grafton, 'The Jewish Book in Christian Europe: Material Texts and Religious Encounters', in Andrea Sterk and Nina Caputo (eds), *Faithful Narratives: Historians, Religion, and the Challenge of Objectivity* (Ithaca: Cornell University Press, 2014): 96–114; Richard I. Cohen, Adam Shear, and Elchanan Reiner (eds), 'Christian Hebraism and the Rediscovery of Hellenistic Judaism', *Jewish Culture in Early Modern Europe: Essays in Honor of David B. Ruderman* (Pittsburgh: University of Pittsburgh Press, 2014): 169–80; with Joanna Weinberg, *"I Have Always Loved the Holy Tongue": Isaac Casaubon, the Jews, and a Forgotten Chapter in Renaissance Scholarship* (Cambridge, MA: Belknap Press of Harvard University Press, 2011); 'In No Man's Land: Christian Learning and the Jews', *Worlds Made By Words* (Cambridge, MA: Harvard University Press, 2009): 176–87.

10. Stephen Burnett, *Christian Hebraism in the Reformation Era (1500–1660): Authors, Books, and the Transmission of Jewish Learning*, Vol. 19, Library of the Written Words (Leiden and Boston: Brill, 2012).

11. Eric Nelson, 'Hebraism and the Republican Turn of 1776: A Contemporary Account of the Debate over Common Sense', *William and Mary Quarterly*, 70: 4 (October 2013): 781–812; *The Hebrew Republic* (Cambridge, MA: Harvard University Press, 2010); '"Talmudic Commonwealthsmen" and the Rise of

Republican Exclusivism', *Historical Journal*, 50: 4 (December 2007): 809–35.

12. On the question of the influence of Hebrew words on the English language during the early modern period, see Naomi Tadmor, *The Social Universe of the English Bible: Scripture, Society, and Culture in Early Modern England* (Cambridge: Cambridge University Press, 2010).

13. On this point, see Warren Boutcher, '"Who taught thee Rhetoricke to deceive a maid?": Christopher Marlowe's *Hero and Leander*, Juan Boscan's *Leandro*, and Renaissance Vernacular Humanism', *Comparative Literature*, 52: 1 (Winter 2000): 11–52. In this article, Boutcher focuses on the importance of vernacular translation to late Renaissance humanist culture in England. He argues that vernacular translation eclipsed translation between Latinate and vernacular texts in ways that reflected the diplomatic, commercial nature of humanist endeavours in the period.

14. Burnett, *Christian Hebraism*, 6.

15. Burnett, *Christian Hebraism*, 114.

16. Frank Manuel, *The Broken Staff* (Cambridge, MA: Harvard University Press, 1992), 3.

17. Robert Wakefield, *On the Three Languages* (1524), ed. and trans. G. Lloyd Jones, *Medieval & Renaissance Texts & Studies*, Vol. 68, The Renaissance Society of America Renaissance Texts Series, Vol. 13 (Binghamton, NY: SUNY Binghamton, 1989): 116.

18. See Wakefield, *On the Three Languages*, 90 for discussion of Hebrew as the divinely inspired language, and 100 and 106–8 for Wakefield's discussion of how God communicates in Hebrew.

19. See Wakefield, *On the Three Languages*, 72 and 74.

20. Sixteenth-century physician and author Andrew Borde (1490–1549) describes the Hebrew spoken by contemporary Jews as barbarous. Andrew Boorde, *The first boke of the introduction of knowledge made by Andrew Borde, of a physycke doctor. A compendyous regiment; or, A dietary of health made in Mountpyllier* (London: William Copland, 1555): 221. Robert Wakefield describes Hebrew as the lost

Jewish vernacular that 'belongs to us [i.e. Christians]' (see *On the Three Languages* 178).
21. See Adelman's full account of the play's substantial investment in what she terms a proto-racial discourse in "Her Father's Blood: Race, Conversion, and Nation in *The Merchant of Venice*', *Representations*, 81: 1 (Winter 2003): 4–30.
22. See the introduction in Adelman, *Blood Relations*.
23. See chapter one of Adelman, *Blood Relations*, for a further discussion of this point with reference to John Foxe's attempts to justify Christian claims to national priority and elect status.
24. John Huarte, *The Examination of Mens Wits. In which, by dicouering the varieties of natures, is shewed for what profession each one is apt, and how far he shall profit therein. Trans. From the Spanish by M. Camilio Camili and from the Italian by Richard Carew* (London: Adam Slip for Richard Watkins, 1594).
25. Huarte, *The Examination of Mens Wits*, 185.
26. Huarte, *The Examination of Mens Wits*, 189.
27. Thomas Coryat, *Coryat's Crudities* (1611), Vol. 1 (Glasgow: James McLehose & Sons, 1905): 371–2.
28. Coryat, *Coryat's Crudities*.
29. Jonathan Gil Harris, *Untimely Matter in the Time of Shakespeare* (Philadelphia: University of Pennsylvania Press, 2009): 103.
30. See chapter three in Harris, *Untimely Matter*.
31. Harris, *Untimely Matter*, 103–4.
32. John Stow, *A Survey of London, by John Stow: Reprinted from the Text of 1603*, ed. Charles Lethbridge Kingsford, 2 vols (Oxford: Clarendon Press, 1908), 1: 9.
33. I am thinking in particular of Shapiro's highly influential and critically lauded *Shakespeare and the Jews*.
34. On this point, see Deeana Copeland Klepper, *The Insight of Unbelievers: Nicholas of Lyra and Christian Readings of Jewish Texts in the Later Middle Ages* (Philadelphia: University of Philadelphia Press, 2007).
35. See Burnett, *Christian Hebraism*, 25–6 for an account of some of the difficulties Christian Hebraists faced learning Hebrew from Jewish tutors, difficulties that stemmed from

fundamental differences in how and when the language was acquired. Jews learned to write Hebrew from a young age by relying on their substantial prior familiarity with spoken Hebrew. Christian Hebraists found it extremely difficult to learn in this fashion since they lacked the requisite fluency in spoken Hebrew. Language instruction from Jewish tutors was therefore often less effective.

36. See Wakefield, *On the Three Languages*, 174ff., where Wakefield argues that knowledge of Hebrew will facilitate disputation with Jews on theological matters. Wakefield claims that once Christians can better grasp Hebrew Scripture, Jews will no longer be able to claim that Christians misunderstand the true sense of the text.

37. Ironically, it was the embrace of Hebrew's universality that prompted many Christian Hebraists, including Wakefield, to declare that Hebrew was an essentially Christian language, one from which contemporary Jews were imagined to be woefully estranged. The self-conscious attempt to distinguish between biblical Hebrew and the Hebrew vernacular spoken by early modern Europe's Jews – often described as an abominable corruption – is a common feature of Renaissance discussions of Hebrew such as Wakefield's *Oratio* (see Wakefield, *On the Three Languages*).

38. See Wakefield, *On the Three Languages*, 66 and 80, for Wakefield's discussion of his collaboration with Jewish scholars and the assistance he received from Jewish grammarians.

39. See Judith Olszowy-Schlanger, 'Robert Wakefield and the Medieval Background of Hebrew Scholarship in Renaissance England', *Hebrew to Latin, Latin to Hebrew: The Mirroring of Two Cultures in the Age of Humanism; Colloquium Held at the Warburg Institute*, London, 18 October 2006, pp. 61–88. Olszowy-Schlanger discusses the extent of Wakefield's fluency in Hebrew and argues that in many cases his treatment of Hebrew sources in the *Oratio* derives from having directly read them in Hebrew rather than via the published work of Hebraists like Reuchlin.

40. My account of the humanist turn towards Hebrew and Hebraism under Henry VIII in the pages that follow draws

on the work of Alastair Hamilton, 'Humanists and the Bible', *The Cambridge Companion to Renaissance Humanism*, ed. Jill Kraye (Cambridge: Cambridge University Press, 1996): 100–17; Frank Manuel, *The Broken Staff: Judaism Through Christian Eyes* (Cambridge, MA: Harvard University Press, 1992); G. Lloyd Jones, *The Discovery of Hebrew in Tudor England: A Third Language* (Manchester: Manchester University Press, 1983).

41. In 'Humanists and the Bible', Alastair Hamilton discusses another important Continental precedent set in fifteenth-century Italy – the humanist imperative to learn Hebrew in order to convert the Jews. He lists Giannozzo Manetti as the first such humanist. Manetti served at Florence as an ambassador and worked as an apostolic secretary to Pope Nicholas V in Rome, acting as a member of the royal council of King Alfonso of Naples. In 1442 with the help of Jewish scholars, Manetti started to read through the Hebrew Bible and assemble a collection of manuscripts. His ambition in translating the Bible was to improve on the Vulgate, and he enabled readers to compare different versions of the text. In the copy of the Psalter he presented to the king of Naples, he provided his own translation of the Hebrew beside two translations attributed to Jerome, one directly from the Hebrew and one from the Septuagint. He discusses the differences between them in his *Apologeticus*.

42. Jonathan Woolfson, 'Robert Wakefield', *Oxford Dictionary of National Biography* (Oxford: Oxford University Press, 2004).

43. Burnett, *Christian Hebraism*, 52.

44. See Lloyd Jones, *Discovery of Hebrew*, 94–5. According to Jones, the only Hebrew book at Oxford in this period was a copy of Reuchlin's 1506 *De rudimentis hebraicis*.

45. See also T. E. Bridgett, *Life of Blessed John Fisher* (London: Burns & Oates, 1888); F. van Ortroy (ed.), *Vie du bienheureux martyr, Jean Fisher* (Brussels: Polleunis et Ceuterick, 1893); *Analecta Bollandiana*, 10 (1891): 121–365, and 12 (1893): 97–287; E. Surtz, *The Works and Days of John Fisher 1469–1535* (Cambridge, MA: Harvard University Press, 1967);

Maria Dowling, *Fisher of Men: A Life of John Fisher, 1469–1535* (New York: Palgrave Macmillan, 1999); Richard Rex, *The Theology of John Fisher* (Cambridge: Cambridge University Press, 1991); B. Bradshaw and E. Duffy (eds), *Humanism, Reform and the Reformation: The Career of Bishop John Fisher* (Cambridge: Cambridge University Press, 1989); Richard Rex, 'St John Fisher's Treatise on the Authority of the Septuagint', *Journal of Theological Studies*, new series, 43 (1992): 55–116; J. Fisher, *Opera Omnia* (Würzburg, 1597).

46. See Desiderius Erasmus, *A booke called in latyn Enchiridion militis christiani, and in englysshe the manuell of the christen knight* (London: Wynkyn de Worde for Johann Bydell, 1533). See also Manfred Hoffmann, *Rhetoric and Theology: The Hermeneutic of Erasmus* (Toronto: University of Toronto Press, 1994).

47. Those works were seized by the crown when Fisher was indicted for heresy.

48. Lloyd Jones, *Discovery of Hebrew*, 98.

49. The medal is currently on display at the British Museum and featured on the website at http://www.britishmuseum.org/research/collection_online/collection_object_details.aspx?objectId=948583&partId=1. The companion volume to the exhibit discusses the medal. See Jonathan Bate and Dora Thornton, *Shakespeare: Staging the World* (London: British Museum Press, 2012). The medal's Hebrew inscription reflects imperfect and, in parts, illegible Hebrew, and the meaning of certain words is unclear. The inscription reads: 'Henry VIII, faithful king of [?], and the people of England and Hiberniai under the head and superior messiah.' Hiberniai is likely a Hebraicisation of Hibernia (Ireland). The least clear word following 'king' is comprised of three badly formed Hebrew letters that may be gimel, lamed, and zayin, which would read nonsensically as 'guz', or may represent the letters gimel, vav, and lamed, which would read as 'gol' or Gaul (France). I extend a special thanks to Ari Lieberman for helping me with this translation.

50. This medal is also on display at the British Museum and is featured on their website at http://www.britishmuseum.org/

research/collection_online/collection_object_details.aspx?obj ectId=952989&partId=1&searchText=Edward+VI+coronati on+medal&page=1. The Latin inscription on the coin's face reads:

EDWARDVS . VI . D . G . ANG . FR . ET . HI . REX . FIDEI . DEFNS . ET . IN . TERRIS . ANG . ET . HIB. ECCLE. CAPVT. SVPREMVM . CORONATVS . EST . M.D.XLVI . XX . FEBRVA . ETATIS . DECIMO.

(Edward VI, by the grace of God, King of England, France, and Ireland, defender of the faith, and the supreme head on earth of the Church of England and Ireland, crowned 20 February, 1546, at the age of ten years.)

51. The manuscript is located in the British Library's collections, Cotton MS, Otho C x, fols. 184r–198r. Cited in the *DNB* entry on 'Robert Wakefield' by Jonathan Woolfson.
52. The following is drawn from Lucien Wolf, 'Jews in Tudor England', *Essays in Jewish History*, ed. Cecil Roth (London: Jewish Historical Society of England, 1934).
53. Cited in Wolf, 'Jews in Tudor England', 62–3.
54. Cited in Wolf, 'Jews in Tudor England', 63.
55. See Wolf, 'Jews in Tudor England'.
56. See J. Christopher Warner, *Henry VIII's Divorce: Literature and the Politics of the Printing Press* (Woodbridge: Boydell Press, 1998). On the precedent set by Lorenzo de Medici in the 1470s and 1480s, see Quentin Skinner, 'Political Philosophy', *The Cambridge History of Renaissance Philosophy*, ed. Charles B. Schmitt and Quentin Skinner (Cambridge: Cambridge University Press, 1991): 426–30.
57. See Henry Ansgar Kelly, *The Matrimonial Trials of Henry VIII* (Palo Alto, CA: Stanford University Press, 1976).
58. Burnett, *Christian Hebraism*, 47.
59. See Burnett, *Christian Hebraism*, 32.
60. On this point, see L. Syson, 'Circulating a Likeness? Coin Portraits in Late Fifteenth-century Italy', *The Image of the Individual: Portraits in the Renaissance*, ed. Nicholas Mann

and Luke Syson (London: British Museum Press, 1998): 113–25.
61. See Jerry Brotton and Lisa Jardine, 'Exchanging Identity Breaching the Boundaries of Renaissance Europe', in *Global Interests: Renaissance Art Between East and West* (Ithaca: Cornell University Press, 2000): 11–62.
62. Roland Greene, *Post-Petrarchism: Origins and Innovations of the Western Lyric Sequence* (Princeton: Princeton University Press, 1991).
63. Miriam Jacobson makes this point in *Barbarous Antiquity: Reorienting the Past in the Poetry of Early Modern England* (Philadelphia: University of Pennsylvania Press, 2014).
64. Thomas Wilson, *The three orations of Demosthenes chiefe orator among the Grecians* (London: Henrie Denham, 1570): preface.
65. John Clapham, *Philosophicall treatise on the quietness of the mind, Taken out of the morall workes written in Greeke by the most famous philosopher & historiographer, Plutarch* (London: Robert Robinson for Thomas Newman, 1589). William Barker, *The Bookes of Xenophon, containing the disciple, schole and education of Cyrus, the noble king of Persie* (London: Reynold Wolfe, 1552).
66. *The Romane Historie Written by T. Livivs of Padva*, trans. Philemon Holland (London: Adam Islip, 1600): 'To the Reader'.
67. Ibid.
68. Ibid.
69. For an elaboration of this argument based on Holland's epistle, prefatory comments, and marginal notations in his translation of Livy, see Peter Culhane, 'Philemon Holland's Livy: Peritexts and Contexts', *Translation and Literature*, 13: 2 (Autumn 2004): 168–86.
70. *Ovid's Metamorphoses: The Arthur Golding Translation of 1567*, ed. John Frederick Nims (Philadelphia: Paul Dry Books, 2000): 426.
71. Raphael Lyne observes that readers are encouraged to approach Ovid's poem 'without moralizing mediation', in *Ovid's Changing Worlds: English 'Metamorphoses', 1567–1632* (Oxford: Oxford University Press, 2001): 45.

72. *Ovid's Metamorphoses*, 427.
73. *Ovid's Metamorphoses*, 427.
74. Joseph Wallace, 'Strong Stomachs: Arthur Golding, Ovid, and Cultural Assimilation', *Renaissance Studies*, 26: 5 (November 2012): 733.
75. John Calvin, *Institutes of the Christian Religion*, trans. John Dawes (London, 1561), fol. 137v (4,17,40). On this point, see William J. Bowsma, *John Calvin: A Sixteenth-Century Portrait* (Oxford: Oxford University Press, 1988): 99.
76. See Wallace, 'Strong Stomachs', 738–9. Wallace's article parses the fuller implications of Golding's emphasis on metaphors of digestion and the theological climate of his era. See also Michael Schoenfeldt, *Bodies and Selves in Early Modern England: Physiology and Inwardness in Spenser, Shakespeare, Herbert, and Milton* (Cambridge: Cambridge University Press, 1999) for an in-depth discussion of the implications of bodily digestion in the context of Renaissance literary readership. See also p. 740 of Wallace's article for a discussion of the sixteenth-century Reformed Italian theologian Peter Vermigli's perspective on the problem of cohabitation with non-believers, published in 1555, which recommends a more insular set of imperatives for Protestants to avoid the problem of moral and spiritual 'contamination' by unbelievers. John Calvin's response evidences a very different set of ideas about the value to be derived from encountering non-believers that was in many ways the opposite of Vermigli's insularity.
77. This insignia represents the motto of the Order of the Garter.
78. Alison Games, *The Web of Empire: English Cosmopolitans in an Age of Expansion* (Oxford: Oxford University Press, 2009).
79. Games, *Web of Empire*, 10.
80. Games, *Web of Empire*, 7.
81. Games, *Web of Empire*, 10.
82. This text is titled 'Princely Preservatives or the Helmet of Health', an unpublished and undated manuscript probably written in 1623 or 1624 while Sturtevant was in prison for unpaid debts. The manuscript is housed in the Bodleian Library, MS Rawlinson D.318, fols 49–72. William Sherman discusses

this text in the only sustained scholarly study devoted to Sturtevant's career and work. William H. Sherman, "Patents and Prisons: Simon Sturtevant and the Death of the Renaissance Inventor', *Huntington Library Quarterly*, 72: 2 (June 2009): 239–56.
83. Sturtevant dedicates this unpublished manuscript to King James I. BL, MS. Royal 18.A.xxvi., fols 1–8.
84. Simon Sturtevant, *Metallica* (London, 1612).
85. The unpublished manuscript, dedicated to Prince Henry, is titled *Virgills Gnomologie: Conteyning his principall Sentences and best appliable speeches: Selected for his Highnes use by Simon Sturtevant*. British Library, Add. MS. 15234, fols 1–10. Sherman cites and discusses this text on pp. 244–5.
86. The two works are *The Latin Nomenclator* (London: Valentine Simms, 1597) and *Anglo-Latinus Nomenclator Graecorum Primitiuorum, E Ioan. Scapula[e] Lexicon desumptorum* (London: Valentine Simmes, 1597).
87. Sturtevant's career was spent inventing devices and securing patents for them, one of which landed him in debtors' prison for failing to work the patent and deliver on its promised results. William Sherman's study of Sturtevant's career locates him within the economy of debt that pervaded late Elizabethan England, in which men from across a wide spectrum of social backgrounds and status groups found themselves spending time in the English prison system for unpaid debts. Sherman outlines the details of Sturtevant's patent woes in 'Patents and Prisons', 249ff.
88. Sturtevant, *Dibre Adam, or Adams Hebrew dictionarie: a rare and new invention for the speedie atteyning, and perfect reteyning, of the Hebrew, Chaldee, and Syriack. Where (by the distinct motion of 66 characters) al the Dictionarie words of the Language of Canaan are truly represented, and cleerly written* (London, 1602): 7.
89. Catholics, particularly Spaniards, were frequently typecast by the English as complacent, lazy and rich. This was particularly the case in the years following Elizabeth's defeat of the Spanish Armada.

90. Sturtevant, *Dibre Adam*, 18.
91. James Shapiro makes this point about Sturtevant's dictionary in *Shakespeare and the Jews*, 41.
92. Sherman, 'Patents and Prisons', 244.
93. Elia Huttero [Elias Hutter], *Derekh ha-kodesh Lo ya'v renu tame ve-hu lamo holekh Derekh ve-evilim lo vitu Hoc est Via Sancta Quam non praeteribunt immundi, cum sit pro illis: Imo nec viatores, nec stulti aberrabunt. Sive Biblia Sacra Eleganti Et Maivuscvla Charactervm Forma* (Hamburg: John Saxon, 1587).
94. Sturtevant cites the names of several classmates and instructors at Cambridge who oversaw the development of his method and contributed to its current form. He also posits the possibility that more than one author may lay claim to a single invention.
95. Sherman, 'Patents and Prisons', 246–7.
96. Sherman, 'Patents and Prisons', 243. On this point Sherman cites John Considine, *Dictionaries in Early Modern Europe: Lexicography and the Making of Heritage* (Cambridge: Cambridge University Press, 2008): 95.
97. Alison Games, "The Mediterranean Origins of the British Empire', *The Web of Empire: English Cosmopolitans in an Age of Expansion, 1560–1660* (New York: Oxford University Press, 2008).
98. Games, *Web of Empire*, 9.

CHAPTER 2

PARTI-COLOURED PARABLES

Catalysed by the Protestant return to the original texts of the Bible, the sixteenth century saw a sharp rise in the study of the Jewish Bible and the Hebrew language by Christians. Engagement with the Torah along with its oral and written commentaries in this period exposed to view the vast array of historical and cultural-linguistic strata that underwrote both New and Old Christian Testaments. The multivocality of biblical writings was made graphically evident in the progressively elaborate multi-language bibles produced in this period, the most baroque of which was the London Polyglot published in 1657 featuring nine different language-texts on every folio page. The multi-vocal potential of biblical texts is something to which Shakespeare's dramatic writings also keenly attuned. In act 1, scene 3 of *The Merchant of Venice*, Antonio and Shylock begin to negotiate their loan, and Shylock recounts a story from the Book of Genesis featuring Jacob's unlikely success breeding his uncle's livestock.

> When Laban and himself were compromised
> That all the eanlings which were streaked and pied
> Should fall as Jacob's hire, the ewes being rank

> In end of autumn turned to the rams,
> And when the work of generation was
> Between those woolly breeders in the act,
> The skillful shepherd peeled me certain wands,
> And in the doing of the deed of kind
> He stuck them up before the fulsome ewes,
> Who then conceiving did in eaning time
> Fall parti-coloured lambs, and those were Jacob's.
>
> (1.3.75–85)

Shylock's account of Jacob breeding Laban's 'parti-coloured lambs' sparks a dispute with Antonio that stands as the only instance of biblical-exegetical debate to appear anywhere in Shakespeare's dramatic writing. But debate is perhaps too strong a word for what happens in this episode, since Antonio clearly does not view this as much of a contest. In response to Shylock's lengthy deliberation, Antonio determines that the meaning of the biblical story is clear enough and singular. 'This [i.e. Jacob's success at breeding cattle] was a venture sir that Jacob served for, / A thing not in his power to bring to pass, / But swayed and fashioned by the hand of heaven' (1.3.88–90). He is eager to move on to the more practical matter at hand, and sees Shylock's comments on Jacob and Laban as a diversionary tactic aimed at justifying charging interest on loans. He concludes by dismissing Shylock's account of Genesis 30, remarking to Bassanio, 'The devil can cite Scripture for his purpose' (1.3.95).

A great many scholars and editors, several of which I discuss shortly, have agreed with Antonio, citing and glossing Shylock's speech here as evidence of usurious motives. But Shylock does not make it easy to take this dismissive view. His normally terse style of speech is abandoned here in favour of an effusive deliberation on the skilled workings of Jacob who, despite terrible odds, successfully breeds his uncle's 'streaked and pied' cattle. This chapter turns with great interest to Shylock's account of this biblical story.

This narrative, which details the exploits of Jacob and Laban at Haran, stands as an important moment of self-explication for Shylock, one that is admittedly and perhaps wilfully misunderstood by Antonio. Audiences, however, might not and indeed ought not look past it. By appealing to Scripture, Shylock adopts a discourse that is itself parti-coloured, figurative of the complex mixture of commonality and difference that characterises Christians' and Jews' distinctive attempts to elaborate these stories' meaning. Shylock points towards these complexities when he uses the term 'compromise' ('Laban and himself were compromised'), a word that originally meant settling conflicting claims between parties.[1] The appeal to 'compromise' here underscores the presence of conflicting viewpoints. Rather than look dismissively past those conflicts or past Shylock's unique explanation of the parable, as Antonio does, this chapter turns instead to its particulars and the scriptural language in which it is embedded, which offers an important window into Shylock's motivations within the play, and which in Shakespeare's own era signalled the presence of multiple theological traditions and voices.

However, this chapter also marks a shift away from historical questions about the context of origin for *The Merchant of Venice*, and a movement instead towards questioning what this play comes to mean if we include Jewish voices in deliberations about the meaning of Jewishness in the play. It is the central insight of this book that Shakespeare's Jews are most productively understood when we consider them as Jews and not as ciphers for other things. 'Jew' is, after all, the very category that this play's early printed texts insistently assigns to Shylock. In this chapter I consider the ways in which Jewish identity is constructed discursively in the play through biblical exegesis, in particular via exegetical discussions of the parable of the parti-coloured lambs. Through centuries of interpretative engagement, the Genesis Jacob cycle of stories has been given both theological and practical life within the Jewish tradition by a great many voices. As I discuss in the pages that follow, the interpretive possibilities that follow from these stories include a rich Jewish aspect that has been all but ignored within the Shakespearean critical tradition.

A full and productive discussion of how *Merchant* has helped shape responses to the question of what it means to be Jewish – questions that have contributed to and, in many ways, generated the play's long historical afterlife – can only take place by setting aside the undue limitations of strict early modern historicist readings of this play. Such readings fail to account for how people and communities have responded to the play from within their own worlds, just as they fail to acknowledge the impact the play has had on conversations about Jewish identity among Jews, including Jewish writers who adapted the play in the nineteenth and twentieth centuries.[2] Rather than confining the discussion to what Shakespeare's early modern audience knew about Jews, or to early modern rabbinical insights on the biblical passages that Shylock cites, this chapter instead emphasises the temporally expansive nature of the central question posed by the book: is Shylock Jewish? That very question, the one that resides at the apex of this book project and comprises its title, asks how Jews themselves understand and come to define their ethnography. It is a question that necessarily includes a wide range of responses. In this chapter, I invoke a range of rabbinic commentaries in my discussion of the meanings assigned to the parable of Jacob and the parti-coloured lambs, and subsequent chapters engage with a more expansive legacy of Jewish responses to this play.

In this chapter, I turn to Jewish discussions of the biblical stories that Shylock references, both the ones he explicitly cites and those that Shakespeare's play-text evokes more subtly, with the aim of fleshing out these aspects of *The Merchant of Venice* in their full dimensionality. There is, in one sense, nothing new in my turn to theological commentary to help explain elements such as character motivation in *Merchant*. The Bible was at one time in the late nineteenth and twentieth centuries the most common inter-text that *Merchant* scholars would discuss to explain the play's structure and characters. However, the interpretive glosses being brought into discussions of the play have, until now, been exclusively Christian ones. It still bears remarking that Judaic approaches to the Genesis Jacob cycle routinely invoke a set of moral questions markedly different from the ones that preoccupy Christian exegetes. Within the last hundred years, only two brief critical accounts have turned to Judaic insights to help determine why Shylock, whom Shakespeare explicitly identifies as a Jew, might be reading these verses in a manner that is distinctive and does in fact cut striking parallels with rabbinic commentaries.[3] Both Julia Reinhard Lupton and Stanley Stewart have usefully referenced the Jewish-exegetical dimension of biblical citation in *Merchant* in their work on this play. However, neither scholar has explored this topic's fuller relevance to the characterisation of Shakespeare's Jewish moneylender, or discussed how the contents of Jewish accounts of these stories fit in with broader structures of meaning in the play. It was *Measure for Measure* that scholar Louise Schleiner once described as 'Shakespeare's most theological play' when she wrote that 'in no other play do the central characters evoke specific biblical passages and theological concepts to explain their crucial deeds; in no other are the allusions so prominent; in no other do they define so distinct and consistent a pattern.'[4] However, as I will soon make clear here, it is *The Merchant of Venice* that most explicitly foregrounds not only religious differences, but also the distinctive hermeneutic strategies and ways of life that follow from them. For Shylock, those patterns of citing and reading express a distinctive moral universe that is recognisably Jewish.

Both Christians and Jews regard Jacob as a figure of immense typological and nationalistic significance who foretells the elect status of the chosen people. From a Christian perspective, so-called Old Testament figures like Jacob – figures from the Torah that were transformed through Christian exegesis – carry deep but also murky moral significance because of their Judaic origins. The 1611 King James Bible translators' introduction begins by appealing to a story from the Jacob cycle that is very near to Shylock's chosen biblical parable. They cite Genesis 29: 10 in which Jacob sees Rachel for the first time and proceeds to roll the massive stone from the mouth of the well, helping her provide water for her father's sheep.

> Translation it is that openeth the window, to let in the light; that breaketh the shell, that we may eat the kernel; that putteth aside the curtaine, that we may looke into the most holy place; that removeth the cover of the well, that wee may come by the water, even as Jacob rolled away the stone from the mouth of the well, by which meanes the flockes of Laban were watered. Indeed, without translation into the vulgar tongue, the unlearned are but like children at Jacobs well (which was deepe) without a bucket or some thing to draw with.[5]

Jacob is here made to stand for the translators and their facilitating activity. Like Jacob watering Laban's flocks, the King James translators give the vernacular masses access to life-sustaining waters. That process is figured as an immersion in the deep waters of Judaic Scripture, and in fact it is the Hebrew text of the Pentateuch that affords those waters with the degree of depth referenced here. That same depth inheres in the figures who inhabit biblical stories, in individuals like Jacob who signify in unavoidably complex, parti-coloured ways because they carry echoes of ancient Judaic meaning that can never be entirely dismissed or extinguished, if indeed the point is to extinguish their rich, ancient pedigree rather than draw from those depths, as the KJV translators imply.[6]

Christian typological readings of the Hebrew Bible frequently draw on the depth and complexity referenced in the 1611 KJV introduction, even as they attempt to smooth over the ambivalent potential of stories like Jacob and Laban at Haran in favour of Christianised readings. In *The Merchant of Venice*, Shakespeare dwells in a number of significant ways on the ambivalent potential of those stories by deliberately prying apart pat, synthetic readings, instead re-emphasizing their ambivalent dimensionality. Twice in act 1, scene 3 Shylock makes clear that he invokes a pre-covenantal version of the biblical story of Abraham. He declares, 'This Jacob from our holy Abram was' (1.3.69), and later, 'O father Abram, what these Christians are, / Whose own hard dealings teaches them suspect / The thoughts of others!' (1.3.157–9). By referencing 'Abram' the spelling of Abraham that deliberately leaves off the 'h' marking the post-covenantal period of Abram's life, Shylock deliberately counters the typological prerogative to read biblical stories in a way that revises their Judaic meaning. Where the story of Jacob is concerned, that means a direct challenge to the Christian tendency to read Jacob as a Christ figure who claims Jacob's originally Jewish birthright for a new, Christian nation.[7]

Shylock makes clear that he sees himself as a present-day incarnation of the original, unrevised 'Old' Jacob descended from 'Abram', the Jacob of the Torah and not the New Testament. He positions himself at the very outset of the scene as a legitimate successor to the original nation of the elect – from his perspective, the Jewish nation. By insisting on a distinctly pre-Christian reading of these verses, Shylock qualifies and challenges the play's supposedly Christian moral architecture in no uncertain terms. Within many critical discussions of this scene, however, Shylock's story about Jacob and the parti-coloured lambs is described – or interpreted – through Antonio's eyes, in which Shylock merely adopts the language of sanctity while concealing predatory motives. Generations of scholars have approached the meaning of the biblical Jacob stories that Shylock invokes by focusing on their Christian resonances with a to understanding how a Jewish character fits into the play's Christian scheme.[8] In focusing solely on Christian typological readings of these biblical scripts, these accounts beg rather than probe the question of whether *Merchant* is, in fact, a Christian allegory at all. The text of Shakespeare's play is far from clear on this question; in fact, it insists at various points on alternate vantage points and on rapid shifts between distinctive readings of these same religious scripts.

A variety of scholars, some of them very apt readers of the play, have even gone a step farther and read Shylock's citation of the parable of Jacob and the parti-coloured lambs as Shylock's attempt to justify usury, as Antonio later claims. M. Lindsay Kaplan's 2002 *Texts and Contexts* edition of the play glosses Antonio's question 'Was this inserted to make interest good?' in just this way with the note, 'brought in to justify the practice of usury".[9] While 'justifying usury' is certainly the way that Antonio views Shylock's motives, far more surprising is the fact that so many scholars and editors have overwhelmingly accepted Antonio's characterisation of Shylock's intentions here. In the 2011 Arden Third Edition of *The Merchant of Venice*, editor John Drakakis discusses usury as the play's major theme.[10] In his view, Shylock's characteristic speech patterns and tendency towards repetition 'require to be read symptomatically as evidence of the propensity to a devilish duplicity that owes its scriptural origin to St. Matthew's gospel'.[11] Drakakis' comments, which appear in his introduction to the play, illustrate a problem that has become pervasive within critical interpretations of scriptural citation in *Merchant*: the unquestioning ascription of devilishness to Shylock following Antonio's designation of him as a 'devil who cites Scripture for his purpose', and the insistence that Shylock's meaning can be successfully grasped through New Testament Scripture. Throughout his commentary on the play, Drakakis consistently interprets Shylock's motivations through the explicitly anti-Semitic remarks of the play's Christian Venetians.

> In the Venice of Shakespeare's play two opposed kinds of money-lending prevail: that which is 'natural' and is practiced by Antonio, who, out of friendship, can say to Bassanio, 'My purse, my person, my extremest means / Lie all unlocked to your occasions' (1.1.138–9); and that which is 'artificial' and practiced by Shylock, who lends 'not / As to thy friends, for when did friendship take / A breed for barren metal of his friend? (1.3.127–9)[12]

What Drakakis does not specify, but which readers who know the play intimately will undoubtedly notice, is that the line 'when did friendship take a breed for barren metal from his friend' is Antonio's, not Shylock's, though Drakakis' comment here makes it appear as if the lines are uttered by Shylock, or can at least be made to speak for him. In effect, Drakakis silently shifts the moral and theological centre of the play onto Antonio, suggesting that we, the play's interpreters and audience, should also accept Antonio as the arbiter of Shylock's motivations.[13] Elsewhere, Drakakis expands more fully on the reasons why. 'Shylock is not primarily a realistic representation, not a "Jew" in the strictly ethnological sense of the term, but both a subject position *and* a rhetorical means of prising open a dominant Christian ideology no longer able to smooth over its own internal contradictions, and therefore a challenge and a threat.'[14]

The suggestion that Shylock is not a realistic ethnographic representation – 'not a "Jew"' but something more akin to a textual function – is particularly problematic when one considers how explicitly Drakakis treats Antonio as a 'real' character capable of uttering meaningful statements that do ostensibly express a subject position and real agency. Drakakis' critical strategy implicitly validates rather than seeking to critically evaluate the power imbalance between Christian

Venetians and the Jewish Shylock that Antonio instantiates in this scene and throughout the play, in which Shylock signals only depravity relative to Christian virtue. In fact, those power imbalances endow the act of watching and interpreting with a great deal of moral complexity and significance for audiences, since to interpret Shylock through the eyes and words of Christian Venetians is to fail to take his words seriously on their own terms. To tacitly accept Antonio's designation of Shylock as a 'devil' is to assign Shylock no agency and to refuse, a priori, to allow him to speak from anything other than a position of a moral foil – the depraved 'letter' relative to Antonio's Christian 'spirit'. And to see him that way is to effectively refuse to allow Shylock to speak at all.[15]

'Usury' is foremost among the words that have been used to describe Shylock's villainy, giving rise to various critical musings about his character's illicit motivations. But the word 'usury' is never uttered in *The Merchant of Venice*, least of all by Shylock. In fact, Shylock heartily rejects a variant of the word – 'usurer' – as Antonio's term for what he does. 'He [Antonio] was wont to call me usurer' (3.1.44–5). The term that Shylock prefers, which he deploys repeatedly throughout the play, is 'usances', which can refer to simple money lending but also has other connotations in an early modern English context, some of which I address later in this chapter. It bears emphasising that justifying usury, the very thing scholars have accused Shylock of doing, is itself an oxymoronic concept. 'Usury' already implies a breach of moral protocol; if a lending practice is usurious, there is no justifying it morally. Shakespeare's contemporaries understood this point, and early modern Christian moralists often took pains to foreground it. The renowned seventeenth-century logician and bishop George Downame reasoned in 1604 that 'although letting [i.e. lending] in it selfe be a lawfull contract, yet usurie in it selfe is simply and utterly unlawfull.'[16]

Even more to the point, if Shylock simply intends to provide a scriptural justification for charging interest, why does he not appeal directly to the relevant biblical verses from Deuteronomy on lending in this scene, verses that were well known to Christian audiences and with which he is evidently familiar?[17] Why does he appeal instead in this instance to a seemingly unrelated, morally obscure story from the Jacob cycle? Deuteronomy 23: 20–21 clearly stipulates where and under what conditions it is lawful to charge interest on monetary loans. 'You shall not deduct interest from loans to your countrymen . . . but you may deduct interest from loans to foreigners.'[18] In no case, however, do the deuteronomic prescriptions offer a justification for usurious or excessive interest rates.

Shakespeare's inclusion of the parable of the parti-coloured lambs in *The Merchant of Venice* signals his clear concern with procreation and generational flourishing. One of the defining features of the Genesis Jacob cycle is its insistence at various points on the promise of proliferation for the descendants of Israel intended to reflect their elect status. Jacob's success with the rods in Genesis 30 is itself a performance of this type of reproductive prowess, and in his recounting of the parable, Shylock repeatedly emphasises sexual reproduction and 'the work of generation' 'between these woolly breeders', who do 'the deed of kind' (1.3.79–81). The sexual coupling that takes place in these verses does, as Shylock notes, result in the successful reproduction of kind, and a proliferation of speckled, spotted and streaked animals that constitute Jacob's 'hire'. But Shylock's account is also emphatic about the cause of all this multiplication and reproduction. It is 'the skilful shepherd' who

> peeled me certain wands,
> And in the doing of the deed of kind
> He stuck them up before the fulsome ewes,
> Who then conceiving did in eaning time
> Fall parti-coloured lambs, and those were Jacob's.
>
> (1.3.81–5)

Shylock dwells on the actions of the clever shepherd, and his description of what Jacob does in this scene deploys active verbs suggestive of his agency – he 'stuck' the rods up before the ewes, he 'peeled me certain wands', actions that contrast with the ewes and their offspring, who more passively 'fall' parti-coloured. The final line of Shylock's summary of what happens – 'and those were Jacob's' – is an assertion of who exactly generates the success of this episode: Jacob. Both the cattle and the agency responsible for their successful reproduction are Jacob's. The cause of Jacob's success is a particular kind of generative power, one akin to craftiness and skill, not mere copulation. In Shylock's account, a form of creativity different and more crucial to his success than brute sexual reproduction effects the multiplication of Jacob's stock. Shylock's response to Antonio's question 'is your gold and silver ewes and rams?' (1.3.92) is 'I make it breed as fast' (1.3.93). Shylock views his own skill with money as a close cousin to Jacob's breeding skills, which he views as legitimate means of advancement. The skill at the heart of Jacob's success story is what interests Shylock, the same attributes and talents that he identifies in his present-day ability to make his financial assets flourish.

It is early on in the negotiations with Antonio that Shylock first identifies Jacob as an exemplar, someone whose skills he believes match his own. 'Mark what Jacob did' (1.3.73), he proclaims as a preface to his lengthy exegesis. With those four words, Shylock succeeds in indicating that it is through Jacob's example that he intends to illustrate his own intentions. While Antonio and Bassanio await his decision on the loan, Shylock recounts the story of Jacob at Genesis 30 in which he skilfully breeds Laban's parti-coloured cattle. Shylock's ability to make things – in this case ducats – multiply evidently strikes him as a reflection of Jacob's success multiplying Laban's speckled animals. Shylock's association of his own skills with Jacob's is rendered even more emphatic in the text of the 1600 First

Quarto and 1623 First Folio editions, where Shylock identifies himself *as* Jacob, substituting 'I' for 'aye' at line 70.[19] Where modern editions of the play (here I cite the Oxford World Classics edition) read 'ay, he was the third', which can be paraphrased as 'yes, he [Jacob] was the third', the 1600 Q1 text reads 'I, he [i.e. Jacob] was the third', which can be read as 'I, as Jacob, was the third'.[20] When Shylock narrates Jacob's breeding experiment, he deploys a series of these grammatical shifts to the possessive, such as the one at line 81, where Jacob 'peeled *me*' (rather than 'peeled *him*') 'certain wands' (1.3.79). The identification between Shylock and Jacob is reinforced further when Shylock comments that he is 'debating of my present store' as he considers the loan proposal (1.3.50). One of the meanings of 'store' is livestock, as in a store of horses or cattle, and in Genesis 30, Jacob deliberates over which of the common stock of cattle that he shares with Laban will serve as his salary.[21]

As Shylock appropriates the biblical Jacob's story, he presents himself as a present-day Jacob ostensibly confronting *his* present-day Laban in Antonio. The impetus to identify with biblical figures and their moral predicaments is itself recognisably Judaic, and represents an approach to resolving present-day problems that is synonymous with midrash. Midrash (or the vernacular 'drash') refers to the act of interpreting and glossing a text; however, it also signals a more specific set of hermeneutic practices in which present-day problems are addressed through an appeal to authoritative biblical stories. By presenting himself as a present-day Jacob, Shylock does more than provide a narrative illustration of his intentions; he actually positions himself to 'coordinate the narrative and prescriptive dimensions of Torah', as Julia Reinhard Lupton has argued, by applying those foundational stories to the exigencies of his own life. In her work on *The Merchant of Venice*, Lupton has argued that this coordinative tendency demonstrates a midrashic hermeneutic, one that informs Shylock's behaviour from the very outset of the scene.[22] Shylock's mode of reading manages to serve an important prescriptive function, since midrash excels at 'tell[ing] [individuals] how they were supposed to conduct themselves at the critical turnings of life'.[23] For observant Jews, this mode of interpretation provides ethical orientation in the world that is central to determining appropriate responses to everyday moral quandaries that are both mundane and immensely significant. Those predicaments in fact constitute a space of moral questions in which individuals must routinely find an orientation, enabling them to construct coherent, meaningful identities in the world with the help of biblical stories.[24]

In actuality, a wide variety of Jewish cultural behaviours encourage midrashic responses, including the practice of naming children after characters from the Torah. Biblical names are intended to provide a set of situational and moral parameters that can inform present-day decision-making. Children are often named 'Sarah' or 'Joseph' because some aspect of their conception or birth corresponds to that of their biblical namesake. The ritual practices of holiday celebrations also perform this same coordinating function; the Seder meal at Passover re-enacts the events of Exodus, reinforcing the sense that present-day celebrants participated in those biblical events, and conversely, that biblical stories have an important bearing on present-day discussions of freedom. The Seder itself, whose literal meaning is 'order', requires an ordering of the present via the story and moral quandaries evoked through the Book of Exodus.[25]

In a less traditional religious context, that same midrashic interpretive pattern remains present in a variety of works of fiction authored by Jews in the twentieth century, several of which I discuss in Chapter 4 of this book. Whether serving the ends of religious orthodoxy or more secular expressions of Jewishness, midrash relies on a shared register of biblical narratives that are both familiar and regarded as authoritative. Those stories, figures, and moral scenarios are then read creatively by individuals who interpretively 'turn' them to suit the needs of the present day.

By identifying himself as a present-day Jacob and reading his present predicament through Jacob's story, Shylock manages to deftly transpose Jacob's moral questions and conflicts onto his own immediate circumstances. Shylock's speech is a particularly significant act of self-explication that allows us to get to know him through his own dialogic engagement with figures who signify importantly to him, as the biblical Jacob clearly does.[26] In effect, by understanding Shylock's Jacob – a Jacob that, I argue shortly, is significantly informed by Judaic exegesis – we understand Shylock's motivations more successfully on their own terms, and can also better contextualise Antonio's slanderous account rather than accepting it as an objective account of Shylock's worth.

Two thousand years' worth of rabbinic exegesis has helped construct a distinctive and recognisable ethos for Jacob over the *longue durée*, one that contrasts in notable ways with Christian responses to these same verses. Despite the vast cultural and historical differences between a medieval Rashi and a modern Menahem Kasher, the integrity and coherence of the rabbinic or 'Jewish' Jacob rest on the inherently dialogic structure of midrashic commentary. Rabbinic scholar Michael Chernick explains that 'the tradition they [the rabbis] were creating was multi-vocal, argumentative, intellectually restless, and concerned with all aspects of life. Returning to that tradition over and over meant hearing its voice and adding one's own.'[27] Volumes of commentary penned by such authorities as Rashi and Maimonides converse not only with the text of the Torah but also (within the limits of chronological possibility) with one another's interpretive reasoning on particular words, passages and grammatical structures, all the while addressing the exigencies of their own interpretive communities. This type of engagement with the Torah and its exegetic legacy describes the basic essence of midrash, characterised by discursive engagement with both authoritative scriptural narratives and practical present-day questions.[28]

Rabbinic exegetes frequently interpret Genesis 30 as a contest among kinship groups that carries strong providential implications, with Laban figuring Syrian or Aramean people and Jacob the people of Israel or the Jewish nation. When Shylock utters 'cursed be my tribe if I forgive him [i.e. Antonio]' (1.3.48) in act 1 scene 3, he calls attention to the long history of ethnographic interaction between Jews and neighbouring non-Jewish groups scripted in the Pentateuch. Those stories detail deep-seated enmities and affinities; in effect, they script out a whole host of authoritative precedents whose moral tones rabbinic commentators routinely graft onto contemporary socio-political relationships between Jews and non-Jewish 'others'. For commentators, the relevant point of distinction is Jacob's monotheism, which is frequently contrasted with the polytheistic practices of Laban's clan. In the *Guide for the Perplexed*, medieval Torah scholar Maimonides (1138–1204) describes Laban as an idolater, a designation that for him goes hand-in-hand with the sense that Laban was also 'a perfectly wicked man'.[29] In the Hebrew text of chapter 30, verse 27, Laban uses the word *nihashti* (learned by divination), saying to Jacob, 'I have learned by divination that the Lord has blessed me on your account.'[30] Some English translations from the Hebrew render *nihashti* as 'learned from experience' or 'observed the signs', which commentators interpret as a reference to divination or idolatry. The medieval Torah commentator Abraham ibn Ezra (1089–1164) remarks that the Hebrew *nihashti* means '"I have divined", for Laban was an enchanter and had *teraphim*'.[31] *Teraphim* are material instruments of sorcery according to ibn Ezra – the same idols that Rachel later steals from her father and conceals in her luggage as she and Jacob flee from Haran and which *The Merchant of Venice* invokes through Jessica's theft of her mother Leah's turquoise ring.

By focusing on stories that have been interpreted as contests between nations of differing faiths, Shylock references a series of primordial ethnographic rivalries that he transposes onto his and Antonio's loan negotiations in act 1, scene 3. Shylock pronounces early on in act 1, scene 3, 'If I can catch him [Antonio] upon the hip, / I will feed fat the ancient grudge I bear him' (1.3.43–4). 'Catching Antonio upon the hip' alludes to a wrestling move, once more reinforcing the link between Shylock's own story and that of Jacob, who wrestles with an angel in Genesis 22 and receives the name 'Israel' from the Hebrew for 'he who wrestles with God'. Shylock's reference to an 'ancient grudge' in this speech appeals in broad terms to a distant, shared biblical past, one that pre-exists whatever immediate conflicts these two men have generated within the play. Their grudge is 'ancient' not because of the recent incident that Shylock reports of Antonio spitting on his 'Jewish gaberdine' in public, but rather because Shylock views the present scene through a biblical rivalry rooted in an ethnographic identification with his 'tribe'.

The ethnographic enmity of Shylock's line 'I hate him [Antonio] for he is a Christian' (1.3.39) is clear enough, and made even clearer when we consider the tribal enmities that recur throughout the Book of Genesis and the Jacob cycle of stories. By appealing selectively to those relationships, Shylock positions himself in this instance as Jacob, the adherent of a true faith, while casting Antonio in the role of Laban the idolater. Shylock thereby stakes his claim to moral and religious priority as the descendant of 'Abram', and positions himself as the opponent of an idolatrous con man.

When we encounter Shylock's Jacob, the Jacob of Genesis 30, he is at the stage in his biblical cycle of stories where he has already left his parents' home and made a new home and family for himself among Laban's kin. In the verses that chronicle Jacob's breeding experiment, Jacob manages to elicit a near-miraculous outcome extremely favourable to him but unfavourable to Laban. The two men strike an agreement to divide their cattle and go their separate ways, but during the breeding season Jacob manages to make his own share of the flock – the speckled and spotted animals – breed far more abundantly than the solid-coloured animals that are to be Laban's share. This outcome goes against the natural genetic tendency of the cattle to produce more plain-coloured offspring than speckled. Unlikely success is a dominant theme in this biblical story, but both rabbinic and Christian commentaries focus less on the unlikeliness of Jacob's feat than on the means through which he obtains it. Is his success generated through divine providence? Through human effort? As it turns out, these questions become centrally important to both Jewish and Christian readings of these stories, though there is substantial disagreement about what exactly transpires.

Rabbinical commentaries on Genesis 30 display a marked interest in the dynamics of what Jacob manages to accomplish by virtue of his own ingenuity. Going into great detail, they elaborate on the skilful interventions that make Laban's sheep breed slower and less abundantly than Jacob's; they discuss the correct work ethic for situations in which an employee must tend to his employer's as well as his own flocks; and they venture opinions about the precise terms of Jacob and Laban's initial agreement. One commentator explains, 'We may learn from Jacob that an employee who works faithfully receives his reward in this world in addition to the portion stored up for him in the World to Come.'[32] Indeed, the emphasis in many of the Hebrew commentaries that discuss Jacob's feat rests on effort, work, and worldly progress.

Rabbinic accounts of Jacob's success stand in marked contrast to Christian approaches to these same biblical verses. Although not all of the Christian commentaries are as explicit as Antonio that 'this was a venture Jacob served for, a thing not in his power to bring to pass', the debate about who exactly was responsible for the multiplication of speckled cattle remains a consistent point of discussion for Renaissance Christian commentators. For these exegetes, the moral status of Jacob's actions in the cycle as a whole is problematic and stands in need of substantial and often lengthy justification. The Christian commentaries are full of what Arnold Williams refers to as 'hair-splitting distinctions' which attempt to excuse Jacob of the various sins he commits: lying, dishonouring his father, tricking his brother, etc.[33] 'The means which Jacob used, was not artificial or fraudulent, but natural, not depending on man's skill, but God's blessing', writes theologian Andrew Willett (1562–1621) in his 1608 *Hexapla in Genesin*.[34] 'Although then that nature had her work, we cannot say that nature wholly did it.'[35]

Antonio's comment to Shylock that 'this was a venture sir that Jacob serv'd for / A thing not in his power to bring to pass, / But sway'd and fashion'd by the hand of heaven' (1.3.86–8) echoes the basic concern expressed by Christian exegetes about the imagined dangers of ascribing too much agency to Jacob in this story. Early modern Christian commentators place a great deal of emphasis on divine intercession as the most and perhaps only satisfying way of absolving Jacob of the moral offences he commits. Andrew Willett's 1633 edition of *Hexapla in Genesin & Exodum* devotes a whole subheading in *The Explanation and Solution of Doubtful Questions and Places* to the question of 'Whether Jacobs device were by miracle or by the workes of nature'.[36] In the same spirit, theologian Henry Ainsworth (1571–1622), in his 1616 edition of *Annotations Upon the First Book of Moses*, writes that only through God's intervention did Jacob's cattle manage to breed abundantly. 'Naturally the cattel would bring forth others like themselves, and so Jacobs part should be few. But by Gods extraordinary providence, it fell out otherwise.'[37] Early modern English commentators worry a great deal over the problem of moral responsibility in these verses. Did God make Jacob commit these actions, or did he perform them of his own volition? And if he performed them of his own volition, how can we regard him as a moral exemplar? Throughout these discussions, divine agency and providential design are emphasised far more than Jacob's own role in making the speckled and spotted cattle breed. Jacob's success is a morally virtuous one only insofar as it is orchestrated by divine will. Where it appears to reflect Jacob's natural abilities, the story instead inspires anxiety.

Embedded in a number of the cultural scripts that accompany this story in Renaissance Europe is a related concern about human agency and the power of the imagination to re-shape material forms. In the popular sixteenth-century book *The Secret Miracles of Nature* written by the Dutchman Lemnius Levinus (1505–68), Levinus cites this parable as an example of the mind's ability to affect matter in mysteriously powerful, sometimes unwitting ways.

> Whilst a man and woman embrace, if the woman think of the man's countenance, and look upon him, and thinks of anyone else, that likeness will the child represent [. . .] Jacob used that stratagem, who was afterwards called Israel, laying rods he had pilled off the rinds from, before them everywhere, and so he made the greatest part of the flock spotted and party-coloured.[38]

This same insight, attributed to Galen, is repeated in English Jesuit preacher Thomas Wright's (1561–1623) early seventeenth-century volume on rhetoric and emotion, *The Passions of the Minde*. Wright discusses the power of women's imaginations to alter the appearance of unborn offspring.

> Galen also reporteth, that a woman beholding a most beautiful picture, conceived and brought forth a beautiful child by a most deformed father, we have also in the Scriptures the like experience in Jacob, who to cause his ewes conceive speckled lambs, put sundry white rods in the channels where the beasts were watered, and thereby the lambs were yeaned party-coloured.[39]

For both writers, the salient issue and source of anxiety is not material forms per se, but rather human agency and the ability to influence material forms 'naturally' according to ordinary, everyday human practices.

Several rabbinical commentaries on Genesis 30 also rehearse Galen's theory of reproductive mutation; however, among rabbinical writers there is a far more positive evaluation of the lambs' natural workings. The French medieval Torah commentator Rabbi Shlomo Yitzhaki (1040–1105), more commonly known as Rashi, remarks:

> Many are amazed at what is reported in our verse, and say that it can only be described as an out of the ordinary phenomenon. Really, what Scripture describes is indeed one of the wonders of nature. However, it is a natural law. Even a woman who is created in the image of the angels affects her fetus by what she looks at while she is pregnant.[40]

In Rashi's view, the manipulation of a foetus is a 'wonder of nature' to some, but actually looks to him like a 'natural law'. His comment reflects the broader tendency within rabbinical commentary to emphasise the natural aspects of seemingly 'wonderful' occurrences. This is particularly the case for the episodes surrounding Jacob's multiplication of speckled cattle, where there is a concerted focus on the skill involved both in the production of the cattle and in Jacob's ability to broker the initial arrangement with his uncle. To this same end, the medieval Jewish scholar Nahmanides, also known as Ramban (1194–1270) writes of Jacob's use of the peeled rods:

> As soon as they [Laban and Jacob] agreed that his hire would be these colours it was permissible for Jacob to do whatever he could to cause them to give birth in this manner. Perhaps Jacob had made a condition that he may do with them whatever he wants since Laban did not know of the ramifications of this measure, nor did Laban's shepherds sense anything when they saw the sticks in the gutters once a year during the days of Nisan.[41]

Nahmanides concludes that Jacob's stratagem is permissible because it abides by the rules governing their arrangement, rules to which both parties agree in advance. But the real reason Jacob succeeds in Nahmanides' view is that he is smarter than Laban and his sons. He finds a way around the obvious constraints, and sees options that neither Laban nor his sons are able to anticipate, despite Laban's mystical divinations. The real substance of Jacob's success consists of his intelligent resolution of a practical problem, just as the moral substance of the episode consists of a skill-based resolution to a complex issue, rather than a passive submission to supernatural force.

When Antonio pronounces, 'This was a venture sir that Jacob serv'd for, / A thing not in his power to bring to pass, / But sway'd and fashioned by the hand of heaven', he insists that Jacob's success is praiseworthy solely because it reflects divine providence. The success is God's, not his. This was also the meaning accorded to these verses by John Calvin. In his sermon 'entreating of the free election of God in Iacob, and of reprobation in Esau', Calvin asks: if it was preordained that one son would be rejected and one accepted, why did God not ordain for Jacob rather than Esau to be born first? Calvin's explanation is that God was actively reinforcing the mightiness of the meek and the humble, 'that men should bring nothing of their owne, to the end to say: I have attained such and such a good thing. I have gotten it by my owne industry.'⁴² God's reason for choosing one over the other, in Calvin's view, is ultimately mysterious and not for humans to know. 'The Church springeth from the pure grace of God: & so that all the praise of our salvation must wholly be reserved to himself.'⁴³

According to the Calvinist view echoed in Antonio's statement, Shylock misreads the true meaning of the scriptural passage, claiming undue credit for a miraculous feat. It is important, however, to recognise Shylock's very different claim here that he grounds in these same biblical verses. Shylock's view of things, following Jacob's, suggests that what he actually seeks is an opportunity to ply his trade in a self-respecting way. He does this through Jacob's own insistence on the altogether natural quality of the work that he, like Jacob, performs, which has made him wealthy. Shylock pronounces:

> Signior Antonio, many a time and oft
> In the Rialto you have rated me
> About my moneys and my usances.
> Still have I borne it with a patient shrug,
> For sufferance is the badge of all our tribe.
> You call me misbeliever, cut-throat dog,
> And spit upon my Jewish gaberdine,
> *And all for use of that which is mine own* [emphasis mine].
> (1.3.103–10)

Shylock's underlying point in this speech is that he seeks a chance to exercise his skills in a self-respecting way, one that does not involve being spat on or insulted in public. In a pragmatic sense, Shylock appears in act 1, scene 3 to be doing what Charles Spinosa aptly summarises as 'getting by according to the abilities God has given him.'[44] Those very abilities constitute the 'use of that which is mine own', a use that for Shylock carries not only physical and financial but also moral resonances.

The interpretive gloss on Genesis 30 that Shylock proffers is rooted in a desire to be seen and recognized by Antonio and also by the play's audience as a legitimate moral agent. It implores Antonio to appreciate his skills fairly for the added value they bring to him and his friends. In Genesis 30, Jacob is a model of economic responsibility and a good provider for his family. He observes his growing household and surveys the practical resources needed to sustain his flourishing flock of cattle, women and children. He asks, 'And now, when shall I make provision for mine own household?'[45] He points towards the years of service he has rendered Laban and the growing family for whose sake he agreed to serve. 'Give me my wives and my children, for whom I have served you, that I may go; for well you know what services I have rendered you.'[46] His question about providing for his own family is one that rabbinical commentators dwell on at great length. While Jacob is without question the object of divine entitlement in the Hebrew commentaries, of equal importance is Jacob's much more ordinary entitlement through hard work and his commitment to supporting his family. In the end, this represents the greatest point of contrast between Laban's and Jacob's moral motivations according to commentators. Laban is depicted as someone who thrives thanks to the labour of others, notably Jacob, while Jacob is someone who thrives by virtue of his own toil and willingness to put his shoulder to the grindstone.[47] Fifteenth-century Spanish Torah scholar and physician Isaac Caro (1458–1535) writes about this verse, 'There are shepherds who feed but do not keep guard, and shepherds who keep guard but do not feed. I will both feed and keep guard. Beloved is labor, for all the prophets engaged in it.'[48]

An appeal to Jacob's work ethic would also have elicited a flash of recognition if not approbation from Shakespeare's audience members. Christian and Jewish interpreters of these stories both greatly admired Jacob's willingness to care for and protect his family. Jacob is consistently associated with the positive sense of thrift in an economic context through the successful management of his expanding household. Early modern English commentaries such as *The Mirrour of Religious Men*, published in 1611, praise Jacob's ability to provide for his kin in active and responsible ways. In that publication, theologian James Maxwell (1581–1635) remarks that 'the children of Jacob are taught not to live Idlely and without some lawfull calling or trade, and rather to embrace the condition of service then to spend their time in sluggishnes, idlenes, and sinne.'[49]

Jacob's divine entitlement and his wealth are made possible because of his hard labour; the two are, in an important sense, coterminous. Where Jacob has acquired his wealth by breeding cattle, Shylock has acquired his by managing his money, a skill in which he takes great pride and which he esteems as highly as Jacob's skill at animal husbandry. Evidently Shylock does not consider his financial practices to be a form of unnatural multiplication or theft, as Antonio insinuates. He takes pains to distinguish Antonio's word for what he does – 'He [Antonio] was wont to call me usurer' (3.1.44) – from his own self-described successes, which he terms 'well-won thrift' (1.3.47). At the end of his account of the parable of the parti-coloured lambs, after he describes how 'the skillful shepherd peeled me certain wands' and Jacob effects the prolific multiplication of speckled and spotted cattle, Shylock remarks that 'This was a way to thrive, and he was blest; / And thrift is blessing, if men steal it not' (1.3.86–7). It is Antonio's belief that Shylock's vocation is unnatural, a belief reflected in his pronouncement, 'If thou [Shylock] wilt lend this money, lend it not / As to thy friends, for when did friendship take / A breed for barren metal of his friend?' (1.3.128–30). However, Shylock maintains that his own success with money is legitimately obtained, just as Jacob's was with the cattle. Thrift can be a blessing so long as it is not stolen. Like Jacob, Shylock finds himself surrounded by naysayers who would discredit his success as ill gained. However, those dissenting voices do not discount the logic of Shylock's reasoning that Jacob's way constitutes a way to thrive, nor should they prevent *us* from examining the logic of his thrift more attentively than Antonio does.

Shylock's appeal to thrift as a 'blessing' so long as 'men steal it not' represents a significant and rich moment in the play, though editors have often read the term 'thrift' as an expression of Shylock's penny-pinching materialism here.[50] The sense of thrift as frugality or parsimony, however, is actually a secondary and later meaning. The *Oxford English Dictionary* lists the primary, older meaning of thrift as 'success, prosperity, or luck'.[51]

Shylock appeals to thrift on two separate occasions in act 1, scene 3. Initially, he describes an unpleasant past encounter with Antonio. 'He hates our sacred nation, and he rails, / Even there where merchants most do congregate, / On me, my bargains and my well-won thrift' (1.3.45–8). Shylock's emphasis in these lines rests on the 'well-won' nature of his success, a success that he takes pains to figure as legitimately gained. On the second occasion where he refers to thrift, he makes a similar argument about the legitimacy of his efforts to thrive. 'This was a way to thrive, and he was blest: / And thrift is blessing, if men steal it not' (1.3.86–7). For Shylock, the 'way to thrive' in Venice is evidently bound up with the strategies of Jacob and, in particular, the Jacob whose exploits are detailed in Genesis 30. Within that story, financial success is really the least important aspect of a much more comprehensive notion of success or thriving. Shylock's vision of thrift imagines the well-lived life predicated upon the intelligent resolution of situational problems. That kind of applied intelligence aims not to passively receive the fruits of divine promises, but rather, in a much more Jacob-like fashion, to prove clever enough to successfully actualise them.

When Shylock appeals to Genesis 30's parable of the parti-coloured lambs as he negotiates the loan with Antonio, he calls attention to a cautionary tale about injustice and the exploitation of a righteous man. Shylock may well be advancing a counter-argument as he cites this episode, as Stanley Stewart has claimed, that opposes Antonio's implied suggestion about charging interest on loans. Antonio's view of moneylending insists that it be lent out according to the Christian formula involving no fee, a practice that would destroy and stigmatise Shylock's livelihood.[52] By arguing that he represents a present-day Jacob faced with the moral quandaries of Jacob at Haran, Shylock deftly references a series of questions about structural inequities among kin and the logistics and ethics of managing them that are also central to the way these biblical stories have been interpreted by rabbinical commentators. Through the biblical inter-text, Shylock references the moral quandary he faces loaning money to Antonio, which involves deciding how to set the terms of a financial arrangement with someone who, like Laban, has dealt dishonestly with him in the past, but with whom he also shares a common ancestry and history.

In the episode from Genesis 30 that Shylock details at length, Jacob is on the brink of establishing his independence from Laban as he negotiates the terms of his leave-taking. Jacob's divinely sponsored wealth and hard work have made him rich and have also, by extension, enriched Laban and his sons. One rabbi offers a precise tabulation of the wealth that Jacob generates once he enters into Laban's service, accounting that added value at four thousand extra pieces of cattle every month.[53] That substantial added wealth does not go unnoticed. Laban readily acknowledges that Jacob has had an auspicious effect on his personal prosperity. 'I have learned by divination that the Lord has blessed me on your account.'[54] While Laban is keen to profit from Jacob's good fortune and hard work, Jacob is cast as a morally upright figure stuck navigating the rough waters of his uncle's attempts to cheat him. Those attempts are elaborated in detail in several rabbinic commentaries, including Isaac Caro's. Caro remarks that at verse 28 when Laban asks Jacob to appoint his wage, the word he uses, *nak'bah* (appoint), is also akin to *neke'vah* (female), signifying that Laban imagined he had discovered a weakness for women in Jacob that he then aimed to exploit. Caro quotes the Zohar's elaboration of this story to the effect that Laban had a third daughter whom he sought to marry off to Jacob. Where Laban proposed to offer that daughter for seven more years of Jacob's service, Jacob's sense of religious piety prevailed and he refused the arrangement.[55]

Laban's interest in Jacob is, according to many commentaries, motivated from the start by financial imperatives. The hospitality that he extends to Jacob when Jacob shows up in Haran empty-handed is due to a mistaken belief that Jacob was already a rich man. To that end, the Classical midrashic homiletic text *Genesis Rabbah* recounts that Laban pats Jacob down when he first greets him to see whether there is gold or silver concealed on his body. He finds none, and then invites Jacob to remain as a guest in his home, believing all the while that a sizeable caravan of his valuables would arrive shortly thereafter.[56] A related midrash about this verse recounts an anecdote wherein Laban pats Jacob down as he moves to kiss him, expecting to find gold hidden on his person. When gold fails to materialise, he waits until Jacob returns home and digs up a patch of ground next to where he stood. Lo and behold, he finds gold and silver buried there.[57]

If Laban is an idolater whose polytheistic practices contrast with Jacob's monotheism, his morally dubious exploitation of Jacob is further complicated by the fact that he is

Jacob's maternal uncle. How does one deal with a kinsman who is also one's boss, particularly when that individual persistently behaves in an unethical and exploitative way? Genesis 30 suggests at the difficulty of such a predicament and the complexity of equitably dividing up property held in common. In the arrangement that Jacob strikes with Laban in Genesis 30, the two men agree to separate their respective cattle according to colour and marking, with Jacob proposing to take all speckled, spotted and brown-coloured offspring. As Shylock mentions, this is how the two agree to be 'compromised'. Laban then removes all of the speckled, spotted and brown animals from the herd, bringing them three days' journey away from Jacob. He leaves Jacob with a flock of solid coloured animals from which to breed his future parti-coloured herd. This arrangement virtually guarantees a smaller share for Jacob and is fraught from the outset with mutual suspicion and unfair advantage.

Those same types of arrangements, with their attendant deceptions and retroactive changes, had long characterised Jacob's work contracts with Laban, most emphatically in the wedding-night substitution of the elder and less desirable Leah for the younger and more beautiful Rachel. Several rabbinical commentators contextualise the breeding experiment against these prior deceptions, describing it as an occasion for Jacob to correct for the past inequities he suffered at the hands of Laban. According to Nahmanides, after Laban changes Jacob's wages ten times, an angel reveals to Jacob that God has seen what Laban has been doing to him. In the prophetic dream, Jacob is shown the multiplication of parti-coloured offspring that indicates the precise manner in which God would grant retribution to him.[58] The eighteenth-century commentary *Or HaChayyim* proposes a related midrash in which Laban possesses charms that help him see into the developing fetuses of the cattle, leading God to interfere on Jacob's behalf. 'For I have seen all that Laban is doing to you ... The God who judges fairly has taken from one and given to the other [i.e. Jacob].'⁵⁹

Midrash HaGadol, a fourteenth-century commentary, insists that there is no foul play involved in Jacob's breeding experiment. Instead, it argues that Laban had repeatedly changed Jacob's wages and Jacob was therefore compelled to resort to schemes of his own to extricate himself from further service to Laban. The commentary cites 2 Samuel 22: 27, 'thou wilt shew thyself unsavoury', as evidence of the legitimacy of this rationale.⁶⁰ In *Or HaChayyim*, the Moroccan rabbi Chayyim ibn Attar (1696–1743) elaborates on the bad-faith negotiations between Laban and Jacob that set the stage for Jacob's subsequent stratagem. Laban was crafty and removed every animal that had any white in its hide. Jacob had asked Laban to remove the speckled and spotted but not the streaked cattle prior to the breeding experiment, thinking that he would be left some animals with white in them to encourage parti-coloured offspring. But Laban deceitfully removed even the streaked animals. Following from this plan, Jacob's wages would be reduced almost to nothing. Jacob therefore had to resort to the stratagem with the rods.⁶¹ Ibn Attar further reasons that Jacob resorted to using the rods only to recuperate his losses. Shepherds in his position who took an active responsibility for breeding their employers' flocks were conventionally paid two-thirds of the flock's offspring. Citing Maimonides, ibn Attar asserts that even after the miraculous outcome, Jacob never obtained the two-thirds portion that shepherds in his position were due.⁶²

Rabbinical commentators routinely endeavour to contextualise Jacob's behaviour in the parti-coloured lambs episode against Laban's deceptions. There is good reason to read Shylock's actions through this same set of concerns for the broader structural inequalities of his relationship with Antonio. By implying that he is Jacob to Antonio's

Laban, Shylock in effect makes a claim that he is a righteous man who has been wronged by a manipulative kinsman who stands to benefit substantially from his skilled labour. When Shylock first mentions the biblical inter-text and proposes that, 'When Jacob grazed his uncle Laban's sheep – / This Jacob from our holy Abram was', he does so after a bizarre performance in which he cannot seem to remember the details of the loan that Bassanio wants. Bassanio must remind him several times of the number of ducats and duration of the loan, after which Shylock finally enters into the deliberations and proposes his terms. There are many ways to read Shylock's strange behaviour here, but it is worth considering it as evidence of a particularly Jacob-like strategy in the context of Jacob's dealings with Laban.[63] Given the complexity of the negotiations between Jacob and Laban over the division of the cattle, and in light of their history of retroactively altered contracts and last-minute substitutions, Shylock might very well anticipate a substantial amount of deception, doublespeak, and injustice at the hands of Bassanio and Antonio. Like Jacob, he stands on the other side of a religious divide from the person with whom he negotiates a contract's terms, a religious divide that he characterises from the outset as an 'ancient' struggle for advantage.

Shylock understands that those religious differences have significant ethical implications, as they do in the biblical story. The implication worth drawing out here is that Shylock's strange behaviour at the outset of the scene, where he transitions rapidly from confident plotter ('cursed be my tribe if I forgive him') to absent-minded bumbler ('how many months do you desire?' 'I had forgot – three months, you told me so') may well be deliberate, since it offers him the opportunity to survey and test the terms of the loan before committing to it. Asking about the terms of the bond and pretending to forget about the most salient elements (how much, for how long) constitute ways of probing the consistency of the loan's terms as well as the 'sufficiency' of the people he is about to engage in a loan contract. Just as Shylock muses aloud at the beginning of the scene about the details of Antonio's fleet and the likelihood of its safe return, here he reveals a similar concern for the worthiness of these credit-seekers. Shylock appeals to the biblical story to position himself in what he believes to be a superior, more knowing position with *his* Laban. Through Jacob's example, Shylock has the foresight to anticipate a degree of dishonesty that he imagines will help him construct a more airtight contract with Antonio.

Several rabbinical commentaries read Jacob's predicament in Genesis 30 as an instance of making the best of a bad situation. Where Jacob fell victim to Laban's schemes, he was forced to devise an effective counter-scheme in order to avoid perpetual enslavement. For his part, Laban is satisfied with the status quo arrangement so long as Jacob remains a subservient member of his household, with his skills and luck helping to subsidise Laban's steadily increasing stores of cattle and grandchildren. However, once Jacob decides to split his cattle from the common stock, both Laban and his sons react angrily, as though Jacob had cheated them of their property.

> Now he heard the things that Laban's sons were saying: 'Jacob has taken all that was our father's, and from that which was our father's he has built up all this wealth.'[64]

The same uneasy mixture of dependency and resentment evidenced by Laban in Genesis 31 is dramatised in *The Merchant of Venice*, where a Christian businessman is compelled to seek credit from a Jewish moneylender whom he despises. In the biblical story, Jacob's labour and his near-miraculous ability to generate affluence are commodities that Laban attempts to marshal for his own personal gain and that of his household. If there is an equivalent in Shakespeare's play, it is Shylock's ability to make ducats multiply, a skill for which he was evidently renowned in Venice.

Those very abilities elicit contempt from Antonio both during their encounter and in Shylock's report of their previous interactions where Antonio had interfered with his business opportunities ('he brings down the rate of usance with us in Venice'), and the encounter where Antonio reportedly disrespects him by spitting on him in public and hurling slanderous epithets – 'misbeliever', 'cutthroat dog'. Antonio continues to scorn Shylock even as he asks for the loan, insisting that 'I am as like to call thee so again, / To spit on thee again, to spurn thee too' (1.3.126–7). And yet as Shylock points out, Antonio stands in obvious need of his financial assistance, and this fact leads Shylock to feel entitled to be treated like an equal.

> Shall I bend low, and in a bondsman's key,
> With bated breath and whispering humbleness,
> Say this:
> 'Fair sir, you spit on me Wednesday last,
> You spurned me such a day, another time
> You called me dog, and for these courtesies
> I'll lend you thus much moneys?'
>
> (1.3.120–5)

Shylock's complaint here is framed as a plea for equitable treatment and recognition, treatment that in effect recognises the bond of kinship that unites them via their ancient biblical ancestry. Shylock is acutely sensible of the lowly, subservient position that he is expected to occupy in Shakespeare's Venice. But in ancient Haran, he and Antonio are kin. Antonio reminds Shylock of his inferior, despised status at every opportunity. Shylock's complaint is that he is required to treat Antonio as his superior, addressing him in a serf's deferential tones, as the phrase 'bondsman's key' suggests.[65] Shylock's speech gives voice to an acute awareness of the unequal distribution of power between them. If Shylock understands his own situation through the dynamics of Jacob's biblical predicament, then what he seeks to accomplish is a levelling of the playing field that currently stands so heavily weighted in Antonio's favour.

Early on in the negotiations with Antonio, Shylock references an earlier episode from the Genesis Jacob cycle when he appeals to Jacob's 'wise mother' Rebecca. He cites Rebecca as the key to jockeying for position within his family, which ultimately allows him to claim the firstborn child's blessing that was rightfully due to his brother Esau.

> When Jacob grazed his uncle Laban's sheep –
> This Jacob from our holy Abram was,
> As his wise mother wrought in his behalf,
> The third possessor; ay, he was the third –
>
> (1.3.68–71)

Shylock's comment emphasises lineage, and positions Jacob as the 'third possessor' of wealth that is figured genealogically through Abram and then Isaac. Shylock describes Jacob's own possession of Abram's wealth in this speech by emphasising the story of Rebecca, the twins' mother who actively prefers Jacob to Esau. In Genesis 27, Rebecca manages to work against the grain of the affective patriarchal preferences that govern her household, plotting against her old, blind husband Isaac's clear favouritism for Esau, the rough-hewn, warlike hunter. It is Rebecca's agency that brings about the procurement – typically referred to as a theft – of Esau's birthright. The distinction between procurement and theft here hinges centrally on seeing things from Rebecca and Jacob's position rather than from Isaac and Esau's. In Rebecca's view, she is simply helping to restore God's blessing to the son who clearly deserves it. Rabbinic commentators confirm this view, describing Rebecca as very much aware that the blessing and the birthright are rightfully due to someone of Jacob's disposition and character – someone clever, studious and committed to upholding the religious traditions of the forefathers.[66] Rebecca, who is described as having conversed with God about her two sons, understands that the possession of the blessing is too important to be decided on the basis of birth order or Isaac's taste for Esau's venison. Rebecca therefore performs her work 'wisely' in the sense of seeing to it that Jacob and not Esau becomes the 'third possessor' after Abraham and Isaac.

Rabbinic commentators describe the Jacob–Esau rivalry as a primordial contest in which only one brother and one nation can emerge with God's blessing to fulfil the promise of Abraham. The crucial factor in belonging to the chosen nation, however, is not merely the fact of being chosen by God; one's chosen-ness in the Jacob cycle crucially depends on the kind of agency that Rebecca exercises in the deception of Isaac. Although Rebecca's actions appear subversive, she in fact facilitates an outcome that was entirely in keeping with God's vision.

The sense of obeying or accepting God's will in this part of the story is quite different from any kind of passive acceptance of a pre-scripted ordinance. Rebecca's involvement displays active, strategic planning; she must devise a clever way to implement a plan. In order to bring blessings to fruition, human agency must cooperate with divine prescription. Shylock's reference to this episode dwells insistently on those practical, pragmatic successes that Rebecca managed to bring into effect; he emphasises Rebecca's 'wisdom', which in its practical applications constitutes a vital skill. It is through the exercise of that skilful wisdom, which Shylock insists that Rebecca 'wrought', i.e. worked at, that she and Jacob succeed in actualising providential designs and generate a successful outcome.[67]

Throughout the Genesis Jacob cycle, Jacob's success in his endeavours owes a great deal to clever innovations upon what look like firmly established rules and conventions. Isaac's affective preference for Esau is an apparently fixed principle determining his fate, and yet Jacob manages to circumvent that obstacle and succeed despite poor odds. If Shylock draws a moral lesson from how 'Rebecca wisely wrought' the deception of Isaac, he must imagine himself succeeding despite poor odds, odds that translate readily to Shylock's own predicament as a Jew living and working in Christian Venice pleading before a Christian audience. Shylock's material circumstances in Venice come with a series of significant, even prohibitive structural inequities. He is a Jew working in finance in the Christian diaspora, and is reviled for it. He has a daughter whom he worries will become drawn to the Venetian revelry taking place just outside her bedroom window. By appealing to a later episode from the Genesis Jacob cycle – the story of Jacob and the multiplication of cattle – Shylock appeals to a narrative that speaks directly to structural inequalities and to long odds.

What Shylock manages to offer is a detailed account of his view of things through scriptural citation that encodes his moral outlook within a rabbinic view of episodes from Genesis. Although Shylock's account of his motivations remains closely bound up with a midrashic strategy that is easily misread (evidenced by the frequency with which scholars misread it), Shylock's attempt to explain himself would not have appeared quite so strange to Shakespeare's contemporaries; in fact, it echoes the accounts of sixteenth-century European Jewish apologists who produced detailed accounts of Jewish customs, rites and practices. There was an avid market for such accounts in sixteenth- and seventeenth-century England, along with travel narratives that included stories about Jews in far-off lands.

Seventeenth-century Venetian Rabbi Leone Modena (1571–1648) wrote one such text, *Historia de gli Riti Hebrei*, in which he offered a detailed explanation of the customs and mores of European Jews. The account was specifically aimed at an English audience, and was composed for King James I and translated into English in 1650 by Edmund Chilmeade under the title *The History of Rites, Customs, and Manner of Life, of the Present Jews Throughout the World*. According to Modena, all Jews derive their core teachings from the Torah and the Talmud; however, Modena also acknowledges early on in the book that the particulars of cultural practice can and do vary from community to community. He attributes this variation to cultural transfer and Jews who 'borrowed the name and manner of use' from their local non-Jewish neighbours.

> Now as these usances have sprung from the Dispersion of the Jews into divers and severall Countries, and have consequently borrowed the Name, and Manner of Use, from the several Inhabitants: so on the other side we are to take notice, that as well in the Particulars of the Law Written by *Moses;* as in that other, received from the Mouth of the *Wise men,* there is very little, or no difference at all, betwixt any Nation of the Jews, how remote, or far distant soever their habitations be: Onely in those things, that are of the third sort, concerning usances, and Customes, there is no small Variety to be observed amongst them.[68]

Modena uses the term 'usance' to describe the diversity of practices among Jews living in the diaspora. This understanding of usances as things concerning customary habits points up the importance of those very practical, routine elements of ethical experience – habits in the sense of practices and styles of dress, rituals, and professional choices that condition daily life and which vary among nations.

During his negotiations with Antonio, Shylock also appeals to 'usances' rather than 'usury', a word that does not appear anywhere in the text of *The Merchant of Venice*. Like thrift, usance is a term that is easily construed in an unflattering way, particularly in a modern context where it is likely to be confused with usury. In fact, the primary meaning of usance is very different from usury and does not explicitly refer to any sort of financial practice. The *OED* lists its meaning as the one Modena appears to signal in *The History of Rites* – custom, wont, or habit.[69] In early modern England, 'usance' was evidently often tied to national customs and ways of life, including ways of life among Jews.

Lending money at interest in many parts of early modern Europe was a characteristically Jewish livelihood, a way of living often born of necessity rather than choice for Jews who found themselves excluded from professional guilds. Italian physician and Rabbi David de Pomis (1525–93) had personally suffered the loss of his professional medical licence subsequent to Pope Paul IV's bull forbidding Jewish physicians from working for Christians. In 1587, de Pomis published *De Medico Hebraeo Ennerato Apologica*, a piece of Jewish apologetic writing that argued for the reinstitution of Jewish physicians and defended both the integrity of the Jewish faith and the practice of lending at interest. In it, de Pomis reasons that moneylending represents a way to thrive amid the difficult circumstances of life in the diaspora, and the Jewish practice of lending to Christians arises out of necessity rather than malice. 'If the Jews do "bite" with usury [i.e. charge usurious interest rates], this is not by permission of the law, but by a cogent necessity which, as it is thought, may make this excusable.'[70] Although de Pomis does not excuse the practice of usury, he does provide some clarification about the motives behind it, motives which foreground the presence of a strong work ethic blunted by the constraining circumstances of life in exile.[71]

Shylock echoes de Pomis' appeals to cogent necessity and permissibility when he exclaims, 'Signior Antonio, many a time and oft / In the Rialto you have rated me / About my moneys and my usances' (1.3.103–5). What he claims to seek is a chance to practise his profession in a self-respecting way, one that does not involve being spat on or insulted in public. It is clear that Shylock regards what he does as self-respecting even if Antonio does not, and his appeal to 'usances' may very well refer to customary habits that Antonio saw fit to mock, as in the very Jewish gabardine that Antonio spat on in the marketplace.

Shylock may also be referencing the financial practice known in early modern England as lending at usance, which involved trading in foreign currencies. When a lender extends credit at usance, they agree to assume the risk of transporting a sum of money – for example three thousand ducats – from Venice to London. The lender charges a fee for moving the money as well as a currency exchange fee. It is the exchange fee that constitutes the most profitable aspect of the arrangement, since currency values would be fixed in advance by the lender at a rate beneficial to him but typically out of line with standard values. The intervening time between loan and repayment – either a month at usance or two for double usance – would offer a further opportunity for lenders to speculate on foreign currency markets and profit tidily. Shylock may be hinting at this practice when he brings up a Dutch unit of currency – the doit – in his appeal to Antonio, 'I would . . . supply your present wants and take no doit of usance for my moneys' (1.3.134–6). This may also help clarify his somewhat obscure reply to Antonio's question about whether or not he intends to charge interest on the loan. Shylock's response is, 'No, not take interest, not as you would say / Directly interest' (1.3.73–4). If in fact Shylock earns his living through currency speculation, then what he does is something other than directly charging interest on loaned money.

If Shylock makes his living selling 'usances' in the early modern sense of the term, he practices a form of speculation based on predictions of future currency markets. That kind of speculation requires a mode of calculative, practical intelligence that sees beyond what three thousand ducats are worth today and imagines what they might be worth in a month's time. Within an early modern context of reference, Shylock's ethos bears a striking resemblance to prudence, the cardinal of all practical virtues.[72] Aristotle thought that being able to reason about ends and form mindful intentions with regard to the future was essential to the exercise of prudential intelligence. Those ideas enjoyed significant currency in Shakespeare's era, where prudence, a cardinal moral virtue, was understood to be a distinctly practical skill-set. In a 1634 treatise entitled *Prudence, the First of the Foure Cardinall Virtues*, the writer Miles Sandys (1601–36) defines prudence as 'a habite of the understanding, according to the true reason of consulting, and doing those things which are good, or evill, during man's life. He is Prudent', Sandys explains, 'who can well consult concerning those things, which are good, and profitable for himself or others, not alone for some particular part, but for the whole course of well living.'[73] Sandys' definition relies heavily on Aristotle, for whom practical intelligence is always connected to the overall project of living well. Aristotelian *phronesis* and early modern prudence are linked to ideas about the good life as well as strategies for how to go about achieving it; these virtues form the basis of practical reason because they deal with human action in contexts where individuals are faced with difficult choices within shifting, contingent circumstances.

Shylock's reference to usances, with their connection to speculating about the future value of currency, recalls some of the practical aspects of *phronesis*, including the ability to think about long-term consequences. The ability to think in the long term is something that *The Merchant of Venice* dramatises in a central way via the Bassanio–Antonio–Portia plot. Bassanio has squandered all of his financial resources and he must approach first Antonio and ultimately Shylock in order to finance his romantic mission to Belmont. In contrast to Shylock's careful assessment of risk and gain ('ships are but boards, sailors but men'), Bassanio's pursuit of Portia stands out as risky, even feckless in light of the *bon vivant* lifestyle (dinner parties, etc., . . .) to which Bassanio appears accustomed, but which he is unable to fund when we first encounter him.

The deliberate contrasting of long-term planning with short-term enjoyment is also a central theme within the Genesis Jacob cycle, and the Jacob–Esau story in particular. In the first of the two deceptions he effects involving the theft of his brother's birthright, Jacob says to Esau, 'First sell me your birthright.'[74] Esau has come in from the fields starving and smells the mess of pottage cooking on the stove. In exchange for a bowl of the lentil stew, Esau renounces his birthright. This verse raises a crucial point for rabbinical commentators. The crux of the matter is the translation of the Hebrew *kayom* – this day – which can mean 'first', as in Jacob's 'first sell me your birthright', but which can also be rendered as the phrase 'as the day', or 'today', thus 'sell me today thy birthright' in the modern King James translation. The question raised by this passage is about the possibility of alienating or selling a birthright. In Abraham ibn Ezra's commentary, the birthright in question is not a form of property as such; instead, ibn Ezra reasons that it refers to the priestly responsibility for offering sacrifices that represents an elder son's rightful inheritance. In ibn Ezra's account, Jacob is a poor man, and the priestly responsibilities constitute the only real wealth he is able to pass down to his children. The priestly responsibilities would only take effect after Isaac's death.[75] They therefore constitute a kind of future entitlement, in contrast to the immediate satisfactions of the mess of pottage.

If a birthright can be sold, it represents a promise of future entitlements, something whose value can only be enjoyed sometime beyond the moment that a transaction occurs. When Jacob says 'sell me as the day thy birthright', his words can be understood to mean 'as of today, sell me your birthright . . . even if the law is later changed, you will not have any claim to it, since the deal will have been closed today.'[76] This is ibn Ezra's reasoning on what transpires, with a distinct emphasis on futural aspects of the transaction. Jacob exhibits a form of forethought of which Esau is evidently incapable. In this episode, along with a number of pivotal moments of the Genesis Jacob cycle, Jacob responds quickly, thinking on his feet about how to respond to a new situation in a way that strategically positions him to advantage for the future. There is a Yiddish term that effectively captures this quality – *seychl* – which denotes a combination of street smarts and taking the long view of things. Esau does not have much *seychl*, according to the way he is described by rabbinical commentators. In the episode where he despises his birthright, Esau is described as so overcome by his physical appetite that he is unable to even articulate what he wants. When he emerges from the field hungry and smells Jacob's stew on the stove, he can't seem to recall the word for lentils, only the word for something red. Commentary places considerable emphasis on Esau's ravenous appetites, suggesting that the high value he places on his physical desires is the reason he gives up his birthright so easily. Nahmanides speculates that Esau's name was a kind of nickname given to him because of the pottage incident. When he comes in famished from the fields and smells Jacob's cooked lentils, he can scarcely articulate the request for a bowl of stew. Instead, he says something akin to: 'give me the red thing'. 'The dish was either reddened by the lentils which were red, or it had been compounded with some red substance, and Esau, not knowing what it was, called it *edom* (red). *Therefore was his name called Edom* since they mocked at him for having sold an honourable birthright for a small dish.'[77]

In other commentaries Esau's short-term appetite is expressed in midrashic elaborations on his scepticism about the possibility of a life to come.

> 'Does the future world exist? Or will there be a resurrection of the dead? Will Abraham who has died, and who was more precious than any other, return again?' Jacob thereupon retorted: 'If there is indeed neither a future world nor a resurrection of the dead, of what use is the birthright to you? Sell me first thy birthright.'[78]

In this account, Esau is characteristically unable to delay immediate gratification in favour of future rewards or the promise of future entitlements. Many rabbinical commentators describe Esau as powerfully, at times self-destructively driven by his physical appetites. In one account, he must wait around for the mess of pottage to finish cooking, all the while complaining about Jacob's choice of lentils over quick-cooking venison. Some exegetes even claim that Esau willingly relinquishes his birthright, gives it up, in effect, for a mere bowl of lentil stew, never having valued it in the first place.[79] Rashi comments that the lentils were actually a mourner's meal for Abraham who had died that day. He reads Esau's failure to recognise the deep symbolic significance of the dish as symptomatic of his spiritual ignorance.[80]

Where Esau is continually associated with base appetite and short-term interests in the rabbinical commentaries, Jacob is characterised as studious, crafty and future-oriented. The most important of these futural concerns is the promise of renewing God's covenant and fathering the Jewish nation. Rabbinical commentary emphasises God's preference for Jacob over Esau, particularly Jacob's interest in books and study in contrast with his warlike brother. Rashi describes Jacob as a devoted Torah scholar, a reading that is historically inaccurate, but which nevertheless succeeds in emphasising an important ethical contrast between the two brothers. Within the biblical narrative, this contrast reveals itself while the twins are still *in utero* struggling within their mother. In Rashi's account, the word 'struggled', which appears in the biblical text to describe the unborn twins' contest in the womb, is akin to running. Whenever Rebecca passed the Torah academies of Shem and Eber, Jacob ran and struggled to be born, but when she crossed a pagan temple, Esau struggled to be born.[81]

As the twins grow up, their heated rivalry only intensifies, and its stakes grow higher and more determinative. After Jacob lays claim to Esau's privileges and blessings, the two ultimately reunite and form a covenant following a long and hostile estrangement. The Genesis Jacob cycle runs thick with related stories about covenants and treaties that the nation of Israel establishes with surrounding peoples, those who do not share their religious affiliations or ways of life, including the covenant established between rival brothers who grow up to father rival tribes or nations. Some of these episodes serve as cautionary tales that warn of the dangers of assimilation or of being surrounded by hostile enemies; others warn of the dangers of retribution at the hands of the sons of Israel. But the notion of covenant also entails assuming responsibility for oneself as an answerable member of the community. Within the Jewish tradition, *brit* or *brit milah*, otherwise known as a briss, is the ceremony that quite literally enacts an individual's entry into a bond or covenant with God. And as anyone familiar with a briss ceremony is aware, it is not a ceremony to be taken lightly, nor is it reversible or subject to retroactive modifications.

In *The Merchant of Venice*, Antonio sees the bond as a mere financial arrangement, something that will 'expire' at the end of three months' time. But for Shylock, it appears to represent something more closely approximating the Hebraic sense of bond as *brit* or covenant. Antonio's focus, and the focus of Bassanio and his Venetian entourage, is on more diverting matters such as wooing beautiful heiresses, midnight elopements, and dinner parties. Conversely, for Shylock the bond is something he clings to and refuses to relinquish to the bitter end, nearly forfeiting his life in pursuit of it. It is a bond that he views as lying near to Antonio's heart and which he thinks Antonio ought to have taken more to heart. The investment that Antonio does end up making in the loan, prompted by Shylock and consisting of a pound of his flesh, is one that in fact is very dear to him. Shylock discounts that flesh as 'not so estimable, profitable neither, / As flesh of muttons, beeves, or goats' (1.3.163–4). But to Antonio, it is indisputably priceless. By asking Antonio to stake something precious, Shylock in effect compels Antonio to enter into the bond with the same degree of seriousness, the same *gravitas* with which he himself views this contest.

If, in Shylock's view, Antonio is like Laban, then he is also like Esau, and as Esau, he radically underestimates the future value of his own flesh while discounting the possibility that the future may bring about a downward turn in his fortunes. Or, perhaps he has a different motivation for issuing Antonio the loan. In the next chapter, I explore the possibility that Shylock stands to lose a great deal too in agreeing to the loan. In the biblical story, Jacob's wives and children represent the fulfilment of future promises of generational thrift repeated throughout the Genesis Jacob cycle. The real stakes of the story and its implicit risks are the women and children of Jacob's entourage. The scene depicted in Genesis 30 is one of fertility, success, and multiplication, just as the story of Jacob's wands is a story of the miraculous ability to make something barren multiply. And like Jacob, Shylock has, in at least one important sense, thrived where Antonio has failed: he has a daughter. In the following chapter, I turn to Jessica and discuss her enormous significance to the contest between Christians and Jews in *The Merchant of Venice*.

Note

1. *OED*, s.v. 'compromise'.
2. The most useful recent discussions of the value of reading Shakespeare through our own worlds are James R. Siemon's *Word Against Word* (Amherst and Boston: University of Massachusetts Press, 2002), and Michael D. Bristol's 'How Many Children Did She Have?' in John Joughin (ed.), *Philosophical Shakespeares* (New York: Routledge, 2000): 19–34, and 'Macbeth the Philosopher: Rethinking Context', *New Literary History*, 42 (Autumn 2001): 641–62.
3. Both Julia Reinhard Lupton's article 'Exegesis, Mimesis, and the Future of Humanism in *The Merchant of Venice*', *Religion and Literature*, 32: 2 (Summer 2000): 123–39, and Stanley Stewart's 'Shylock and Jacob, the Patriarch', *Cithara*, 46: 1 (November 2006): 24–38 have examined this aspect of the play. Lupton notes a correspondence between Shylock's approach to the Genesis episode and a rabbinic-midrashic hermeneutic. Stewart's discussion of George Granville's eighteenth-century revival of *Merchant* focuses on relevant ethical distinctions between Shylock and Antonio. He identifies those distinctions in Shylock's biblical citation, and takes up a select few rabbinic source materials in his discussion.
4. Louise Schleiner, 'Providential Improvisation in *Measure for Measure*', *PMLA*, 97: 2 (March 1982): 227–36, esp. 227.
5. 'To the Reader', *The Holy Bible Conteyning the Old Testament and the New* (London: Robert Barker, 1611), no page.
6. See Harold Fisch, *The Dual Image: The Figure of the Jew in English and American Writing* (London: World Jewish Library, 1951) for a discussion of the lingering significance of Judaic meaning for Hebrew biblical figures in early modern England. Janet Adelman also addresses this topic throughout *Blood Relations: Christian and Jew in The Merchant of Venice* (Chicago: University of Chicago Press, 1998).
7. John Scott Colley makes this point in 'Launcelot, Jacob, and Esau: Old and New Law in *The Merchant of Venice*', *Yearbook of English Studies*, Vol. 10 (1980): 181–9, esp. 186.

See also William G. Madsen, *From Shadowy Types to Truth: Studies in Milton's Symbolism* (New Haven, CT: Yale University Press, 1965): 1–48 for a discussion of Renaissance Christian typological readings of Jacob. On the implications of Genesis narratives about elder and younger sons for English primogeniture in the seventeenth century, see Michael Austin, "The Genesis Narrative and the Primogeniture Debate in Seventeenth-Century England', *Journal of English and Germanic Philology*, 98: 1 (January 1999): 17–39.

8. The tendency to read Shylock's biblical citation through a Christian interpretive prism is particularly prominent in nineteenth- and early twentieth-century criticism of the play. See, for example, Karl Elze, *Essays on Shakespeare* (London: Macmillan, 1874): 73; William W. Lloyd, *Critical Essays on Plays of Shakespeare* (London: George Bell, 1875): 103; Richmond Noble, *Shakespeare's Biblical Knowledge and Use of the Book of Common Prayer* (New York: Octagon Books, 1970): 270; Elmer Edgar Stoll, *Shakespeare Studies: Historical and Comparative in Method* (New York: Macmillan, 1927): 323 *From Shakespeare to Joyce: Authors and Critics; Literature and Life* (Garden City, NY: Doubleday, 1946): 123; Harold R. Walley, *Essays in Dramatic Literature: The Parrott Presentation Volume* (Princeton: Princeton University Press, 1935): 237; Cary B. Graham, 'Standards of Value in *The Merchant of Venice*', *Shakespeare Quarterly*, 4: 2 (1953): 145–51; and Leah Woods Wilkins, 'Shylock's Pound of Flesh and Laban's Sheep', *Modern Language Notes*, 62: 1 (1947): 28–30. For examples from the later twentieth century, see Nevill Coghill, 'The Theme of *The Merchant of Venice*', *Twentieth Century Interpretations of The Merchant of Venice: A Collection of Critical Essays* (Englewood Cliffs, NJ: Prentice-Hall, 1970): 108–13; Barbara K. Lewalski, 'Biblical Allusion and Allegory in *The Merchant of Venice*', *Shakespeare Quarterly*, 13: 3 (1962): 347–3; John Scott Colley, 'Launcelot, Jacob, and Esau: Old and New Law in *the Merchant of Venice*', *Yearbook of English Studies*, 10 (1980): 191–9; and Joan Ozark Holmer, *The Merchant of Venice: Choice, Hazard,*

and *Consequence* (New York: St. Martin's Press, 1995). The fullest recent discussion of the biblical inter-text in relation to *Merchant* is Marc Shell's 'The Wether and the Ewe: Verbal Usury in *The Merchant of Venice*', *Kenyon Review*, New Series, 1: 4 (Autumn 1979): 65–92. Lars Engle's 'Thrift Is Blessing: Exchange and Explanation in *The Merchant of Venice*', *Shakespeare Quarterly*, 37: 1 (Spring 1986): 20–37, esp. 28–32 devotes a section to discussing Shylock's use of the Genesis Jacob inter-text, and prefaces it by contending that Shylock's citation of a 'powerful multivalent sub-text . . . is full of danger for him in an exegetical argument with a Christian in a Christian state' (29). Engle notes that Shylock's biblical citation contains a number of particularities, which he describes as omissions, but he never probes the potential for reading those differences as a distinctly Judaic account of these biblical episodes.

9. M. Lindsay Kaplan (ed. and intro.), *The Merchant of Venice: Texts and Contexts* (Boston: Bedford St. Martin's, 2002): 39.
10. John Drakakis (ed.), *The Merchant of Venice*, Third Series Arden Shakespeare (New York and London: Bloomsbury Press, 2010): 1–159, esp. 1–50.
11. Drakakis, *Merchant*, 45.
12. Drakakis, *Merchant*, 46.
13. Although Drakakis acknowledges at several points in the introduction that Antonio's perspective is subjected to some measure of critique within the play, he fails to acknowledge that such a critique also has an important source-point in Shylock's own words. Drakakis' discussion effectively discounts Shylock and continually bypasses his words and actions in favour of other voices that ostensibly carry greater legitimacy.
14. John Drakakis, 'Historical Difference and Venetian Patriarchy', *The Merchant of Venice*, ed. and intro. Martin Coyle (New York: St. Martin's Press, 1998): 181–213, esp. 186.
15. See Alexa Huang and Elizabeth Rivlin's introduction to their recent collection, *Shakespeare and the Ethics of Appropriation* (New York: Palgrave Macmillan, 2014). Huang and Rivlin assert the relevance of ethics to discussions of appropriation, and of course they refer to the appropriation of Shakespeare's

work and not on the appropriation within Shakespeare of other texts. However, their point about the relations of power and authority that underwrite appropriation, and their assertion that such appropriations are, at heart, ethical acts, has enormous relevance to my discussion here of Antonio's appropriation of the biblical text that Shylock interprets in this scene of the play.

16. George Downame, *Lectures on the XV Psalme* (London, 1604): 300.
17. Shylock references these verses obliquely at 1.3.134–8, pronouncing 'I would be friends with you, and have your love, / Forget the shames that you have stained me with, / Supply your present wants, and take no doit / Of usance for my moneys; and you'll not hear me. / This is kind I offer'. His indirect reference to kinship ('This is kind I offer') as the basis for refusing to charge Antonio monetary interest on the loan gestures towards the deuteronomic prohibition observed by Jews in which interest can only be charged to strangers but never to fellow Jews.
18. Deuteronomy 23: 20. Unless otherwise specified, all biblical citations are drawn from *Tanakh: The Holy Scriptures, the New JPS Translation According to the Traditional Hebrew Text* (Philadelphia: Jewish Publication Society, 1985). I use this edition in order to provide a modern English translation that emerges out of the Judaic rather than the Christian reading of the Hebrew text.
19. Shell makes note of this point in his 'Wether and the Ewe', 68.
20. William Shakespeare, *The Most Excellent Historie of the Merchant of Venice* (London: Thomas Heyes, 1600); William Shakespeare, *Mr. William Shakespeares Comedies, Histories, and Tragedies* (London: Jaggard & Blount, 1623). Marc Shell makes this point about variations between editions in his 'Wether and the Ewe', 65–92, esp. 68.
21. *OED*, s.v., 'store'.
22. Lupton, 'Exegesis', 125. On this point, Lupton also cites Jacob Neusner, *A Midrash Reader* (Minneapolis: Fortress, 1990).
23. Neusner, *Midrash*, 76.
24. I borrow the phrase 'orientation in a space of moral questions' from the philosopher Charles Taylor, *Sources of the Self:*

The Making of Modern Identity (Boston: Harvard University Press, 1992).

25. Many of the rituals surrounding Jewish holidays facilitate and, indeed, require a sense of participation among present-day celebrants in biblical events. The Passover Seder scripts out first-person participation in the events of Exodus by calling on participants to repeat, '*I* was led out of Egypt'.
26. This insight is articulated by Mustapha Fahmi in 'Shakespeare: The Orientation of the Human', *Harold Bloom's Shakespeare*, ed. Christy Desmet and Robert Sawyer (New York: Palgrave, 2001): 97–107.
27. Michael Chernick, "Turn It and Turn It Again:' Culture and Talmud Interpretation', *Exemplaria*, 12: 1 (2000): 63–103.
28. I point here to Jacob Neusner's lucid discussion of the structure and aims of midrash in *A Midrash Reader.* In Neusner's account, the primary function of midrash consists of its coordination of narrative and prescriptive dimensions of Torah.
29. Maimonides, *The Guide for the Perplexed*, trans. M. Friedlander (New York: Dover, 1956): 236.
30. Genesis 30: 27.
31. *Ibn Ezra's Commentary on the Pentateuch*, trans. H. Norman Strickman and Arthur M. Silver (New York: Menorah Publishing, 1988): 289.
32. Menahem Kasher (ed.), *Encyclopedia of Biblical Interpretation: A Milliennial Anthology*, trans. Hyman Klein (New York: American Biblical Encyclopedia Society, 1959), 4: 112. I cite frequently from Kasher's encyclopedia, which represents an important compendium of Hebrew biblical commentaries spanning Classical through modern periods of rabbinic exegesis. Noted rabbinic scholar Menahem Mendel Kasher (1895–1983) is the author of the *Torah Shelemah*, a pioneering multi-volume compendium of the Written Law of the Pentateuch and Oral Law of the Talmud and Midrash, as well as extensive commentaries that include previously undiscovered midrashic texts.
33. Arnold Williams, *The Common Expositor: An Account of the Commentaries on Genesis, 1527–1633* (Chapel Hill, NC: University of North Carolina Press, 1948): 169.

34. Andrew Willet, *Hexapla in Genesin* (London: Thomas Creede, 1608): 320.
35. Willet, *Hexapla*, 321.
36. Andrew Willet, *Hexapla in Genesin & Exodum* (London: John Haviland, 1633): 275.
37. Henry Ainsworth, *Annotations upon the First Book of Moses, Called Genesis* (Amsterdam: Giles Thorp, 1616), Gen. 30: 32.
38. Lemnius Levinus, *The Secret Miracles of Nature* (London: Jo. Streeter, 1658): 11.
39. Thomas Wright, *The Passions of the Minde in General*, Vol. 15, *Renaissance Imagination*, ed. William Webster Newbold (New York: Garland, 1986): 140.
40. *Rashi: Commentaries on the Pentateuch*, trans. Chaim Pearl (New York: Norton 1970): 295.
41. *Ramban (Nachmanides) Commentary on the Torah: Genesis*, trans. Charles Chavel (New York: Shilo, 1971): 376–7.
42. John Calvin, *Thirteene Sermons of Maister Iohn Calvine, entreating of the free election of God in Iacob, and of reprobation in Esau*, trans. John Fielde (London: Thomas Man and Tobie Cooke, 1579): 18.
43. Calvin, *Thirteene Sermons*, 21.
44. Charles Spinosa, 'The Transformation of Intentionality: Debt and Contract in *The Merchant of Venice*', *English Literary Renaissance*, 24: 2 (1994): 394.
45. Genesis 30: 30. Parallels between wives and cattle are drawn out nicely in the Hebrew text; Leah's name means 'ewe lamb' and Rachel's means 'wild cow'. There is a great deal of wordplay between cattle and female name references in this part of the Jacob cycle. For example, when we first meet Rachel in Genesis 29: 9, we are told that 'Rachel came with her father's flock, for she was a shepherdess'. The Hebrew is 'ki roach hu', which translates as 'she was a shepherdess', and also 'she was grazing' – the word 'roach' can mean either shepherd or the verb 'to graze'.
46. Genesis 30: 26.
47. He works seven additional years for the privilege of marrying Laban's youngest daughter, Rachel.

48. On this point, Kasher cites Isaac Caro's comments in *Toldot Yitzhak*. Kasher, *Encyclopedia*, 4: 108.
49. James Maxwell, *The Mirrour of Religious Men* (London: E. White, 1611): 105.
50. In the Arden Third Series, Drakakis cites Shylock's use of 'thrift' here as 'the act of thriving or prospering . . ., but in this context meaning profit or material gain'. See note 85 to 1.3.86, John Drakakis (ed.), *The Merchant of Venice* (2010). M. Lindsay Kaplan supplies both thriving and profit as meanings to 'thrift' in the 2002 *Texts and Contexts* edition of the play. John Russell Brown notes 'But usury was equated with theft' in the 2007 Arden Second Series edition.
51. *OED*, s.v. 'thrift'.
52. Stanley Stewart, 'Shylock, Jacob, and the Patriarch', *Cithara*, 46 (November 2006): 24–38.
53. Kasher cites the Zohar as well as *Genesis Rabbah* on this point. Kasher, *Encyclopedia*, 4: 242.
54. Genesis 30: 27.
55. Kasher cites Caro's elaboration of the Zohar in *Encyclopedia*, 4: 242.
56. *Genesis Rabbah*, 70: 13, cited in Rabbi Chayim ben Attar, *Or Hachayim: Commentary on the Torah*, trans. Eliyahu Munk (Jerusalem: Eliyahu Munk, 1995): 1: 246.
57. On this point, see *Genesis Rabbah*, cited in Kasher, *Encyclopedia*, 4: 108.
58. Ramban (Nahmanides), *Commentary on the Torah: Genesis*, trans. Charles B. Chavel (New York: Shiloh, 1971): 380–1. Nahmanides bases his interpretation on the word 'Vehineh' in 30: 10, which he asserts always indicates a dream.
59. *Or Hachayim*, 263–4.
60. Quoted in Kasher, *Encyclopedia*, 4: 242.
61. *Or Hachayim*, 260–1.
62. *Or Hachayim*, 248–9.
63. Some well-known approaches to Shylock's speech in the opening section of act 1, scene 3 include Mark van Doren's, which casts Shylock as a miser or verbal hoarder: 'He is always repeating phrases, as misers do.' Mark van Doren,

'The Merchant of Venice: An Interpretation', *Shakespeare* (New York: Henry Holt, 1939): 96–105, esp. 84. C. L. Barber has argued that Shylock's speech patterns here reflect an inhuman, mechanical mind. C. L. Barber, *Shakespeare's Festive Comedy: A Study of Dramatic Form and Its Relation to Social Custom* (Princeton: Princeton University Press, 1959): 180. John Gross surmises that Shylock's speech reflects the language of bookkeeping and double entries. John Gross, *Shylock: A Legend and Its Legacy* (New York: Simon & Schuster, 1992): 66.

64. Genesis 31: 1–2.
65. M. Lindsay Kaplan points out that the term 'bondsman's key' references a serf's tone of voice. Kaplan, *Texts and Contexts*, 40.
66. There is a variety of evidence in the commentaries suggesting that Rebecca facilitates the deception of Isaac out of prudent apprehension of the relevant differences between her two sons and a clear vision of Jacob as the deserving recipient of God's blessing. Kasher cites *Genesis Rabbah*'s explanation of Jacob's blindness in old age at Genesis 27: 1, in which God makes Isaac's sight dim in order to prevent him from recognising the deception. Kasher, *Encyclopedia*, 4: 39. Kasher also cites *Lekah Tov*, an eleventh-century midrashic commentary by Rabbi Tobiah Eliezer: 'Rebekah said to Jacob: If Esau receives the blessings, what will happen to the Five Books of the Torah which the world is going to receive through the medium of your descendants?' Quoted in Kasher, *Encyclopedia*, 4: 43.
67. Michael Bristol first made this point during a presentation of our work for the Shakespeare and Performance Research Team at McGill University in March of 2009.
68. Leo Modena, *The History of Rites, Customs, and Manner of Life, of the Present Jews Throughout the World*, trans. Edmund Chilmeade (London: J. L., 1650): 3.
69. *OED*, s.v., 'usance'.
70. David de Pomis, *De Medico Hebraeo* (Venice, 1587), in H. Friedenwald, *The Jews and Medicine* (Baltimore: Johns Hopkins University Press, 1944): 2: 404.

71. The sixteenth century saw even more direct rabbinical arguments in favour of charging interest as a matter of general practice. Both Isaac Abravanel's and Abraham Farrisol's commentaries on the Torah elaborate on the idea that economic actualities make lending at interest entirely sensible. See Benjamin Ravid, 'Moneylending in Seventeenth Century Jewish Vernacular Apologia', *Studies on the Jews of Venice* (Burlington, VT: Ashgate, 2003): 279–80.
72. Prudence in the modern sense has come to carry very nearly the same negative connotations as thrift. It is often confused with prudishness, a faintness of heart in the face of risk. Certainly, prudence falls short of what most modern people would identify with wisdom. Its negative connotations have effectively managed to taint the term such that it has become less and less used as a form of praise or key term for discussing intelligence, practical planning, and long-term strategising. To wit, Terence Irwin, the editor of the Hackett edition of Aristotle's *Ethics*, chose to translate Aristotle's Greek term *phronesis*, which is, properly, prudence, as intelligence. He explains:

> A good translation for *phronesis* would be 'wisdom' if that were not already needed for *Sophia*. 'Intelligence' is misleading to the extent that we associate it with an intellectual ability that someone might have without any wisdom in planning his life . . . 'Prudence' might be preferable in so far as it suggests good sense about one's own welfare; but we tend to associate prudence with a rather narrow-minded caution, and we do not assume that a prudent person is necessarily reflective or deliberative at all.

Aristotle, *Nicomachean Ethics*, trans. and intro. Terence Irwin (Indianapolis: Hackett Publishing, 1999): 412.
73. Miles Sandys, *Prudence: The First of the Foure Cardinall Virtues* (London: W. Sheares, 1634): 50.
74. Genesis 25: 31.
75. Ibn Ezra, *Commentary*, 252.

76. Yaakov Culi, *Torah Anthology*, trans. Aryeh Kaplan (New York: Maznaim Publishing, 1977): 2: 468.
77. Nahmanides, *Commentary: Genesis*, 317.
78. Kasher cites his *Torah Shelemah* on this point. *Encyclopedia*, 4: 17.
79. Kasher cites the Zohar on this point to the effect that Esau hated his birthright from the start, and the meal constitutes only a formal conclusion to the agreed-upon trade. *Encyclopedia* 4: 18–19.
80. Rashi, *Commentary*, 55.
81. Rashi, *Commentary*, 54.

CHAPTER 3

STOLEN DAUGHTERS AND STOLEN IDOLS

In act 1, scene 3, Antonio readily agrees to the terms of Shylock's bond and risks a pound of his own flesh in the process. When Bassanio objects to these steep stakes – 'I'll rather dwell in my necessity' (1.3.152), he pleads, Antonio insists that he is more than willing to accept Shylock's unusual conditions, and feels confident in his ability to make good on the debt.

> Why fear not, man, I will not forfeit it;
> Within these two months, that's a month before
> This bond expires, I do expect return
> Of thrice three times the value of this bond.
> (1.3.153–6)

Some critics have characterised Antonio's ready acceptance of Shylock's terms here as an indication of his Christ-like self-sacrificial qualities (in act 1, scene 1 he offers his 'person' as well as his 'purse' to Bassanio), or of a venturing economic spirit eager to accept risk, an ethos that found growing support in the later decades of the sixteenth century and well into the seventeenth.[1] In the previous chapter, I looked to the Genesis Jacob cycle to suggest a different set of motives, arguing that Antonio exhibits an Esau-like inability to plan for future eventualities, radically discounting the future value of his own flesh in order to supply Bassanio's 'present wants'. Evidently Antonio feels very good about his ships' prospects today because his friend really needs a loan today; but Shylock, in a much more Jacob-like capacity, takes the long view in calculating risk and gain, and sees that 'ships are but boards, sailors but men' (1.3.21). In act 2, Shylock comments on his servant Launcelot's departure from his household in a way that reflects this same prudent regard for risk, which he contrasts with Bassanio's profligacy. 'Therefore I part with him [Launcelot], and part with him / to one that I would have him help to waste / his borrowed purse' (2.5.48–50). Shylock's remark rings with a Jacob-like disapproval of short-term wastefulness as he bids Launcelot good riddance and bequeaths him to Bassanio, whose household he imagines squandering the very credit that he, Shylock, had just extended.

In Chapter 2 I described the complex and substantial investments that Shylock makes in the loan negotiations with Antonio, and the considerable significance of the exegetical dispute to Shylock's own motivations and perspective in the play. By contrast, this chapter begins by considering not Shylock's intentions, but Antonio's and those of his Christian friends. What is the motivational scenario underwriting Antonio's easy, confident acceptance of Shylock's terms? And why do Antonio and Bassanio approach Shylock in particular for a loan of three thousand ducats? By beginning with a question about Antonio and Bassanio's intentions in act 1, scene 3, this chapter moves from the pound of flesh at the heart of the commercial bond among men to a different pound or, rather, several pounds of flesh that, I will argue, are even more central to Antonio's motivations than the loan and equally central to the play, in the form of Shylock's daughter Jessica.

Although Jessica occupies what is clearly the more minor of the play's two romance plots, her story remains pivotal to the unfolding of *Merchant*'s action, including the bond plot and trial. Jessica has immense value to her father; it is when he learns of her absconsion that his quest for vengeance reaches its characteristically bloodthirsty peak. In this chapter, I explore Jessica's value to both Jews and Christians in *The Merchant of Venice*, where she functions as a key figure within the play's ongoing negotiation of tribal conflict. Jessica's character is particularly compelling within that conflict because of her liminal position. She is poised between ethnological and theological worlds for much of the play, neither willing to remain affiliated with the Jewish 'blood' of her father nor able to convincingly be defined by the Christian 'manners' that she seeks to adopt through conversion. If Shylock's practical decision-making is centrally shaped through midrashic appeals to Judaic scriptural stories, to what extent is Jessica, who yearns for an exit from her father's household, also able to effect an exit from the moral universe that constitutes her father's and, presumably, her own Jewishness?

In this chapter, I discuss how this aspect of Jessica's predicament is developed in the play through appeals to two episodes from the Genesis Jacob cycle: the abduction of Dinah featured in Genesis 34, and the story of Rachel who steals her father's idols from Genesis 31. Both biblical inter-texts have important structural and thematic parallels with *Merchant*'s Jessica: both feature young women positioned at the liminal margins of ethnological communities, and both address problems that follow from inter-faith marriages. By examining rabbinic and Renaissance English constructions of these biblical stories, this chapter explores how these texts develop the profound marginality of *Merchant*'s Jessica, who remains suspended between Jewish and Christian worlds for much of the play. In keeping with Chapter 2, this chapter considers in detail the distinctions between Christian and Jewish perspectives on Jessica's biblical inter-texts, and also considers how the meaning of Jessica's moral predicament in the play shifts as we consider alternative ways in which those inter-texts have been translated, interpreted and refashioned over time.

Act 1, scene 3 of *The Merchant of Venice* features a curious episode in which Shylock 'debates of his present stores' and reveals to Antonio that he does not have the money on hand to stake Antonio's loan. He must go to a third party, Tubal, a 'wealthy Hebrew of my tribe', in order to raise the sum. In view of the fact that Shylock is a professional moneylender, the moment represents an odd turn. Why would Shylock need to consider his reserves and then appeal to a third party in order to stake the loan?

To pose the same question in even more practical terms, exactly how much money does three thousand ducats represent within the play? Is it a large or a small sum, or somewhere in between? If three thousand ducats represents a moderate sum, falling somewhere between large and small, this might explain why Shylock must first deliberate of his 'present stores' before deciding whether he is able to stake the loan. Perhaps Tubal serves as the backer for large loans and Shylock extends only smaller loans from his own private reserves. But three thousand ducats may also be an inordinately large sum – the equivalent of millions of dollars today, far in excess of what a small-time agent like Shylock possesses in liquid assets. And so Shylock might have to appeal to a third party, someone unusually wealthy or accustomed to lending large amounts, to generate these funds. If this is the case, and Antonio and Bassanio both know it – Antonio's stature as a prominent local businessman familiar with Shylock's 'bargains' suggests that he would know such a thing – why do Antonio and Bassanio then approach Shylock for the loan rather than appealing directly to Tubal?

The inclusion of Tubal's name in the loan scene is a small textual detail, but it raises the intriguing possibility that Antonio and Bassanio may have another motivation for approaching Shylock, and might be after something even more crucial than three thousand ducats. In that same scene a small but significant event takes place that offers a suggestive clue: Bassanio asks Shylock 'if it please you to dine with us' (1.3.30), and invites him to supper. Although the invitation is an easily overlooked moment in a scene containing a host of complex negotiations, it soon acquires a great deal of importance to the progression of *Merchant*'s various plots by providing Jessica with an opportunity to abscond and Lorenzo with a chance to steal her from her father's home, along with her father's valuables.

A Christian motivational scenario that includes the premeditated seduction or theft of Shylock's Jewish daughter from his household is in no way precluded by Shakespeare's text. Jessica identifies her romance with Lorenzo as a means to her Christian conversion, but their romance has an altogether different aim when we consider it – and Jessica – as part of the ongoing tribal conflict between Christians and Jews that pervades the play. If, as Shylock claims early on in act 1, scene 3, the loan constitutes a kind of wrestling match in which Christian and Jew each struggle for advantage, by laying claim to Jessica, Lorenzo seizes Shylock's most valuable asset and effectively 'catches Shylock on the hip'. As the events in the play unfold, it becomes clear that this initial seizure facilitates a more comprehensive seizure of all of Shylock's assets, financial and familial, culminating in the trial scene where he is ordered to resign his wealth to his lost daughter and new 'son'. If we consider those events forensically, working backwards from that final moment where 'justice' is restored through the total expropriation of the Jew's wealth, the seizure/theft/appropriation of Jessica acquires a pivotal importance as an opening move that sets up the final outcome in which all of Shylock's assets are handed over to Christians. We might even consider the bond plot as a mere ruse to facilitate that final outcome. Whether or not Antonio's ships end up coming in, the loan negotiations provide an opportunity to invite Shylock to dinner and get him out of the house so that his daughter can escape. Predictably, the loss of his daughter elicits Shylock's rage and the subsequently vindictive pursuit of a pound of Antonio's flesh. The final outcome of the bond plot at trial, in which all of Shylock's wealth is consumed by Christians, occurs regardless of whether or not Antonio's mercantile venture succeeds; if we impute sufficient conspiratorial intelligence to Antonio and his friends, the loan may well represent a clever scheme designed to set in motion a sequence of events culminating in the seizure of Shylock's fortune. If such a plan underwrites the action of *Merchant of Venice*'s main plot, then its key component is the theft of Shylock's daughter.

At various points *The Merchant of Venice* encourages readers to consider the implications of romance as a form of stealing. In both of *The Merchant of Venice*'s love plots, the language of love is tightly bound up with the discourse of theft. Portia and Jessica are each figured as rich prizes to be stolen. Bassanio makes clear from the start that Portia is a 'lady richly left' and that his motives for pursuing her – and her appeal – are bound up with her affluence. He names the Classical Jason as he describes courting her, where she is figured as a golden fleece. '[H]er sunny locks / Hang on her temples like a golden fleece, / Which makes her seat of Belmont Colchos' strand, / And many Jasons come in quest of her' (1.1.169–72). Jason's success, of course, derives from *stealing*, not just taking his prize. This same sub-text of romantic conquest-as-theft is rehearsed with even greater intensity and frequency in the Lorenzo–Jessica romance. Lorenzo remarks to Gratiano that 'She [Jessica] hath directed / How I shall *take* her from her father's house, / What gold and jewels she is furnished with' [emphasis mine] (2.4.29–31), spelling out the material gains he stands to receive by eloping while simultaneously invoking theft as the means of acquiring them. And in fact, if we consider Jessica's removal from Shylock's home as part of a Christian plot to expropriate Shylock's fortune, the parallel between Jessica and Portia, the wealthy Belmont heiress, becomes even clearer since it is through both women that male suitors stand to become rich. Lorenzo reinforces the link to Jessica as a stolen commodity two scenes later in a joking quip where he suggests that he has been too busy stealing a wife to keep apace of his current meetings with his friends. 'Sweet friends, your patience for my long abode / (Not I but my affairs have made you wait): / When you shall please to play the thieves for wives / I'll watch as long for you then' (2.6.21–4), suggesting that his friends all share in the joke about stolen daughters. Finally, Jessica herself revisits the issue of theft and romantic conquest in act 5 by offering a gloomy reiteration of her union with Lorenzo in which she casts herself as a poor stolen soul. 'In such a night / Did young Lorenzo swear he loved her well, / Stealing her soul with many vows of faith, / And ne'er a true one' (5.1.17–19). This moment of self-reflection for Jessica, which I discuss in greater detail shortly, is tinged with regret over how her story has unfolded as she acknowledges the pattern of theft that has determined their courtship, which she here describes as a form of foul play. Her tone is regretful, suggesting that she had previously failed to understand the economic implications of her elopement or fully grasp the economic motive driving Lorenzo's plot to possess her.

The insinuations of theft that inhere in Jessica and Lorenzo's romance manage to effectively evoke a sense of conspiracy within the play among the Venetian Christians. Lorenzo's friends cooperate to coordinate Jessica's escape, appearing to be in on the joke about romantic conquest providing an occasion for stealing prized daughters. Gratiano gestures towards the newly arrived couple in Belmont in act 3, scene 2 by rehearsing the same golden fleece imagery that Bassanio initially uses to describe Portia. 'Nerissa, cheer yond stranger, bid her welcome … What's the news from

Venice? / How doth that royal merchant, good Antonio? / I know he will be glad of our success; / We are the Jasons, we have won the fleece' (3.2.235–9). In this instance, it is Jessica who represents the prize that has been claimed by Gratiano's band of friends, who stand together as the triumphant heroes who have stolen her from her father's home.

Antonio also merits being considered as part of the collusion. Later in the play, he reiterates the language of courtship-as-theft to describe what has happened to Jessica, figuring her as a meaningful prize that has been wrested from the home of her Jewish father. During the trial scene, his proposed resolution for punishing Shylock handily combines the two forms of property – money and daughter – before effectively confiscating what remains of Shylock's stores. As he recommends that Shylock forfeit all of his wealth and reallocate it to himself and Lorenzo, Antonio's description of Shylock's punishment explicitly calls attention to the fact that Shylock's daughter has been stolen by a Christian suitor.

> So please my lord the duke, and all the court,
> To quit the fine for one half of his [Shylock's] goods,
> I am content: so he will let me have
> The other half in use, to render it upon his death unto the
>   gentleman
> That lately stole his daughter.
>
> (4.1.376–81)

This proposed resolution forces Shylock to place his assets aside 'in use' under Antonio's supervision until Shylock's death, at which point they will be rendered up to Lorenzo, whom Antonio names here as the man who 'lately stole his daughter'. This speech explicitly reiterates the theft motif by recalling that Jessica was stolen from Shylock's household, reminding Shylock that not only his money, but also his daughter have been expropriated. The culmination of this scene's humiliations involves Shylock forfeiting all of his wealth, which Antonio's speech here makes achingly clear also includes Jessica.

In his final lines during the trial, Antonio recommends that Shylock not only 'record a gift / (Here in the court) of all he dies possessed / Unto his son Lorenzo and his daughter' (4.1.384–6); he will also have to become a Christian. Although these lines superficially suggest at a restoration of some form of financial justice and familial integrity, with Shylock's money routed towards his estranged daughter and new 'son' Lorenzo, that restoration is belied by the total loss of his financial and familial assets. By citing Jessica as part of the penalty, Antonio's proposal makes clear that Shylock's Jewishness is subjected to a conclusive attempt at erasure specifically through the erasure of any hope of future generational flourishing. In the contest between rival Christian and Jewish nations who continue to seek advantage, struggling to 'catch' one another 'on the hip' throughout the play, in the end it is Shylock who is pinned and utterly humiliated, and that defeat is in no small part both plotted and effected through the loss of his daughter.

In the 1560 Geneva Bible's marginal gloss on Genesis 30: 23, fertility and reproduction are interpreted as signs of divine favour. 'Because frutefulnes came of Gods blessing, who said, Increase and multiplie; bareness was counted as a curse.'[2] Throughout the Genesis Jacob cycle of stories, wealth is measured through the generation of offspring who in Genesis 22: 17 are explicitly prophesied to become as numerous as stars in the sky and grains of sand on the shore. The promise of continued national flourishing is fulfilled in Genesis through conventional tokens of wealth: camels, horses and sheep, but also, more importantly, wives and children. In the parting view we have of Jacob leaving Haran in Genesis 31, there are camels, horses, asses, wives, and children: the whole glittering entourage speaks to Jacob's well-won thrift. Wealth and fertility carry providential meaning, and Jacob's sons in particular signal divinely sponsored success that serves the ends of nation building. Jacob's twelve sons go on to become the twelve tribes of Israel. In the early modern imagination, those twelve tribes and their descendants were imagined to encompass the entire known world's population.[3]

Like so many of Shakespeare's plays, *The Merchant of Venice* is intently focused on progeny, familial legacy, and relationships between parents and children. It is significant, though, that for all the friendship, prosperity, and sensual revelry exhibited by Antonio and his fellow Venetians, each of these characters remains childless. With the exception of Old Gobbo, Shylock is the sole character in *The Merchant of Venice* with a child of his own. In the context of *Merchant*'s evident concern with reproduction and the flourishing of not only individuals but entire ethnographic communities and 'nations', Shylock evidently has a great deal to lose. Where Antonio has succeeded in expropriating all of Shylock's financial assets, his most impressive triumph resides in his expropriation of Shylock's daughter.

Shylock reacts to Jessica's departure with a cry of betrayal, exclaiming '*My* own flesh and blood to rebel!' (3.1.32). 'I say my daughter is *my* flesh and my blood' [emphasis mine] (3.1.35). He makes clear that he views her absconsion as something more than a mere departure; he figures it as the most intimate kind of bereavement, the loss of his integral bodily property. Shylock's appropriative language when he refers to his daughter in act 2, scene 5, as in line 15's 'Jessica my girl', is of a piece with his concern for his house, reflected in the line immediately following, 'Look to my house' (2.5.15–16). Both house and household members are seen by Shylock as components of his well-won, divinely approved rewards. Shylock both appropriates Jessica in this scene ('*my* daughter') and equates her with the features of his house – 'lock up *my* doors', 'stop up *my* house's ears', 'Let not the sound of shallow fopp'ry enter / *My* sober house' [emphasis mine] (2.5.29, 35–6). Merging architectural features with human physiological ones, Shylock implores Jessica to 'stop my house's ears' – ostensibly he means his daughter's ears. He then quickly corrects his error in the same line, 'I mean my casements' (2.5.34), further conflating the elements of his home with its household members.

Jessica represents a prized, integral piece of flesh for both Jews and Christians in *The Merchant of Venice*. From the perspective of ethnographic rivalry, the romantic sub-plot centres on which group can successfully lay claim to her. Lorenzo and his friends stand to gain a great deal of money through her, and even more if we consider their scheme as a deeper plot to divest Shylock of the vast totality of his wealth and profit from his utter financial ruin. That conspiratorial view gains further ground in the scene where Shylock prepares to go to dinner. He harbours suspicions about the invitation. 'I am bid forth to supper ... I am not bid for love, they flatter me ... I am right loath to go, / There is some ill a-brewing towards my rest' (2.5.11–17). His servant Launcelot Gobbo derides Shylock's fears as silly superstitions. Tellingly, however, Launcelot does form part of the Christian plot that helps design Jessica's surreptitious departure. He speaks asides to Jessica, alerting her to Lorenzo's plan: 'Mistress look out the window for all this: / There will come a Christian by / Will be worth a Jewës eye' (2.5.39–42). In this scene, Shylock repeatedly voices premonitory concerns about Jessica's place in his household, fears that turn out to be all too founded when the dinner invitation becomes a key plot device that enables Lorenzo and his friends to lure Shylock away from his home so that Jessica can abscond.

Hebrew biblical references once more form a key part of the sub-text of this scene and its underlying power struggle. In this scene, Shylock suspects some foul play, and before departing comments, 'By Jacob's staff I swear / I have no mind of feasting forth tonight' (2.5.36–7). In swearing by Jacob's staff, Shylock cites the exploits of Jacob, this time at Genesis 32: 11, 'I am not worthy of the least of all mercies, and of all the truth, which thou hast shewed unto thy servant; for with my staff I passed over this Jordan; and now I am become two bands.' At this point in the story, Jacob engages in strategic preparations before meeting his estranged brother Esau. He prays for divine protection for his large family and retinue. Tellingly, this verse resonates for Renaissance English commentators as an allegory for the merchant's life. In his 1592 *Certaine Plaine, Briefe, and Comfortable Notes Upon Every Chapter of Genesis*, the English theologian Gervase Babington (1550–1610) writes:

> I cannot omit this godly remembrance that Iacob here maketh of his first estate when he came into the country, and of his estate present now when hee doth returne. *With my staff*, saith he, *came I over this Iorden & now have I gotten two bandes*. A notable meditation morning and evening for rich marchantes ... whom God hath exalted from litle too much, ...[4]

Babington's comments offer a 'notable meditation' on humility in which material success is contextualised by recalling its divine origins. Generational flourishing too, he insists, forms part of the wealth that merchants are well served to remember has its true source in God's blessings. Shylock's reference to this biblical verse is punctuated by Launcelot's asides to Jessica in act 2, scene 5, which position Shylock as the butt of a Christian joke. He is the rich merchant who dreamed only last night of moneybags, yet he is unable to see what is coming as his daughter prepares to rob him. Moreover, he appears to lack the requisite humility that Babington identifies at the heart of the passage's moral lesson. The deeper theological implication – that Shylock fails to understand the proper meaning of his own scriptural reference to Jacob's staff, though Launcelot and the audience are poised to see it all too clearly – mirrors Antonio's claim in act 1, scene 3 that Shylock misinterprets and misuses the very scriptural parable that he cites.

Like that parable, however, Jacob's staff has an alternate interpretive tradition within Judaic exegesis, one that forecasts an impending conflict with a dangerous kinsman. Rabbinic commentators read this sequence of events through Jacob's anxious regard for the safety of his family as he prepares to confront his estranged brother Esau.[5] Jacob sends messengers to offer tributary gifts in an attempt to avoid warfare. In verse 7, the messengers return to camp and report back to Jacob. 'The messengers returned to Jacob, saying, "We came to your brother Esau; he himself is coming to meet you, and there are four hundred men with him."'[6] The report inspires fear and Jacob moves to protect his family. One commentator reflects on the literal meaning of the phrase 'to your brother Esau' and explains that the messengers appealed to Esau as 'brother' – i.e. an intimate kinsman – but discovered that they had come instead to 'Esau', an enemy filled with hatred.[7] Jacob fears extermination at the hands of his brother and divides his family into two camps in order to better ensure their protection should the confrontation turn violent.

Shylock's citation of Jacob's staff contributes towards the sense of ancient tribal conflict that undergirds the play and these scenes in particular as he anticipates 'some ill a-brewing' while preparing to dine at Antonio's. In fact, Shylock's anxiety over the fate of his household accurately anticipates the very next scene's events where Lorenzo removes Jessica from his home. Shylock's reaction to the news of her departure in act 3 – 'The thief is gone with so much, and so much to find the thief, and no satisfaction, no revenge' (3.1.86) – emphasises Jessica's tremendous, irreplaceable importance to his household and his view that Jessica represents a piece of his household property that has been stolen. Shylock mourns the loss of 'so much', indicating both the material possessions stolen by Jessica and Lorenzo, and his bereavement over the loss of his only daughter, while his suggestive mention of 'no satisfaction, no revenge' foregrounds the impassioned vengeance that comes to consume him for the remainder of the play, and the irrevocability of his losses, which even revenge cannot remediate.

While Shylock continues to position himself as a Jacob-figure in this scene, *Merchant*'s dramatisation of Jessica's plot – including her status as a stolen commodity who leaves behind bereaved, humiliated, and ultimately vengeful male kin – establishes striking parallels to a later episode of that same cycle of Genesis Jacob stories: the abduction of Dinah, which informs Jessica's plotline throughout the play.[8] In Genesis 34 Dinah, the young unmarried daughter of a now elderly Jacob wanders from her home in what editors and commentators have alternately labelled an abduction or seduction (more on this shortly). Dinah quickly finds herself embroiled in a messy entanglement with Shechem, the son of a neighbouring non-Israelite prince. After seducing her, Shechem expresses a desire to marry Dinah. As part of the negotiations that ensue, the people of Shechem agree to exchange local trade opportunities for the privilege of marrying Israelite women. However, the agreement is conditional; Jacob's sons insist that the Shechemite men must first undergo circumcision. In the end, the pact is revealed to be a ruse, and Jacob's sons attack the men as they recover from their surgery in a vicious slaughter intended to avenge the seduction-cum-theft of their sister.

Through Jessica's storyline, *The Merchant of Venice* appeals explicitly to the plot structures, characters and moral quandaries of the abduction of Dinah narrated in Genesis 34. Both Genesis 34 and Jessica's plot centre on experiences of violation, loss and betrayal in which young Jewish women leave their paternal households and advance towards exogamous marriages in the diaspora, sparking violent retribution that effectively drives the remainder of the action. In both cases, the loss of a daughter is framed as a theft that then prompts vengeful action on the part of her male relatives.

Like Genesis 34, Shakespeare's play introduces a young Jewish woman who opts to depart from her home, although Shakespeare's text details Jessica's desire to permanently break from her faith and family far more explicitly than the biblical text. In both Genesis 34 and *The Merchant of Venice*, the luring of young women from their homes is linked to musical seduction. Shylock warns Jessica explicitly against those dangers. He describes music in terms of its exotic appeal, associating it with Christian revelry and imploring Jessica to stop up her ears against it. 'When you hear the drum / And the vile squealing of the wry necked fife, / Clamber not you up to the casements then / Nor thrust your head into the public street / To gaze on Christian fools with varnished faces' (2.5.28–33). Some rabbinic commentaries on Genesis 34 describe how Shechem, the prince of a non-Jewish neighbouring tribe, attracted Dinah's attention 'by playing music within her hearing'.[9] Shechem's seduction of Dinah is also linked with poetic seduction. Shechem 'seduced her with words', a strategy that successfully draws Dinah out from her familial home and into the arms of a foreigner.[10] Lorenzo and Jessica's exchanges in act 5, scene 1 offer some of *Merchant*'s most notably beautiful poetic language, which strikes a particularly sharp contrast with Shylock's cryptic, far less poetic speeches.

Adding to these elements is the striking structural parallel between Jessica's plot and Genesis 34. Both *Merchant* and Genesis 34 bury seduction/abduction plots centred on young Jewish women and their non-Jewish paramours deep within stories focused on male commercial relationships. If we take seriously the possibility that Shylock's pound-of-flesh imperative constitutes a response in kind to his loss of Jessica (*his* pound of flesh), a figure whom Antonio evidently thinks important enough to mention in the pivotal trial scene, then Shakespeare's play in fact mirrors Genesis 34 quite faithfully. Like Genesis 34, which prominently features trade negotiations that are ultimately revealed to be a ruse to recover a stolen Jewish daughter, *Merchant* nests Jessica's seduction, which is explicitly labelled as a theft, within a story about complex male-orchestrated commercial bonds.

Although the biblical Dinah's story merely bookends the male-centred action in Genesis 34, Dinah's plot represents the moral and thematic heart of that chapter. Even where the story appears to evolve into a narrative focused on trade agreements between Jacob's clan and the neighbouring Shechemites, the story is brutally brought back to Dinah's absconsion, which her brothers figure as rape at the chapter's end. The significance of Dinah's story within Genesis 34, which is brought out by the violence of her brothers' response, emphasises the relative importance of Jessica's storyline within *The Merchant of Venice* and to her father and the play's Christians. Despite the decidedly secondary status of Jessica's romance plot within the play, her absconsion carries significant and irretrievable implications, initiating a sequence of events that encompasses the bond, the pound of flesh, and the trial.

In Genesis 34, Dinah, a young Jewish woman, is the key figure within a story that details cross-cultural encounters between Jacob's clan and the men of Shechem, just as Jessica becomes enfolded into the bond plot between Christian and Jewish men in *The Merchant of Venice*. Even where Genesis 34 appears to move away from Dinah's story and take up trade agreements between Jacob's sons and the Shechemite men, the story is conspicuously and abruptly brought back to Dinah. The final two verses' featured exchange between Jacob and his sons Simeon and Levi punctuates the episode sharply. 'Jacob said to Simeon and Levi, "You have brought trouble on me, making me odious among the inhabitants of the land, the Canaanites and the Perizzites; my men are few in number, so that if they unite against me and attack me, I and my house will be destroyed.'[11] The two sons respond with a pointed question in the final verse: 'Should our sister be treated like a whore?'[12] The exchange between Simeon and Levi and their father raises pressing questions about the role and place of women within ethnographic communities, particularly when young unmarried women are understood to function as familial property and harbingers of their clans' reputation. Jacob's response suggests that it is Simeon and Levi's violent actions that have ruined the Israelites' reputation among foreigners, while Simeon and Levi assert that in fact Dinah's and her family's honour were irretrievably impugned when she was abducted by a Shechemite man.

Jessica's predicament is vital to *The Merchant of Venice*'s concern with thrift-as-ethnographic-flourishing on a number of fronts that include her significance as a progenitor of future Jewish offspring. Unlike Christian religious identity that is transmitted through the male line, Jewishness is passed down matrilineally. Janet Adelman and M. Lindsay Kaplan have both written extensively on the significance accorded to Jewish women's bodies in early modern England, convincingly reading the cultural anxiety about Jewish corporeal taint into Jessica's plot in *The Merchant of Venice*. Both scholars have argued that Jessica is not able to effect a meaningful conversion through religious inter-marriage in the play, despite her claim that her Christian-seeming 'manners' can expunge whatever trace of her father's Jewish 'blood' courses through her veins.[13] Within the play, it is presumably through Jessica's body that Shylock can hope to see the perpetuation of Abraham's line and the 'sacred nation' of which he forms a part. Historically, however, Jewish women have long played a crucial role in perpetuating Jewish family life far beyond physical reproduction. Within traditional families, it is women who are assigned the task of shaping the moral outlook of impressionable young children. They are their children's earliest educators. Mothers induct young boys and girls into cultural and moral norms through conditioning, repetition, and the routine transmission of knowledge at close proximity. This is precisely the kind of formative education that allows Jewish children to learn Hebrew before setting foot in school, and which posed such an intractable barrier to sixteenth-century Christian Hebraists, who sought in vain for formal instructional manuals to teach them what Jewish children were learning at home without textbooks.[14]

Should Jessica be counted among *The Merchant of Venice*'s Jews? Where critical discussions of this aspect of the play, exemplified by Adelman's and Kaplan's work, have in recent years tended to focus on Jessica's Jewish body and emerging notions of race, the question of Jessica's Jewishness is equally pressing and complex when it is framed through questions about her moral orientation and the ethical universe within which she deliberates practical moral questions. What I have been arguing throughout this book so far is that the moral universe of Jewish characters in *The Merchant of Venice* is constructed through Hebrew biblical stories. In looking to the interpretive tradition surrounding Genesis 34, one of Jessica's most important inter-texts, I turn now to the questions of consent and moral answerability that lie at the heart of both Dinah's and Jessica's stories.

In the only scene where Shylock shares a stage with his daughter, he implores her to shut up the windows and resist the urge to listen to the revelry animating the streets below.

> Hear you me Jessica,
> Lock up my doors, and when you hear the drum
> And the vile squeaking of the wry-necked fife
> Clamber not you up to the casements then
> Nor thrust your head into the public street
> To gaze on Christian fools with varnished faces
>
> (2.5.28–33)

Although Shylock's advice can be read as a commanding set of imperatives in which he extinguishes Jessica's will and appropriates her ability to choose ('hear you me' accomplishes a similar function as 'the skilful shepherd peeled me certain wands' from 1.3.81 – both indicate an appropriation of another's actions), the very fact that Shylock leaves Jessica at home to carry out his wishes is telling. That decision enables her escape, allowing her to carry out her own intentions, intentions that, unbeknownst to Shylock, are rebellious.

Shylock's motives in this episode are to have his daughter carry out his will. Behind his back, however, a mocking Launcelot Gobbo supplies contravening advice: 'Mistress look out the window for all this: / There will come a Christian by / Will be worth a Jewës eye' (2.5.40–2). Shylock's servant also conspires against him, though Shylock misapprehends the danger, esteeming Launcelot a mere 'patch' or fool not worth taking seriously.[15] Jessica's final response once Shylock has left the scene makes her own aims clear: 'Farewell – and if my fortune be not crost, / I have a father, you a daughter lost' (2.5.55–6). Clearly Jessica has no intention of obeying her father's wish to 'Do as I bid you, shut doors after you' (2.5.52).

Shylock's advice to Jessica is frequently read as an attempt to cloister her, in keeping with the pervasive discourse of separateness, enclosure and difference that attends his character throughout the play. However, it can equally reflect a desire to have Jessica make prudent decisions on her own behalf. Shylock's error consists of presuming that he knows Jessica's true intentions, and that her loyalty to him is, in fact, true.

Jessica's predicament with Shylock strikes a marked contrast with the play's other father–daughter plot featuring Portia precisely where it concerns the agency given to young unmarried daughters. Portia must obey the terms of her father's posthumous love-test, a test that accords no decisive agency whatsoever to her; instead, it places choice solely in the hands of her prospective suitors, who must obey the terms of her father's decree. Jessica is here given licence to carry out her father's wishes, even if she effectively uses that freedom to instead act on her own desires.

Shylock's comments to his daughter express a concern with Jessica's capacity for moral choice, choice that ultimately bears on his own position as well as his fate within the play. It is Jessica's absconsion that fans the flames of his vengeance towards Antonio, which then catalyses the pound of flesh plot and trial. A daughter's choice of suitor is also the catalysing event of Genesis 34, and it is Dinah's capacity to choose appropriately and consensually that remains a focal point for rabbinic exegetes as well as translators of these verses. English-language translations of Genesis 34 have produced varying accounts of Dinah's level of complicity in the chapter's opening verses. In verses 1 and 2, Dinah leaves the household of her father and brothers, goes out to see the neighbouring tribeswomen and is seduced by Shechem, the son of a local prince. The question of her intention when she leaves her paternal home and the degree of her consent in the affair with Shechem figures prominently in translators' renderings of these passages. The modern King James translation renders them this way:

1. And Dinah the daughter of Leah, which she bare unto Jacob, went out to see the daughters of the land.
2. or the Hivite, prince of the country, saw her, he took her, and lay with her, and defiled her.[16]

Alternatively, the 1917 Jewish Publication Society translation (often referred to as the 'Old' JPS version) renders these verses slightly differently:

1. And Dinah the daughter of Leah, whom she had borne unto Jacob, went out to see the daughters of the land.
2. And Shechem the son of Hamor the Hivite, the prince of the land, saw her; and he took her, and lay with her, and humbled her.[17]

Between these two modern translations, we can already discern two very different versions of the events that transpire between Dinah and Shechem. The modern KJV uses the word 'defiled' to describe what happens to Dinah, while the Old JPS translation prefers the term 'humbled', a considerably milder adjective that may suggest a transgression of social protocol relating to pre-marital sex but not necessarily sexual violation. Other more colloquial modern English translations offer even more decisive descriptions of what takes place. The Kaplan Living Torah translation produced by the twentieth-century American Orthodox rabbi Aryeh Kaplan renders the verse simply and directly as 'He seduced her, slept with her, and raped her.'[18]

Early modern English translations of Genesis 34 offer equally diverse renderings of this scene. The 1560 Geneva Bible, one of the two bibles that Shakespeare himself knew best, uses the term 'defiled' to describe the encounter between Shechem and Dinah. The Geneva translation advertises itself as one that consults with the original Hebrew text. A marginal comment notes that the Hebrew word for what happened to Dinah approximates the English 'humbled'. I reproduce here the 1560 Geneva edition's translation, with its line breaks and verse enumerations intact:

1. And then Dinah the daughter of Leah,
   which she bare unto Iakkob, went out
   to se the daughters of that countrey.
2. Whom when Shechem the sonne of Ha
   mor the Hivite lord of that countries sawe,
   he toke her, and lay with her, & defiled her.[19]

Further marginal commentary in the Geneva text explains, 'This example teacheth that to muche Libertie is not to be given to youthe.'[20] For the Geneva's translators, Dinah's story represents a cautionary tale for women about the dangers of proceeding unaccompanied in public. Dinah is described as a 'youthe' – a young person, and though the consequences she suffers for her indiscretion are 'humbling', the episode is framed through the marginal commentary as an indiscretion associated primarily with youthful naivety.

The 1568 Bishops, the other English biblical text with which Shakespeare would have been most familiar and whose revised text forms the basis for the 1611 King James translation, uses the word 'forced' to describe Dinah's encounter with Shechem. It too announces itself as a translation that consults with the Hebrew, noting, like the Geneva version, the English word 'humbled' in the margins of the text. The Bishops translation of these verses, with its original lines breaks and verse enumerations, reads as follows:

1. Dina, the daughter of
   Lea, which she bare
   unto Iacob, went out
   to see the daughters
   of the lande.
2. Whom when Sichem
   the sonne of Hemor the
   Hivite lord of the countrey sawe, he
   toke her & lay with her, and forced her.[21]

This translation prefers 'forced' to 'humbled' or 'defiled', suggesting that a violation took place in the encounter. This is no mere cautionary tale intended to instruct young people to adopt more prudent behaviour; instead, it represents a threatening story that the Bishops Bible follows with a pointedly condemning, gender-focused commentary. The marginal comment in the Bishops translation reads, 'This vayne curiositie of this woman greevouslye punished', which offers a far sharper, more moralising reading of the story than the Geneva's commentary.[22] In the Bishops Bible, Dinah is described as 'vayne' rather than merely youthful, suggesting at the possibility that it was her moral flaw of vanity – a flaw conventionally associated with women – rather than her inexperience that brought on the 'greevous' punishment that followed. In casting Dinah's as a 'vayne curiositie', the note in the Bishops foregrounds Dinah's perceived moral weakness, consequently casting her story and character far less sympathetically than in the Geneva Bible, where an evil set of consequences befalls an inexperienced adolescent. Where the Geneva Bible describes Dinah as a 'youth', in the Bishops Bible she is explicitly designated as a 'woman', a characterisation that indicates a more mature figure in terms of age and development as well as a more explicitly gendered commentary that implies that this is a story about a wicked woman rather than a hapless youth.

As with the contrast between the modern KJV, JPS, and Kaplan translations, early modern English renderings of these verses provide different accounts of what transpires in Genesis 34 by invoking varying degrees of violence and violation. The Bishops and Geneva translations exemplify how these variations occur even among texts that advertise having consulted with the original Hebrew. Among translations that do not consult directly with the Hebrew, there is even more variation and creative licence among early modern editions. The Douay-Rheims is among the most striking examples. Translated from Jerome's Latin Vulgate, the Douay-Rheims Bible was intended to oppose the Protestant Reformation and its vernacular Bible translations, offering an alternative Catholic Bible to English readers. Its rendering of Genesis 34 radically reconfigures Dinah's seduction, supplying additional material to the narrative that supplements the Hebrew text. The 1609 Douay-Reims Bible, sometimes referred to as the 'Douai Bible' or 'Douai Old Testament' because of its publication at the French University of Douai, translates Genesis 34 in the following way (my transcription here once again reproduces the text's line breaks and verse enumerations):

> And Dina the daughter of Lia went forth to see the[1]
> wemen of that countrie. Whom when Sichem had[2]
> seene the sonne of Hamor the Hevite, the prince of that
> land, he was in love with her, and he took her away, and
> lay with her, by force ravishing the virgin.[23]

In this version, translators insert a plotline into the story in verse 2 that affords Shechem with additional motivation for 'ravishing' Dinah who, we are now told, was a virgin. Straightaway before the two are introduced, we are told that Shechem 'was in love with' Dinah. By foregrounding Shechem's affection for Dinah before their encounter, Shechem is given a set of motivations wholly absent from either the Bishops or Geneva versions. In the Hebrew text there is no mention of Shechem's feelings until verse three, when we are told that Shechem's 'soul cleaved to Dinah the daughter of Jacob, and he loved her.' By foregrounding Shechem's emotional attachment to Dinah, the Douay-Rheims translation develops a rather sympathetic set of interior motives for Shechem's character. He is no longer simply a sexual aggressor; instead, he is a lovesick prince who sweeps the virginal Dinah away, has his way with her, 'ravishing' (rather than defiling or humbling) her in a manner that emulates contemporary courtly romance plots.[24] The story also becomes Shechem's rather than Dinah's as the focus shifts away from their sexual encounter and is reoriented around Shechem's experience, who is represented as her paramour and the episode's protagonist.

The Tyndale-Coverdale Bible, the first to offer a complete translation of the Bible into English and the first English Bible to receive official sanctioning from the Church of England (the 1539 Folio edition contains the royal licence), transforms these verses to similar effect. I have reproduced the textual layout from the 1535 Coverdale Bible here:

> Dina the daughter of Lea, which she
> bare unto Jacob, went out to be-
> holde the daughters of the lande.
> Whan Sichem the sonne of Hemor the He-
> vite (which was lorde of the land) sawe her,
> he toke her and laye with her, and forced
> her, and his herte hanged upon her, and he
> loved the damsel, and talked lovingly with
> her, and spake to his father Hemor: Get me
> this mayden to wife.[25]

It is worth noting that the Tyndale-Coverdale Bible does not enumerate individual verses, and instead blends verses 1–4 into a single narrative paragraph, as was customary in editions that predate the 1560 Geneva Bible. Although the Tyndale-Coverdale Bible does not go so far as to supplement the text in the way that the Douay-Rheims Bible does, the Coverdale edition offers much the same sense of the encounter between Dinah and Shechem as the Douay-Rheims. Without clear verse divisions, the sequence of events in the story becomes less clearly delineated. In the Masoretic Hebrew text, Shechem does eventually proclaim his feelings of love, but he does so after violating Dinah. That sequence becomes key to the retribution that follows and to the story's punctuating conclusion, 'Should one deal with our sister as with a harlot?'[26] In the Coverdale rendering, Shechem's motives follow hot on the heels of his violation of Dinah, with no separation between the two. Coverdale's punctuation of the episode reinforces the commingling of Shechem having 'forced' Dinah with part of the story where his 'herte hanged upon her, and he loved the damsel' – a mere comma separates her violation from his pining. The physical encounter and Shechem's feelings of love are made much more distinct in other translations, but in the Coverdale translation they are merged into a single sentence or thought, calling attention to verses 1–4 as part of a unified narrative about Shechem falling in love with Dinah and attempting to get his father to arrange their marriage, while Dinah's violation becomes only a small component embedded within that story.

In the Hebrew text of Genesis 34: 2, it is the phrase 'va-yishkav attah' that is used to describe the encounter between Shechem and Dinah. As Ilona Rashkow has noted, the term 'va-yishkav', 'and he lay', when followed by 'attah', 'her', is the rough equivalent in English of 'he laid her' rather than 'he lay with her', a formulation which is not used in either the modern KJV or the Old or New JPS translations. There is nothing in the Hebrew text to indicate that Dinah offers herself willingly to Shechem; the text suggests that Shechem violated her, since there is no implied consent, no 'with' in the formulation of this verse.[27]

Rabbinical commentaries on these verses go to great lengths to discuss Dinah's degree of consent in her relationship with a foreign man when she 'goes out' from her home. Overwhelmingly, they characterise the abduction of Dinah as a violation of her will, though there is substantial disagreement among exegetes about what exactly happens during the encounter. The eighteenth-century commentary *Or Hachayim* explains that Shechem expended a great deal of effort attempting to verbally seduce Dinah because she wasn't willing or able to enjoy their physical encounter. Citing the Talmudic dictum that when the wicked derive physical pleasure the righteous experience pain, *Or Hachayim* explains that Dinah felt tortured by sleeping with Shechem even though Shechem may not have actually forced her, hurt her or subjected her to 'perversions'.[28]

The medieval rabbi Nahmanides offers a substantially different opinion. He explains that Verse Two's 'he took her, and lay with her, and defiled her', implies a forced sexual connection, since it uses the word 'va-ye-ah-ne-ha' which translates to the English 'afflicted'. Nahmanides cites a variety of biblical sources to justify his claim, including Deuteronomy 21: 14, 'thou shalt not sell her at all for money, thou shalt not make merchandise of her,' and Judges 20: 5, 'and my concubine have they forced, that she is dead.' He asserts quite plainly that Dinah 'was forced, and she did not consent to the prince of the country.'[29] He then goes on to point out that the word 'umatan'(gift) in verse 12, referring to the silver and gold garments sent to fathers and brothers of a bride, was in this case given as a kind of bribe to Jacob and his sons because Dinah did not consent to have sexual relations with him. In Nahmanides' view, the gifts were intended to procure her male relatives' consent instead. Dinah was already captive in Shechem's house, 'and he [Shechem] feared not her brothers because he was the prince of the country and how could they take her by force out of his house?'[30]

For some rabbinical exegetes, the issue of Dinah's consent is framed as a question about her age at the time of the abduction. How old is she when Shechem lays claim to her? In his eleventh-century Torah commentary, Abraham ibn Ezra states very clearly that Dinah was a minor at the time of her abduction.[31] Commentaries like ibn Ezra's that discuss the question of Dinah's consent through a consideration of her age emphasise that she belongs to a class of persons too immature to offer consent. Consent is then relegated to her guardians who must speak for her since she is insufficiently mature to be answerable for her own decisions. The excessive gifts to her brothers and father after her abduction that Nahmanides details represents an attempt to work out the logic of this idea.

Under this view of Genesis 34, Dinah is categorically unable to accept Shechem's advances, no matter how sweetly she is courted by him. The issue of her complicity in their sexual encounter becomes irrelevant to the greater fact that

Shechem violates a child. One commentator writes: 'Their answer was telling and final. It teaches us that Dinah had been forced, and had not consented to Shechem.'³² Another commentator's observation suggests that consent is really the central issue of the entire Dinah affair. The Hebrew text uses the word 'na'ara' in verse 4, which translates into 'girl', when Shechem says 'get me this girl as a wife'. When, as in the case of this verse, the Hebrew word for girl lacks the final letter 'he', it shows that she has not yet reached puberty.³³ In the Masoretic Hebrew text, Shechem's words for 'get me this girl as a wife' are 'kakh li et ha-yeladah hazot le-ishah,' where 'yeladah' is the word for a female child in modern Hebrew, 'yeled' is a male child and the resonance is unmistakeable.³⁴ One commentator states the matter clearly: 'Dinah was eight and a half years old.'³⁵

Rabbinical commentators and textual editors responsible for translating Genesis 34 into English have dwelt intensively on Dinah, deliberating about her position as a piece of familial property within a patriarchal Jewish household, along with questions of her agency and choice in the affair with Shechem. While there is great concern over Dinah's implication in the world of her male relatives, and concern over the consequences to their reputation when she 'goes out' from her home, in some ways it is the question of Dinah herself and her largely absent thoughts and feelings as she ventures forth in the diaspora that represents the most consuming question for Jewish exegetes responding to Genesis 34.

The Merchant of Venice embeds a telling link to the biblical Dinah in the report of Jessica pawning the heirloom ring belonging to her mother, who is named 'Leah'. Shylock reacts to the news by recalling that 'It [the ring] was my turquoise, I had it of Leah when I was a bachelor' (3.1.114).³⁶ Dinah too has a mother named Leah; in the biblical story, Leah is Jacob's first wife and the elder, less desirable of Laban's two daughters whom Jacob is tricked into marrying. The passing reference to Leah in *Merchant* contributes towards an already dense network of connections linking Jessica to Dinah, in particular the Dinah of early modern English bibles.[37] The 1568 Bishops Bible's rendering of Genesis 34 as a story about women's wickedness finds a suggestive counterpart in the story of Jessica pawning the ring. The inclusion of the monkey is a telling detail in light of the animal's primary allegorical significance in the Renaissance – vanity. The early modern monkey's other allegorical meanings – excessive worldliness, over-indulgence in worldly pleasures, particularly sexual pleasures – are also implied through Jessica's actions in the play when she pawns the valuable ring for a monkey, and is reported to have spent 'in one night four-score ducats' in Genoa, according to Tubal (3.1.99).[38]

The Douay-Rheims Bible's translation of Genesis 34, which paints Shechem as a lovesick paramour, is also part of the sub-text of Jessica's romance with Lorenzo. The glamorising veneer of masculine heroism in *Merchant*, which glosses over its thieving seduction plots, mirrors the Douay-Rheims' preoccupation with Shechem as a courtly romantic paramour who 'ravishes' his damsel. Just as the Douay-Rheims romanticises what other translations as well as the Hebrew text describe as a rape, the language of courtship in *Merchant* contributes towards a glossing over of disturbing aspects of its featured seductions, seductions that include experiences of profound loss and bereavement. When Jessica quips that 'In such a night / Did young Lorenzo swear he loved her well, / Stealing her soul with many vows of faith, / And ne'er a true one' (5.1.17–19), she poignantly suggests that she may have misread Lorenzo's true intentions in an earlier moment of naivety. The word 'steal', which suggests both escape and theft, nicely captures the dichotomy: is Lorenzo her saviour, or has she been duped? In this scene, Jessica therefore manages to both invoke and question those very conventions of romantic courtship that had obscured its darker realities. *Merchant* thereby addresses both the language through which such violations are instantiated – language notably part of the Catholic Douay-Rheims rendering of Dinah's story – while also giving voice to the experiences of those who are, as Jessica claims to have been, momentarily seduced by that language.

Within the complaint that underscores Jessica's speech, Jessica manages to effectively speak back to the conventions of romance – the 'vows of faith' – that gloss over the difficult, uglier truths she subtly references. Those truths may well be emotional ones pertaining to her compatibility with Lorenzo and the strength of the bond that initially draws the two together in 'vows' of marriage. For Lorenzo, that bond is initially forged through a distinctively mercenary interest in Shylock's wealth, a fact he highlights to Jessica in act 5, scene 1: 'In such a night / Did Jessica steal from the wealthy Jew, / And with an unthrift love did run from Venice, / As far as Belmont' (5.1.14–17). His comment succeeds in reminding audiences of his motivating interest in Jessica – her father's wealth – while also ascribing a high level of responsibility and culpability to Jessica for stealing it. In his view of things, 'In such a night / Did *Jessica* steal from the wealthy Jew' [emphasis mine]. In effect, Lorenzo simultaneously recalls the conditions that enabled their relationship – portable assets acquired from her father, and an 'unthrift' or generous love for him. At the same time, he appears to censure Jessica for the morally questionable modes she used to obtain those very things. Lorenzo's comment suggests that even if Shylock is 'merely' a Jew and therefore deserving of being looted, it is nevertheless Jessica who committed the act, since 'On such a night did *Jessica* steal from the wealthy Jew' [emphasis mine]. While Jessica's 'unthrift love' for Lorenzo signals a munificence intended to contrast with the implicit meanness of her father, the phrase 'unthrift love' also contains the alternate meaning of un-thrifty as unable to thrive, making Jessica's love one that Lorenzo here construes as impossible, non-viable, even foolhardy.

The melancholy tone that inheres in Jessica's exchange with Lorenzo in 5.1 may imply that her previous understanding of her predicament and her partner had been incomplete when she made the decision to abscond. The issue of consent, in precisely the sense outlined by rabbinical commentators on Genesis 34, is very much at issue in her story. Commentaries such as Abraham ibn Ezra's, which emphasise Dinah's immaturity, her youth, and her inability to agree to a sexual relationship with or marry Shechem, articulate a predicament wherein Dinah is morally unable to anticipate future consequences with any degree of pragmatic skill. Those discussions of Dinah's age and lack of legal answerability in issues of sexual consent speak meaningfully to the regretful potentialities embedded in Jessica's language in act 5, scene 1. The 1560 Geneva Bible's estimation of Dinah's predicament, 'This example teacheth that to muche Libertie is not to be given to youthe,' echoes aspects of Jessica's exchange with Lorenzo in act 5, scene 1. Both rabbinic exegetes and Geneva commentators interpret Dinah's misadventures with Shechem as signs of her immature sensibility and lack of clear vision in the moment, which contribute to her inability to offer meaningful consent to any sexual relationship or marriage. Significantly, Shakespeare takes up such questions in an era that only just begins to experience the first stirrings of change to basic ideas about what constitutes consent and who is capable of offering it. A full century later, the concept of an age of reason comes to radically reshape legal and institutional practice in both England and America, redefining who can enter into and ratify legal contracts such as marriage, or initiate or revoke religious membership.[39]

The Dinah inter-text in *The Merchant of Venice* indexes important questions about Jessica's ability to enter into a serious romantic relationship and undertake meaningful, consensual religious conversion. Although physically able to flee from her father's house, it is less clear what it means for Jessica to escape from the faith that has defined her way of life under her father's direction. It is possible that Jessica received insufficient moral instruction under her father's care, an option that I discuss later in this chapter. Perhaps Jessica, like Dinah, has not yet grown into a mature sense of personhood plotted along ethnographically defined lines, or developed the mature agency to make concerted alterations to that aspect of herself. Perhaps she does not possess enough prudence or common sense to be able to meaningfully anticipate the implications of inter-marriage, something that her exchange with Lorenzo at 5.1 seems to imply. Through Dinah's story, *The Merchant of Venice* engages directly with questions about what consent and choice amount to for young, unmarried women, questions that represent the explicit focal point of exegetical commentary on Genesis 34 as well as Renaissance translations of these verses.

Within the Jewish tradition, the notion of moral answerability is paramount to full, participatory membership in religious and social life, membership that is initiated in bar- and bat-mitzvah ceremonies where a twelve- or thirteen-year-old is called up to the Torah. It is an act that requires a great deal of education within the tradition as well as a commitment to learning the cantorial rhythms of that week's *parsha*, or portion of the Torah readings. The act of being called to the Torah within the Jewish community indicates that an individual has been sufficiently educated in those traditions to be able to respond – musically and rhythmically – to the Torah as well as *with* the Torah when facing life's imminent moral predicaments. It signals the end of childhood and the beginning of moral and legal answerability for Jews.

Avowedly unwilling to remain bound to the religious community into which she is born, Jessica represents a problematic example of someone who does not offer her consent or have any desire to participate in her own identity-formation as a Jew. Instead, she longs to enter the fold of the Christian community, which she attempts to undertake by marrying Lorenzo, though her conversion is never represented onstage.[40] The manner in which Jessica shifts from Jewish to Christian households, by absconding and stealing from her father to compensate for the lack of a dowry and her fiancé's poverty, renders an already problematic situation even more difficult by positioning her as a disloyal daughter within a culture that overwhelmingly valued female obedience, submissiveness, and silence. In plotting Jessica's absconsion along these lines, *Merchant* draws substantively on a second episode from the Genesis Jacob stories centred on a daughter who, like Jessica, steals her father's valuables. I refer here to the biblical Rachel who in chapter 31 of Genesis steals Laban's idols before fleeing her paternal home. Rachel's story, which details an act of theft committed by a young woman with an ambivalent relationship to both her father's religious traditions and the ethnography of her Jewish husband, helps develop the complexity of Jessica's predicament as a young woman positioned between moral and theological worlds in *The Merchant of Venice*. Where Dinah's story calls attention to issues surrounding consent and moral answerability in Jessica's plotline, it is through Rachel's story that *Merchant* develops these threads by inquiring into what sorts of inner resources effectively make up or constitute moral answerability. Christian and Jewish exegetes and Renaissance English writers who discuss Rachel's theft respond to this question through a concerted focus on moral education, particularly women's moral education. In the remainder of this chapter, I take up Rachel's story and its implications for Shakespeare's Jessica, who is also positioned as a woman who stands to be educated in the ways of the community she seeks to join.

When in act 3, scene 1 Tubal relays the news of how Jessica sold her mother's ring in exchange for a monkey, the play recalls a biblical scene from Genesis where Rachel steals her father's valuables. Genesis 31 narrates the story of Jacob and his family's furtive departure from Haran. As they make preparations to leave, Rachel takes Laban's 'teraphim' or household gods, concealing them in the blankets of her camel's saddle. The *teraphim* that Rachel steals carry an exceptionally high value for Laban, just as Leah's turquoise ring does for Shylock. Laban pursues Jacob and his clan, running them down and demanding to search through their possessions in order to reclaim the objects. Both Jessica and Rachel depart surreptitiously from their paternal homes; in Rachel's case, she leaves Haran, land of her birthplace and site of Jacob's long toil for the privilege of marrying her. Both women steal objects of significant value to their fathers and undergo religious transformations as they move from paternal to matrimonial households.

Rachel's theft offers a discernible template for Jessica's actions in *The Merchant of Venice*: both young women steal from their fathers prior to clandestine departures and exit not only their father's households but also the religious faith that defines them. The moral ambiguities of this biblical episode also help shape Jessica's predicament, ambiguities elaborated in both Judaic and Christian exegetical commentaries that struggle to make sense of what Rachel does. Some rabbis conclude that Rachel's theft of the idols constitutes a violation of the moral prohibition against stealing, a prohibition whose severity is made clear by Jacob's assertion that whomever has committed the offence will be put to death. Other commentators attempt to vindicate Rachel's actions. In one account, the *teraphim* that Rachel steals are invested with the power of speech. The *Genesis Rabbah* commentary contends that Rachel's rationale for stealing the talking idols was to cover up the location of her family as they fled Haran;

otherwise, their whereabouts would have been revealed.[41] Other rabbis explain it as an attempt to steer her father away from the sins of idolatry.[42]

Much of the exegesis on Rachel's actions in Genesis 31 dwells on religious distinctions between her father's and husband's households. This same distinction between Laban's idol-worship and Jacob's monotheism remains a point of emphasis throughout the biblical chronicling of Jacob's exploits at Haran. In Genesis 31: 14 Rachel and Leah complain that they have lost their rightful inheritance. They ask whether they are now to be considered strangers to their father, pointing out that Laban effectively sold them to Jacob and then squandered the proceeds. 'Are we not counted of him strangers? For he hath sold us, and hath quite devoured also our money.'[43] Commentators interpret this complaint as an expression of ongoing kinship with Laban. In seeking a share of their father's inheritance, Rachel and Leah voice an affiliation with his idolatry that they were supposed to have abandoned when they joined Jacob's household. One commentator argues that this complaint led to Rachel's death on the journey to Bethlehem.[44] These observations point towards Rachel's divided loyalties, which lead to a perpetual state of non-belonging. Her sense of exclusion also informs rabbinic exegesis of Rachel's final resting place, which stands apart from that of Jacob and the other Jewish patriarchs and matriarchs. According to one commentary, because Rachel stole her father's idols she could not be buried in the cave of Makhpelah along with Jacob's clan, causing her to be excluded from full belonging in a meaningful material sense.[45]

Jessica voices her desire to become a Christian in no uncertain terms throughout *The Merchant of Venice*, and expresses none of the affiliation with her father's way of life or religious practice that commentators attribute to the biblical Rachel. However, Jessica's status as a would-be convert places her in a similarly marginal position, and *Merchant*'s

Venetian Christians avidly take up the question of her proximity and likeness to Shylock. That likeness is sometimes expressed using physiological language and the discourse of blood, which several scholars have addressed in recent years.[46] The Renaissance preoccupation with lineage and bloodlines intersects in important ways with questions of religious identity and conversion, and those questions emerge with particular force in the wake of fifteenth-century Spanish blood purity laws. The question of blood and the transmission of religious identity has become particularly important to Shakespeare scholars in view of *Merchant*'s emphasis on inter-faith marriage and its suggestive allusions to the progeny that issue from sexual liaisons among partners from differing ethnological backgrounds.

The discourse of blood and biological difference is one of several languages made available in *Merchant*'s treatment of Jessica's conversion, and it offers a valuable way of thinking through how offspring complicate issues of tribal and national flourishing across several of the play's plots. However, *The Merchant of Venice* also interrogates tribal membership in Jessica's storyline via a set of practical moral questions. To what degree are women like Jessica, raised in one faith and converted to another, able to overcome the habits associated with their former way of life? To what degree can one's moral orientation be re-calibrated to suit the demands of a new community and its ethical and spiritual demands, which speak to one's ability to remake oneself in distinctly practical-ethical ways? These same questions recur in discussions of the biblical Rachel who, like Shakespeare's Jessica, shifts religious identity when she moves from her father's to her husband's household, and engages in behaviour that troubles moral norms.

To biblical commentators, Rachel's ongoing expression of affiliation with her father's household and religious traditions mark her as a marginal figure neither fully divorced from her father's ways nor seamlessly integrated into Jacob's monotheistic practice. Renaissance English exegetes call attention to Rachel's mixed heritage and describe it as a lingering influence that could not be overcome. In *Hexapla in Genesin & Exodum* (1633), Andrew Willet writes, 'Rachel was not free from all touch of superstition: both because she had beene a long time trained up under a superstitious father, and could not so easily forget her manner of education, though much qualified with Jacob's instruction.'[47] Willet imagines Jacob as a moral educator attempting to uproot his wife's pagan beliefs and replace them with sounder monotheistic ones; yet despite Jacob's efforts, he is unable to fully displace Rachel's entrenched superstitions. Gervase Babington's 1592 commentary is equally chastising of Rachel's paganism, and emphatic about the lingering effects of her upbringing. He too concludes that Jacob applies tremendous effort to morally reform his wife, to little effect. 'Rachell departing, stole her fathers idols, which he called Gods, a great fault in a good woman: but weaknes sometimes is in the best, and it may not be justified. This itch of superstition though goad men indevour, yet can they not ever utterly extinguish in their deerest, but in long time, if ever.'[48]

Both Willet and Babington dwell on the lingering effects of Rachel's idolatrous upbringing under Laban, which they imagine indelibly affecting Rachel's capacity for moral conduct. Both commentators determine the source of the problem to be the ongoing influence of a belief-system acquired under her father's instruction. Rachel stands as the object of moral reform, at the centre of efforts that are proffered in good faith by her devoted husband with the expectation of improving her. And yet, Rachel also stands as something of a contradiction. Her actions reveal that those attempts have miscarried. Biblical exegesis elaborates on how she has failed to absorb the lesson. Ultimately, Rachel is deemed neither wholly an adherent of the ethical universe of her idolatrous father nor entirely converted to the monotheistic belief-system of her Jewish husband, placing her in a liminal place in between, much like Shakespeare's Jessica.

Renaissance English commentators focus their discussions of Rachel's transgression on the moral-theological origins of her actions – what they term 'superstitions' – that endorse the practice of idol worship. In *The Merchant of Venice*, Lorenzo also distinguishes Jessica through a related set of moral-theological differences. His meditation in act 5, scene 1 on the civilising powers of music dwells insistently on a spiritual life that transcends the brute physical one, and like the biblical Jacob reforming his wife, Lorenzo attempts in this scene to re-educate Jessica and draw her from 'this muddy vesture of decay' (5.1.64). By referencing the spiritual transcendence of the flesh and its depravities, Lorenzo cites tropes widely associated in the early modern world with Christianity's transcendence over Judaic law, epitomised by the Pauline rejection of the Jewish practice of circumcision. Lorenzo's speech characterises Jessica's early life as something that must, like the Letter epitomised by Jewish law, be overcome by a more spiritualised Christian vision. The base materialism or 'muddy vesture of decay' and musical-cum-moral ignorance that Lorenzo goes on to elaborate represent ways of describing – and maligning – Jessica's Jewishness. Lorenzo makes direct and disparaging reference to Jessica's father when he asserts, 'The man that hath no music in himself, / Nor is not moved with concord of sweet sounds, / Is fit for treasons, stratagems, and spoils . . . Let no such man be trusted' (5.1.83–8). His characterisation of the untrustworthy man inured to music's charms recalls Shylock's earlier aversion to music, while the reference to 'stratagems' recalls stereotypical Elizabethan views of Jews as alien, degenerate plotters.

When Jessica fails to heed Lorenzo's lesson, Lorenzo elaborates by likening Jessica to 'a wild and wanton herd / Or race of youthful and unhandled colts / Fetching mad bounds, bellowing and neighing loud' (5.1.71–3). He insists that despite the 'hot condition of their blood' (5.1.74), these colts can be made docile:

> If they but hear perchance a trumpet sound,
> Or any air of music touch their ears,
> You shall perceive them make a mutual stand,
> Their savage eyes turned to a modest gaze
> By the sweet power of music.
>
> (5.1.75–9)

In its emphasis on the mass conversion of an entire herd of hidebound creatures as well as its strategy of moral-theological re-education, Lorenzo's speech crafts an image of widespread religious transformation that expounds Christian eschatological beliefs about the conversion of the Jews, a conversion viewed as the necessary precursor to Christ's second coming. Lorenzo's interaction with Jessica reflects both medieval strategies for conversion centred on moral-theological dispute, historically enacted through humiliating staged disputations between rabbis and Christian theologians, as well as more immediately contemporary Renaissance humanist-inspired encounters with Jews that occasioned far more considerate and collaborative forms of interaction across sixteenth-century Europe. The 'in such a night' exchange between Lorenzo and Jessica in this scene evokes the one-upmanship of theological dispute, and Lorenzo's presumption of the educator's prerogative assumes the discourse of Christian proselytisation even while the loving tone of their exchange softens these confrontational aspects and their attendant power imbalances by reflecting what appears to be a couple with evenly matched wills engaging in a playful lover's spat. Lorenzo approaches Jessica's moral education with great optimism and patience, pronouncing that her savage rhythms can be subdued since she, like the herd of colts he describes, ostensibly has the capacity for moral and spiritual transformation. Through the wild colt analogy, Lorenzo maintains that Jessica's inner mettle can at least temporarily be eclipsed by a more refined spiritual sensibility, since 'music for the time doth change his [i.e. the colt's] nature' (5.1.82). His vision is capacious, delineating a bright, beautifully rendered and inclusive future that hinges, however, on her ability to attune herself to its truths.

Therein lies the rub for Jessica. Lorenzo identifies an immediate problem with her spiritual transformation in Jessica's own unwillingness to heed or, according to his analogy, hear the lesson. In Lorenzo's estimation, Jessica proves an unwitting pupil – her 'spirits are attentive' (5.1.70), suggesting that she is too preoccupied to register his instruction. When read through a Christian eschatological lens, Lorenzo's insistence on Jessica's impending spiritual awakening figures a Christian belief in the imminent necessity of converting the Jews, an imperative greatly troubled by Jews' perceived unwillingness to heed the truth of their own scriptures, which Jessica appears here to reflect. But Lorenzo does not only offer Jessica a theological primer in act 5, scene 1; he also attempts to initiate her into a particular social order with normative moral and behavioural standards for women. In addition to its Christian eschatological message, Lorenzo's speech also emphasises particular – and particularly female – virtues at the very moment when the young couple stand poised on the brink of retreating indoors to the social world of Portia's Belmont. Lorenzo's speech contains a correspondingly practical aspect concerned less with theology and more with manners, mores, and matrimonial roles. Throughout their exchange, he adopts the language of a schoolmaster issuing instructions to his pupil: 'Sit, Jessica. Look how the floor of heaven / Is thick inlaid with patens of bright gold' (5.1.58–9). He directs her attention throughout the scene – 'do but note a wild and wanton herd' (5.1.71); 'you shall perceive them make a mutual stand' (5.1.77). Jessica's resistance, typified by her inability to register the theological lesson and her feisty one-upmanship as she and Lorenzo cycle through a litany of Classical lovers in act 5, scene 1, defies the submissiveness, docility, and silence expected of good wives, which Lorenzo figures through his description of the hot-blooded colt whose 'savage eyes' are turned to a more 'modest gaze'. Presumably, this 'modest gaze' becomes possible once Jessica, *his* wild colt, is domesticated and rendered docile through the civilising harmonies of not only Christian theology but also marriage.

Lorenzo's lesson offers a theological and also a practical moral lesson for his young wife about the kind of conduct that facilitates acceptance within the ordered universe of Christian social life. Where Lorenzo and Jessica's elopement is figured for audiences through Tubal's story about their whirlwind traverse across Italy, Lorenzo's lesson to Jessica in act 5, scene 1 suggests that their wild adventures have come to an end, and it is now time to find some measure of domestic harmony within a highly structured social world, one that requires that the 'wild colt' begin to 'mark the music' and adopt a more 'modest gaze'. The discourse of taming wildness is one that the play explores at various junctures in relation to manners, sociability, and belonging. Most memorably, the term appears in Shylock's reaction to the news of his daughter's departure with Leah's turquoise ring: 'I would not have given it [the ring] for a wilderness of monkeys' (3.1.115). The term 'wilderness' here, which contrasts with the plural 'monkeys', vividly evokes the solitude that characterises Shylock's position from this point on in the play, and which reflects on Lorenzo's later ascription of wildness to Jessica through the wild colt imagery and to her social isolation as a 'stranger' at Belmont. In a slightly different register, Bassanio counsels Gratiano in act 2, scene 2 about the virtues of softening his wild manners in preparation for their trip to Belmont.

> ... hear thee, Gratiano;
> Thou art too wild, too rude and bold of voice;
> Parts that become thee happily enough
> And in such eyes as ours appear not faults;
> But where thou art not known, why, there they show
> Something too liberal. Pray thee, take pain
> To allay with some cold drops of modesty
> Thy skipping spirit, lest through thy wild behaviour
> I be misconstrued in the place I go to,
> And lose my hopes.
> (2.2.173–81)

In this speech, Bassanio invests a high degree of importance in having Gratiano learn to temper his 'wild behaviour' to suit Belmont's refined social climate. In each of these cases, wildness contravenes the accepted moral code associated with social life among the play's Christians, with Belmont and Portia serving as the pinnacle of that decorum, devolving outward towards those on the margins of social acceptability such as Shylock and Jessica.

Similar lessons about decorum were of course being elaborated throughout the sixteenth and seventeenth centuries in Renaissance conduct manuals, many of which aim directly at women readers and the fathers and husbands tasked with their care. Overwhelmingly, such manuals turn to biblical examples to illustrate their lessons, lessons into which morally ambivalent Hebrew biblical characters such as Rachel figure in complex ways. Like Lorenzo's elaboration of celestial harmonies to Jessica, English Renaissance writers devote considerable effort trying to supply a clear didactic framework for the morally problematic actions of Hebrew biblical women. By writing Rachel into conduct books, sixteenth- and seventeenth-century English moralists have her serve an instructive function even where she stands as a negative moral example. *The Monument of Matrones*, first published in 1582 and dedicated to Queen Elizabeth I, is one of the foremost examples of a voluminous conduct manual about women's lives that also directly addresses English women as its reading audience.[49] Author Thomas Bentley (1543–85) compiles devotional readings, meditations, prayers, and advice geared towards the various stages of a woman's life. Divided into seven sections or 'lamps', lamp five of Bentley's *Monument* turns to Rachel and Leah's complaints over their missing inheritance, which he cites as an example of filial ingratitude. Under the section entitled 'Another very necessary prayer to be said of any daughter or maiden child,' Bentley writes:

> Though my parents forsake me, and count me as a stranger, yet give me grace never to forsake them utterlie, nor to saie of them as Leah and Rachel said of Laban their father, We have no more portion or inheritance in our fathers house: but rather make me through the gift of thy grace obedient and verie willing to suffer for thy sake, my parents to worke thine and their willes in me.[50]

Bentley counsels good daughters to refrain from emulating Rachel and Leah who selfishly demand their inheritance from their father. Instead, he advises his readers to adopt the requisite modesty, patience, and obedience even in the face of ungenerous parents that represent the pre-eminent female virtues advanced throughout *The Monument of Matrones*. Rachel's story here constitutes a cautionary example that Bentley urges readers not to follow; however, he locates her story within a didactic text aimed at instilling docility.

Texts such as Bentley's *Monument of Matrones* endeavour to offer a way, through practical moral instruction, for even morally ambivalent figures like Rachel to become morally instructive for good English women. Even though several writers align Rachel's behaviour with 'ungodliness,' indicating her failure to correspond with a neatly defined moral-theological framework, she still emerges as an important example to caution women against rebelliousness. In *The Monument of Matrones*, Bentley prescribes: 'A daughter that is bold or past shame, dishonoureth both hir father, and hir husband, and the ungodlie shall regard her, because she is not inferiour unto them, but both hir father and hir husband shall despise her, because of hir follishnesse.'[51] Bentley condemns excessive boldness in young women, concluding that this behaviour places women in line with 'ungodlie' folk who will recognise in them a kindred spirit, even as their behaviour elicits condemnation from their own fathers and husbands.

With a more directly condemnatory emphasis, the translator Thomas Paynell's (d.1564?) 1561 edition of the thirteenth-century Frenchman Nicolas de Hannapes' text *The Ensamples of Virtue and Vice, Gathered Out of Holy Scripture* enumerates the sins, weaknesses and travesties committed by a long list of biblical women. Included in the litany are Eve, Sarah, Lot's daughters and Rachel. Like Bentley, Paynell also dedicates his text to Elizabeth I, though, interestingly, he also writes and dedicates a series of religious texts to the Catholic Mary in the 1540s and 1550s, including an index of the religious writings of Thomas More in which he pointedly attacks reformed religion.[52] Paynell proves adept at straddling the confessional fence throughout his career, producing and dedicating various works to both Mary and Elizabeth I as well as friends of Elizabeth's father, Henry VIII. But where Paynell proves able to pander to both Catholic and Protestant monarchs, he ironically fails to appreciate Rachel's similar skills at negotiating multiple moral-theological contexts. Paynell identifies Rachel's theft as a clear sin and locates her on the long list of biblical women who deceive their husbands and fathers.

In a section entitled 'Of the deceitfulness of wemen', Paynell condemns Rachel, who with 'inventions beguyled her father, seekynge his idoles'.[53]

Other early modern writers consider Rachel's actions in a more redeeming light. William Lowth's 1581 translation of Barthélemy Batt's (1515–59) prescriptive text on parenting, *The Christian Mans Closet*, parses the question of Rachel's theft by weighing the duties daughters owe their parents against their obligations to God.

> Rachel against her fathers will stole his idols, and hid them away very warily. Saint Augustine saith: Our father is to be beloved, but yet god is to be preferred before our father. And the 70 psalm techeth, in this thing only a child ought not to obey his parents if they shall commaund him any thing against God.[54]

For Lowth, when there is a conflict between duties to one's parents and duties to God, the clear obligation is to God, which may involve forsaking one's parents, as Rachel does. He advises, 'if they [i.e. parents] shal once go about to withdrawe thee from God or to move thee to doe any thing against the will of God, leave father and mother, joyne thy self to God.'[55] In Lowth's view, Rachel's theft is justified even though it violates her ethical obligation to Laban; her primary moral obligation, evidenced when she hides the idols, is to God.

Lowth's conclusion suggests one way of ascribing positive moral meaning to Jessica's deception if we consider Shylock's Jewishness through Lorenzo's narrowly partisan lens, as a source of spiritual depravity.[56] A more comprehensive overview of early modern discussions of Rachel's theft, however, reveals a genuine moral ambivalence towards her behaviour and her character, but a corresponding insistence on using Rachel's example to instil proper moral conduct in young women. Paynell's translation of Hannapes' text includes Rachel's name in the litany of women's deceptions, beginning when 'Adam by the occasion of Eve, was deceyved . . . he by her perswasion and counsell, did eate of the tree forbyden.' After Eve's pernicious influence comes Sarah's faithlessness: 'Sara hearing the promise, that she shoulde conceyve a chylde, laughed within her selfe. But when she was reproved of her mystrust, with a lye she excused her selfe.' He then proceeds to Lot's daughters, who 'with wyne . . . accomplished their purpose', followed by Rachel's theft of the idols, which Paynell roundly condemns.[57] Rachel's forms part of an extensive roster cited by Paynell of rebellious, disingenuous women clearly intended to serve as cautionary tales.

Although Renaissance English writers vary in how they evaluate Rachel's actions, Rachel becomes an important example in the project of educating young women in morally acceptable courses of conduct. Rachel's story and background, however, also resist the kind of containment provided by such conduct manuals. She proves a stubbornly unsettling figure in the eyes of many early modern writers. Rachel's burial site, located at a crossroads en route to Bethlehem regarded as a beacon for wayfarers and itinerants who have not yet arrived at a fixed destination, speaks to her unsettled and unsettling quality, one that Jessica mirrors in her reported travels across Italy after eloping with Lorenzo. Renaissance conduct manuals attempt to offer a way of utilising those examples and transforming them into practical moral lessons for women. Lorenzo's homily on celestial music in act 5, scene 1 offers a neo-Platonic iteration of the message reinforced throughout texts such as *The Monument of Matrones*, which aim to improve women's behaviour by underscoring obedience to a moral system with clearly delineated parameters with an emphasis on quelling wayward impulses. While Lorenzo figures the process of moral improvement as liberation from the bondage of material forms, his language, like the language of contemporary conduct manuals aimed at young women, proposes to improve by mollifying defiant spirits and instilling the docility and submissiveness proper to virtuous wives.

Lorenzo appears to be sincere in suggesting that if Jessica can become a gentle, submissive doe – an imperative that she shows early signs of defying – then she can be transformed and assume a proper place within the ordered Christian universe he maps out in his speech in 5.1, undoubtedly the play's most singularly beautiful and poetic. Jessica's initial logic early on in the play maps out a process of conversion through marriage – 'O Lorenzo, / If thou keep promise, I shall end this strife, / Become a Christian and thy loving wife' (2.3.19–21). In act 5, scene 1, Lorenzo reconfigures Jessica's equation, however, by insisting that such spiritual transformations follow from submitting to an ordered universe within which she must become both modest and meek. Within his vision, spiritual transformation and a woman's domestication through marriage are effectively reduced to one and the same thing; marking the music entails both rising above 'this muddy vesture of decay' and transforming 'savage eyes' to a 'more modest gaze'.

In act 5, scene 1, Jessica bucks up against Lorenzo's authority and the domesticated role that he outlines through his wild colt analogy. Her rebelliousness aligns her in some ways with Portia, another clever and strong-willed wife whom Jessica encounters immediately after they retreat indoors. In her liminal position, however, Jessica is strikingly like the biblical Rachel, particularly once she shows signs of not fitting in at Belmont. Within biblical commentary, Rachel is also described as unable to fully align with a single set of moral or theological norms; instead, she stands as an outsider positioned between ethnographic worlds. Jessica's position as a 'stolen bride' who commits theft in order to elope epitomises this form of liminality and its attendant challenges. Jessica steals from Shylock in a display of disloyalty towards her father that contemporary moralists roundly condemn in young women, even where her strong impulse towards conversion suggests a potentially redemptive motive for that disloyalty. In this case, it is prompted by Jessica's desire to be firmly fixed by a new Christian identity, a desire that the play both validates and problematises. Jessica's desire to integrate into a Christian world poses an important question about what function her rebelliousness is intended to serve. If it offers her a way of disenfranchising from Shylock and her Jewish identity, it seems to also trouble the model of domesticated obedience that Lorenzo equates with spiritual conversion to Christianity.

Rachel's story offers suggestive options for reading Jessica's failure to neatly align with the moral and cultural imperatives of both Jewish and Christian communities. For many biblical commentators, Rachel's story is the site of convergence for multiple ethnological, linguistic, and interpretive traditions. Within the Genesis Jacob narrative, she stands as the object of competing claims. In the early verses of chapter 31, Rachel's brothers, fathers, and husband each assert ownership of her and her sister Leah. Jacob insists that he has earned the right to take possession of his cattle, servants, wives and children. Laban's sons insist on their rightful claim to their father's property: 'Jacob has taken all that was our father's; and from that which was our father's he has built up all this wealth.'[58] Once Laban chases Jacob down, he too outlines an emphatic claim to them, telling Jacob in no uncertain terms that he has stolen his property and kidnapped his daughters: 'The daughters are my daughters, the children are my children, and the flocks are my flocks; all that you see is mine.'[59] In the end, the men gather a heap of stones, which Laban declares will serve as a 'covenant' and a 'witness' before God, effectively acting as a dividing line between the two clans henceforth. 'And Laban declared, "This mound is a witness between you and me this day."

That is why it is named Gal-ed; and [it was called] Mizpah, because he said, "may the Lord watch between you and me, when we are out of sight of each other."[60] Commentators note the two distinct names, Hebrew and Aramaic, for the site of the covenant. This bi-fold naming emphasises two distinct traditions, hearkening once more to the distinct ethnographic identities of Jacob's and Laban's respective clans.[61]

Renaissance English interpretive commentary is equally concerned with the multi-vocality of Rachel's story. In *Hexapla in Genesin Exodum*, Andrew Willet begins his commentary on Genesis 31 by citing rabbinical exegesis. He reiterates Abraham ibn Ezra's position to the effect that Rachel stole the idols so that Laban would not learn the whereabouts of Jacob's family. Willet then proceeds to cite another rabbi, Salomon, by whom he likely meant the medieval rabbi Rashi (also known as Shlomo Yitzhaki), who argues that Rachel stole the idols to 'revoke her father from idolatry'.[62] Willet ultimately rejects the rabbinical explanations, and instead proposes

> ... it is most like that Rachel, though much reformed, and reclaimed from her fathers superstition by her husbands instruction, yet was somewhat touched therewith still: and therefore of a superstitious mind did take away her father idols: and hereof it was that long after this, Jacob reforming his house, caused all the strange gods to be removed.[63]

Both the substance and the composition of Willet's comments teem with dissenting opinions, contesting points of view, and differing interpretive traditions, which speak to the complex and layered nature of Rachel's character and story. Rather than serving as a text that can help individuals negotiate cross-cultural encounters in a diasporic setting, as the story of the parti-coloured lambs becomes for Shylock, the story of Rachel in Genesis 31 enfolds clashing cultural contexts into its fabric. Her story itself becomes the site of contest – particoloured terrain.

Where Shylock's citation of Scripture in *The Merchant of Venice* gives voice to a Judaic moral vision intended to counter Christian assertions, Jessica, by dint of her profound longing to convert and join the Christian community, becomes particularly subject to its exclusions and its partisan moral vision. It is perhaps for this reason that Jessica's final lines in the play are mournful ones. 'I am never merry when I hear sweet music' (5.1.69). Among Renaissance writers, the most commonly cited feature of Rachel's story also draws on a mournful image: the figure of Rachel weeping in Jeremiah 31: 15: 'A cry is heard in Ramah – wailing, bitter weeping – Rachel weeping for her children. She refuses to be comforted for her children, who are gone.' In this verse, the prophet Jeremiah recalls Rachel's death during childbirth on the way to Bethlehem. She dies at Ramah, the site of the ancient Israelites' deportation into exile by the Babylonians that Jeremiah reports. Rachel's story for many Renaissance writers is the story of diasporic lament, the cry of the eternal outsider in her exilic suffering. In this capacity, she gives voice to the role of outsiders who, like *Merchant*'s Jessica, cannot find their way in. The point at which we leave Jessica reflects a melancholy end. But Jessica's ending is dually tragic; her father is also crushed by her departure, and is ultimately crushed by the legal and theological apparatus that come to dominate the conclusion of the trial scene. Viewed internally, from the perspective of Jewish families who lose members to diasporic life, *Merchant*'s Jessica, like the biblical Rachel, speaks to the very acute failings – and feelings – of bereaved kin.

Shylock's response to the loss of his daughter and his property is recounted to us second-hand in the play via Solanio's invidiously construed Christian stereotype intended to mock and demean his suffering. '"My daughter! O my ducats! O my daughter! / Fled with a Christian! O my Christian ducats!"'

(2.7.15–16). Such a report both fits in with the comic structure of the play, whose main target is Shylock and his Jewishness, while also exemplifying the difficulty of peeling back those very layers of discrimination, since they often masquerade as reported fact in the play, as they do in this instance. Some of the most effective responses to such scenes, which reconfigure Shakespeare's comedy into a tragedy, occur when Jewish writers adapt this play and give voice to its tropes of loss, mourning and melancholy, particularly over the loss of daughters to the diaspora and to religious inter-marriage. In the following chapter, I turn to an episode in *The Merchant of Venice*'s history that sees the rewriting of its characters by Jewish writers, in ways that appeal to these same scriptural episodes. Biblical figures such as Dinah play a vitally important role in the literary imagination of nineteenth- and twentieth-century writers who flesh out the moral agency of Jewish women in particular. The spirit of rebellion that underwrites Dinah's and Rachel's stories becomes a significant feature of Jewish adaptations of *The Merchant of Venice* in this period, a development that I discuss in detail in Chapter 4, which turns to Yiddish-language adaptations of *The Merchant of Venic*.

Notes

1. See Benjamin Nelson, The Idea of Usury (Chicago: University of Chicago Press, 1969), 73ff. for a discussion of how Protestant doctrine transforms Renaissance English attitudes towards charging interest. See also C. G. A. Clay, Economic Expansion and Social Change: England 1500–1700 (Cambridge: Cambridge University Press, 1984): 2: 126–95 on the economics of European trade in the sixteenth century, especially England's expanding role in global trade east of the Levant in this period. A number of sixteenth-century English writers offer increasingly positive valuations of merchants and mercantile activity, including John Wheeler in *A Treatise of Commerce* (London, 1601), and Daniel Price in *The Merchant: A Sermon Preached at Paul's Cross on Sunday the 24th of August Being*

the Day Before Bartholomew Fair, 1607 (Oxford, 1608), and of course the charter of the Levant company itself, reprinted in Richard Hakluyt's *The Principal Navigations, Voyages, and Discoveries of the English Nation* (London, 1589): 172–4.

2. *The Bible and Holy Scriptures Conteyned in the Olde and Newe Testament* (Geneva: Rouland Hall, 1560), marginal note Gen. 30: 23–4.
3. On this point, see Colin Kidd, *The Forging of Races: Race and Scripture in the Protestant Atlantic World, 1600–2000* (Cambridge: Cambridge University Press, 2006).
4. Gervase Babington, *Certaine plaine, briefe, and comfortable Notes upon everie Chapter of Genesis* (Thomas Charde: London, 1592), folio 130, note 7 on Genesis 32.
5. See Menahem Kasher (ed.), *Encyclopedia of Biblical Interpretation: A Milliennial Anthology*, trans. Hyman Klein (New York: American Biblical Encyclopedia Society, 1959): 4: 136–44.
6. Genesis 32: 7.
7. Kasher cites Joseph Herman Hertz (1872–1946), British chief rabbi and author of the Torah commentary *The Pentateuch and Haftorahs with Commentary*. Kasher, *Encyclopedia*, 4: 138, 'Commentary'.
8. In identifying the biblical Dinah in Genesis 34 as an important inter-text for Shakespeare's Jessica I follow Janet Adelman, who discusses the relationship between the two in great detail in chapter four of *Blood Relations: Christian and Jew in The Merchant of Venice* (Chicago: University of Chicago Press, 2008): 99–134. The resemblance between the two stories is also discussed by James T. Bracher, 'The Lorenzo-Jessica Subplot and Genesis XXXIV', *Shakespeare 1964*, ed. Jim Corder (Fort Worth: Texas Christian University Press, 1965): 33–42, and mentioned briefly by Joan Ozark Holmer, *Choice, Hazard, and Consequence* (New York: St. Martin's Press, 1995): 83.
9. Kasher, *Encyclopedia*, 4: 174, note 7. Kasher cites the Bahya section of *Bereshith Rabbathi*, an eleventh-century commentary written by French rabbinical scholar Moses ha-Darshan. Ha-Darshan was the founder of rabbinical exegetical studies in France and chief rabbi of the yeshiva at Narbonne. See his *Midrash Bereshit Rabati Nosad 'al*

Sifro Shel Rabi Mosheh Ha-Darshan, ed. Chanoch Albeck (Jerusalem: Meḳitse Nirdamim, 1940). Hebrew.
10. Menahem Kasher (1895–1983) cites his own multi-volume work, the *Torah Shelemah* on this point. First published in 1927, the *Torah Shelemah* is an encyclopedic text that joins the Written Law of the Pentateuch with the Talmud and Midrashim of the Oral Law, along with extensive commentaries. See Kasher, *Encyclopedia*, 4: 175.
11. Genesis 34: 30.
12. Genesis 34: 31.
13. See especially Janet Adelman, 'Her Father's Blood: Race, Conversion, and Nation in *The Merchant of Venice*', *Representations*, 81: 1 (Winter 2003): 4–30, as well as chapter 3 of Adelman's *Blood Relations: Christian and Jew in the Merchant of Venice* (Chicago: University of Chicago Press, 2008): 66–98; also see M. Lindsay Kaplan, 'Jessica's Mother: Medieval Constructions of Jewish Race and Gender in *The Merchant of Venice*', *Shakespeare Quarterly*, 58: 1 (Spring 2007): 1–30.
14. On this point, see the very useful discussion in chapter 2 of Stephen G. Burnett, *Christian Hebraism in the Reformation Era (1500–1660): Authors, Books, and the Transmission of Jewish Learning* (Boston: Brill, 2012): 49–92.
15. John Russell Brown glosses the term 'patch' as *pazze* or fool, in the Arden Second Edition. See *The Merchant of Venice*, ed. John Russell Brown, Arden Second Edition (London: Cengage Learning, 1995): 52.
16. Genesis 34: 1–2. *The Holy Bible: King James Version* (New York: American Bible Society, 1980).
17. *Torah, Nevi'im, u-Khetuvim: The Holy Scriptures According to the Masoretic Text* (Philadelphia: Jewish Publication Society of America, 1917).
18. *The Living Torah = The Five Books of Moses*, trans. Aryeh Kaplan (New York: Miznaim, 1981).
19. Genesis 34: 1–2. *The Bible and Holy Scriptures Conteyned in the Olde and Newe Testament* (Geneva: Rouland Hall, 1560).
20. See the marginal note to Genesis 34: 1–2 in *The Bible and Holy Scriptures*, 1560.

21. Genesis 34: 1–2. *The holie Bible Conteyning the olde Testament and the newe* (London: Richard Jugge, 1568).
22. See the marginal note to Genesis 34: 1–2 in *The holie Bible*, 1568.
23. Genesis 34: 1–2. *The Holie Bible Faithfully Translated into English out of the Authentical Latin* (Doway: Lawrence Kellam, 1609).
24. Ilona M. Rashkow provides a detailed reading of some of the relevant differences in early modern English translations of the biblical story of Dinah in 'Hebrew Bible Translation and the Fear of Judaization', *The Sixteenth Century Journal*, 21: 2 (Summer 1990): 217–33.
25. Genesis 34: 1–2. *Biblia the Byble, that is the holy Scrypture of the Olde and Newe Testament, faithfully translated in to Englyshe* (Southwark: J. Nycolson, 1535).
26. Genesis 34: 31.
27. See Rashkow's discussion in 'Hebrew Bible Translation', 226–8.
28. Hayyim ben Moses, *Or Hachayim: Commentary on the Torah*, trans. Eliyahu Munk (Jerusalem and Brooklyn: Hemed Books, 1995): 1: 283
29. Ramban (Nahmanides), *Commentary on the Torah: Genesis*, trans. Charles B. Chavel (New York: Shiloh Publishing House, 1971): 414.
30. Ramban, *Commentary*, 414–15.
31. *Ibn Ezra's Commentary on the Pentateuch*, trans. H. Norman Strickman and Arthur M. Silver (New York: Menorah Publishing, 1988): 329.
32. Kasher, *Encyclopedia*, 4: 185.
33. Kasher, *Encyclopedia*, 4: 176.
34. This is my transliteration of the Hebrew text of Genesis 34: 4. *The Holy Scriptures: A Jewish Bible According to the Masoretic Texts* (Tel Aviv: Sinai Publishing, 1979).
35. Kasher, *Encyclopedia*, 4: 176.
36. Adelman notes that it was likely that Shakespeare was familiar with Genesis 34, since it constituted a Proper First Lesson, a Hebrew Bible chapter substituted for a lesson, which Shakespeare was likely to have heard at Church. Adelman, *Blood*

Relations, 103, and note 13. Adelman cites Naseeb Shaheen's work on Proper First Lessons in *Biblical References on Shakespeare's Comedies* (Newark: University of Delaware Press, 1993): 210–11.

37. Bracher notes the resemblance between Jessica's monkey and the ornamental D that appears in Genesis 34 in the Bishops Bible.
38. On early modern monkeys, see the recent essay by James Knowles, '"Can ye not tell a man from a marmoset": Apes and Others on the Early Modern Stage', in Erica Fudge (ed.), *Renaissance Beasts: Of Animals, Humans, and Other Wonderful Creatures* (Urbana: University of Illinois Press, 2004): 138–63. For an earlier discussion, H. W. Janson addresses the moralistic significance of monkeys in the sixteenth century, including their iconographical representations in the visual arts in *Apes and Ape Lore in the Middle Ages and the Renaissance* (London: Warburg Institute, University of London, 1952).
39. On the issue of changing notions of consent in seventeenth- and eighteenth-century England and America, see Holly Brewer, *By Birth or Consent: Children, Law, and the Anglo-American Revolution in Authority* (Chapel Hill: University of North Carolina Press, 2005).
40. Not only is Jessica's conversion never staged, Lorenzo's extensive speech about music at act 5, scene 1, which I discuss in detail shortly, implies that Jessica has not yet been converted in any meaningful spiritual sense, since she remains imperceptive of the theological harmonies that Lorenzo uses to figure a Christian moral universe.
41. *Genesis Rabbah*, 74, cited in Kasher, *Encyclopedia*, 4: 119, note 20.
42. See Kasher, *Encyclopedia*, 4: 119, note 20. This view is echoed in Joan Ozark Holmer's critical assessment of Jessica's exchange of the turquoise ring for a monkey, which is explained as a rejection of her father's idolatry. Holmer, *Merchant of Venice*, 127.
43. Genesis 31: 15.

44. According to one commentary, the unfortunate consequence follows from Jacob's assertion in 31: 32 that 'with whomsoever thou findest thy gods, he shall not live.' Kasher cites the eleventh-century commentary *Midrash Aseret Ha-Dibrot* on this point. Kasher, *Encyclopedia*, 4: 123, note 27.
45. Kasher cites the commentary *Mincha Belulah* on this point. Kasher, *Encyclopedia*, 4: 123, note 147.
46. See, for example, Janet Adelman, *Blood Relations* (2008): especially chapter 3, 66–98; M. Lindsay Kaplan, 'Jessica's Mother: Medieval Constructions of Jewish Race and Gender in *The Merchant of Venice*', *Shakespeare Quarterly*, 58: 1 (Spring 2007): 1–30; Lisa Lampert, *Gender and Jewish Difference from Paul to Shakespeare* (Philadelphia: University of Pennsylvania Press, 2004); Janet Adelman, 'Her Father's Blood' (2003): 4–30; Ania Loomba, *Shakespeare, Race, and Colonialism* (Oxford: Oxford University Press, 2002); Mary Janell Metzger, 'Now By My Hood, A Gentle and No Jew: Jessica, *The Merchant of Venice*, and the Discourse of Early Modern English Identity', *PMLA*, 113 (1998): 52–63; Michael Ragussis, *Figures of Conversion: 'The Jewish Question' and English National Identity* (Durham, NC: Duke University Press, 1995); Lynda E. Boose, '"The Getting of a Lawful Race": Racial Discourse in Early Modern England and the Unrepresentable Black Woman', in Margo Hendricks and Patricia Parker (eds), *Women, Race, and Writing in the Early Modern Period* (London: Routledge, 1994): 35–54; and Kim F. Hall, 'Guess Who's Coming to Dinner? Colonization and Miscegenation in *The Merchant of Venice*', *Renaissance Drama*, 23 (1992): 87–111.
47. Andrew Willet, *Hexapla in Genesin & Exodum* (London: John Haviland, 1633): 281.
48. Babington, *Notes*, folio I, comment 8 on Genesis 31.
49. Thomas Bentley, *The Monument of Matrones Conteining Seven Severall lamps of Virginitie, or Distinct Treatises* (London: H. Denham, 1582).
50. Thomas Bentley, *The Fift Lamp of Virginitie Conteining Sundrie Forms of Christian Praiers and Meditations* (London: H. Denham, 1582): 36.

51. Bentley, *Fift Lamp*, 35.
52. See *The Workes of Sir Thomas More Knyght, Sometime Lorde Chancellor of England, Wrytten by Him in the Englysh Tonge* (London: John Cawod, John Waly, and Richard Tottell, 1557). The index is composed by Paynell.
53. Nicolas de Hannapes (1225–91), *The Ensamples of Virtue and Vice, Gathered Out of Holy Scripture*, trans. Thomas Paynell (1561), no page numbers, chapter 128, image #391.
54. Barthelemy Batt, *The Christian Mans Closet Wherein is Conteined a Large Discourse of the Godly Training Up of Children*, trans. William Lowth (London: Thomas Dawson and Gregorie Seton, 1581): 72.
55. Ibid., 72.
56. Lowth's view is paralleled by Peter Milward in 'The Religious Implications of *The Merchant of Venice*', *The Medieval Dimension in Shakespeare's Plays* (Lewiston: Edwin Mellen Press, 1990), 29–45, especially 31. Milward argues that Jessica's sins are forgiven when we read the play through an appropriately Christian allegorical lens.
57. Paynell trans., *Ensamples*, no page numbers, chapter 128, image #391.
58. Genesis 31: 1.
59. Genesis 31: 43.
60. Genesis 31: 48–9.
61. See Kasher, *Encyclopedia*, 4: 128 for an account of the importance of both the Aramaic and Hebrew place-names for the site of the covenant between Jacob and Laban. In footnote 233 Kasher comments on how the location of the heap was on the border between Israel and Ammon. His comments recall how ethnological liminality is also expressed geographically in this episode, while also highlighting the multi-linguistic, polyglot features of those places, which signal differing ethnographies as well as differing ways of life.
62. Willet, *Hexapla in Genesin & Exodum*, 280–1.
63. Willet, *Hexapla in Genesin & Exodum*, 281.

CHAPTER 4

REBELLIOUS DAUGHTERS ON THE YIDDISH STAGE

The phrase *fartaytsht und farbesert!* 'translated and improved!' that is said to appear in the preface to an early Yiddish translation of *King Lear* has long formed part of the lore surrounding Yiddish-language adaptations of Shakespeare. The expression is probably apocryphal – there is no record of its existence in any printed copy of Shakespeare's plays in Yiddish; and yet, *fartaytsht und farbesert* has nevertheless become endemic to the cultural understanding of Yiddish Shakespeare translations among Yiddish-speaking Jews, and something of an inside joke whose self-promotional claim to not only translate but also ameliorate Shakespeare's plays Joel Berkowitz aptly describes as 'an inimitable combination of nineteenth-century American puffery and Jewish ethnic pride'.[1]

For all of its naivety uncannily shored up with chutzpah, its status as folklore rather than historical fact, *fartaytsht und farbesert* manages to distil a vital essence of the spirit of Yiddish adaptations of Shakespeare and the writers who undertook them in ways that confirm but also transcend familiar stereotypes. The spirit of innovation that prompts such adaptations strikes a noteworthy contrast with the English colloquial expression 'new and improved'. Rather than emphasising what is new, 'translated and improved' calls attention to what is old by emphasising the act of bringing authoritative, not new, texts to the attention of present-day audiences. Although many Jewish writers have Shakespeare's cultural capital in mind when they translate his plays into Yiddish in the hopes of ennobling Yiddish as a language, Yiddish adaptations of *Merchant* in fact routinely chart a return to an even more authoritative set of texts – Hebrew biblical stories, which writers rely on to render Shakespeare's play more relevant and meaningful for contemporary Jewish audiences. It is the return to these stories that forms the subject of the present chapter.

In the pages that follow I discuss two adaptations that self-consciously borrow from biblical stories: Meir Jacob Freid's 1897–8 short prose adaptation, *Der koyfmann fun Venedig* and Maurice Schwartz's 1947 hit theatrical adaptation, *Shayloks tokhter*. Both Schwartz's and Freid's works devote considerable attention to *The Merchant of Venice*'s romantic sub-plot featuring Jessica and Lorenzo, and both develop Jessica's role by drawing on elements from the biblical stories of Dinah and Rachel. Freid and Schwartz appeal to scriptural sources of authority in order to address practical questions about the nature of modern Jewish identity, particularly a woman's place within socio-political life.[2] I discuss how and why these writers' interpretive use of biblical stories in adaptations of *The Merchant of Venice* is most productively understood as a form of midrash, which operates by coordinating scriptural episodes with the exigencies of daily life. In fact, as I make clear shortly, a wide range of modern Jewish writers appeal to the biblical stories of Dinah and Rachel to address young Jewish women's evolving relationships to traditional ways of life and Jewish identity in the modern diaspora.

Scriptural stories once represented an integral part of early Yiddish theatre in the form of *purimshpiln*, a word that translates to 'Purim plays' and refers to dramatic works performed during the Purim holiday, a period long associated with carnivalesque revelry in the Jewish tradition. The first known performance of a *purimshpil* involving a scripted play and multiple actors took place in Tannhausen, Germany in 1598.[3] These plays tended to centre on stories drawn from the Torah, including the story of Purim itself featuring the Jewish heroine Esther who saves her entire community of Persian Jews from genocide.[4] It was during the *haskalah* or Jewish Enlightenment of the eighteenth and nineteenth centuries that European Jewish writers began moving away from the *purimshpiln*. A professional Yiddish theatre first began to develop during the 1870s. Yiddish actors during this period tended to be itinerant, and the fate of Jewish communities was often uncertain in Europe, as were professional opportunities for Jewish actors. Anti-Jewish laws such as Tsar Alexander III's May Laws of 1882, which forced Jewish actors off the stage and into exile, precipitated the increasingly westward movement of Yiddish performing arts throughout the nineteenth century. That movement was ultimately responsible for the creation of a dynamic and flourishing Yiddish theatre across cities in North and South America in the late nineteenth and early twentieth centuries, although Yiddish theatre also continued to flourish in parts of Europe through the early twentieth century in Poland and the Soviet Union.[5]

Yiddish actors, playwrights, producers and audiences in the early decades of professional Yiddish theatre shared a common background in religious education that emphasised the study of the Bible, midrashic biblical commentary, and Hebrew. Training in liturgical music was an equally common denominator among the musicians who contributed to Yiddish theatrical productions during this period.[6] Where the origins of early Yiddish theatre remained steeped in religious life and biblical stories, the nineteenth century also ushered in a new linguistic nationalism among Yiddish-speaking Jews that placed Yiddish itself at the forefront of discussions about Jewish cultural and artistic expression. It was during this period that the first Yiddish-language translations of Shakespeare were published, and those translations produced during the late nineteenth and early twentieth centuries often took pains to emphasise the literary merit of Yiddish as a language. Yiddish writers living in Poland, Russia, and other parts of Eastern Europe actively endeavoured to redefine the status of Yiddish from a pidgin dialect to a literary vernacular on a par with French, German and English. Because of the tremendous cultural capital of Shakespeare's writing in this period, his works served a vital role in efforts to burnish Yiddish's reputation and position the language as a medium for culturally and aesthetically sophisticated literary expression.

Yiddish-language adaptations of *The Merchant of Venice* first began to appear in print during the late nineteenth century in Europe.[7] For Jewish writers, translating *The Merchant of Venice* afforded an opportunity to 'improve' Shakespeare's text by redressing Shakespeare's perceived historical myopia.[8] In a foreword to a 1947 Yiddish translation of a Hebrew novelisation of *The Merchant of Venice*, one writer remarks: 'I wished to show the real Shylock and not the character of the medieval legend over which a world genius had stumbled because he had no occasion to meet with and study a living Jew of the Sixteenth Century.'[9] This rationale for adapting *The Merchant of Venice* builds on a commonly held supposition among contemporary Jewish audiences that Shakespeare knew very little about Jewish people and worked instead from a series of inherited medieval stereotypes. This led some Yiddish-language writers to understand their own historical position as uniquely auspicious – a knowing, privileged vantage point for revising and adapting Shakespeare's writing. It is in this spirit that a number of twentieth-century Jewish playwrights adapted *The Merchant of Venice* for the Yiddish stage, undertaking what they perceived to be a process of correcting the historical inaccuracies of the flawed Shakespearean original.[10]

These kinds of editorial ambitions that prompted the Yiddish refashioning of Shakespeare's plays led writers to focus anew on Shylock's role, reimagining it with a view to fleshing out his fuller subjectivity. But Shylock is not the only figure whose subjective motivations and reactions were explored in greater depth in Yiddish-language adaptations of *Merchant*. Jessica's character too became the object of considerable revision and expansion, particularly in her capacity as a woman poised for marriage who chooses to marry outside her Jewish faith. The fate of Jewish daughters who abscond from their father's households represented a pervasive literary trope for Jewish writers in the nineteenth and twentieth centuries both in English- and Yiddish-language writing. That trope became a site where writers as diverse as Sholem Aleichem and Philip Roth deliberated the meaning of Jewish identity in the modern world. As I discuss shortly, it is by narrating this loss that writers began to imagine the subjectivity of Jewish women positioned as inheritors of traditional ways of life, poised to either fulfil its aims or substantively transform them. In crossing the threshold into new worlds outside their father's homes, these women's choices acquire a crucial importance that determines the fate of their fathers' legacies and the future of tradition itself. Absconding daughters become the site of intensive literary exploration in this period because of their unique capacity for abandoning, destroying or reinterpreting traditional Jewish scripts, and responding in vitally important ways to the question of what it means to be Jewish in the modern era.

As the primary spoken language for a vast majority of Ashkenazi Jews throughout Europe and North America, Yiddish served as an important medium through which Jews negotiated cultural and geographical changes in the late nineteenth and early twentieth centuries. Yiddish during this period constituted the language of domestic life – the *mameh loshn* (literally, mother's tongue) or language spoken at home for a majority of Jews of Eastern European descent, even among Jews who spoke two or more languages fluently. Yiddish writing was particularly poignant in reflecting lived attempts to contend with diasporic existence and pressing questions about Jewish identity, cultural heritage, and belonging. For Eastern European Jews who emigrated to North America, Yiddish recalled the old world of the *shtetl* even as Yiddish-speaking immigrants struggled to adapt to new cultural surroundings and languages. It is this complex commingling of old and new frontiers that came to be featured in Yiddish adaptations of *Merchant*, and Jessica's storyline in particular.

In the hands of Yiddish novelists and playwrights, Jessica's plot becomes a narrative of assimilation, which looms as an archetypal crisis of modern Jewish life for many writers in this period. Yiddish fiction in the nineteenth and early twentieth centuries poignantly reflects concerns about the integrity and structure of families in the face of modernity's mounting pressures. The biblical story of Dinah furnishes a familiar and versatile text for exploring the perceived dangers and causes of cultural assimilation. Like Shakespeare's Jessica, Dinah's story centres on religious inter-marriage. Whether she absconds from her father's household voluntarily or by coercion, Dinah's story queries whether it is ever permissible for Jewish women to marry non-Jewish men, a question that writers use to probe the motives of young women poised to begin their lives as wives and mothers who will bear responsibility for raising their own Jewish children.

Meir Jacob Freid, a Jewish writer from Kalvariya who lived and wrote in Warsaw, produced one of the earliest published Yiddish adaptations of *The Merchant of Venice*, and in it Freid does away with the name 'Jessica', changing Shylock's daughter's name to 'Dinah'. His 1897–8 adaptation is a short novelisation thirty pages in length published in leaflet form and sold for three kopecs. Freid published it through Tsukerman's Folksbibliothek located on Nalevki street in Warsaw, the main thoroughfare of Warsaw's Jewish neighbourhood.[11] At the time that he published this adaptation, Freid was already a writer of considerable note and part of the flourishing Yiddish literary scene in Warsaw under the influence of poet Y. L. Peretz. Freid published prolifically in Yiddish, including one of the first best-selling Yiddish books, a historical novel about the Dreyfus Affair that sold over 25,000 copies in its first printing and was subsequently translated into Polish and Russian.[12]

Freid's *Der koyfmann fun Venedig (Shaylok)* was one of several Yiddish adaptations that tellingly recast the title of the play and suggested that Shylock, not Antonio, was the Venetian merchant. The title page illustration features a portrait of Shakespeare that suggests the presence of a skullcap and the religious forelocks known as *peyas*. While Freid innovates in these respects, he closely parallels Shakespeare in others, notably the opening scene, which narrates, 'It was a beautiful morning, and Antonio and his good friends were walking around the Venetian market. But Antonio was inexplicably sad. When his friends tried to comfort him, he became even more melancholy.'[13] In this and several other aspects Freid's version follows Shakespeare's initial plot structure. Bassanio needs a loan; Antonio's funds are all tied up in his ships which should come back to port in two months' time.

In part 3 of the novella, Freid implements an important change to his *Merchant of Venice* by altering Jessica's name to 'Dinah' and supplying her with a set of psychological motivations for her turn towards a Christian man. Freid writes:

> If Shylock had had more *seychl* [prudence, or foresight] and if he'd been less consumed by money, he would have been much more cognizant of the change that had taken place

in his daughter recently. But he didn't want to know, didn't want to understand. He therefore didn't hear what was going on right behind his back ... The practical-minded Shylock had never made it a priority for his daughter to know about her *Yiddishkayt* [Jewishness], so that she could feel bound up with the fate of her nation, its language, or its history.[14]

Dinah leaves her father's home to elope with a Christian and absconds with Shylock's valuables in tow because, Freid emphasises, Shylock had never instilled a firm sense of Jewish values in his daughter. Because of her lack of moral grounding, Dinah becomes vulnerable to the slanderous anti-Semitic invectives of Lorenzo, who 'misleads the reckless Dinah to scorn and hate not only her father, but all Jews.'[15] The lack of any formative education leaves Dinah without a moral compass to direct her. She has no connection to the salient elements Freid identifies with her *Yiddishkayt* or Jewishness – a feeling of being bound up with the fate, the language and the history of her people.

The elements that Freid cites as foundations for *Yiddishkayt* constitute a series of learned practices, making Freid's account markedly different from the discourse of blood and physiology that pervades the text of Shakespeare's *The Merchant of Venice*. Shakespeare's emphasis on blood contributes towards his play's construction of Jewishness as a form of biological contagion that inheres even in the face of religious conversion, as several scholars have discussed.[16] Alternatively, Freid's stress on women's moral education and in particular the kind provided by fathers suggests that Jewishness is far more fragile, that it must be deliberately instilled, and that it is parents' responsibility to instil it. The burden falls on Shylock to transmit *Yiddishkayt* to his daughter, and consequently the blame for failing to instil it also falls on his shoulders.

Insufficient moral education carries grave consequences in Freid's novella. As a result of Shylock's inattentive parenting, Dinah becomes unduly vulnerable to Lorenzo's influence. Freid describes how

> Lorenzo appeared to her [i.e. Dinah] as a king from heaven who had opened before her eyes the gates to paradise, rescuing her from the darkest mud into which her father had brought her, and she followed Lorenzo blindly, believing in his every word, she didn't want to be without him for even a minute; his words were holy to her.[17]

By emphasising the importance of education to moral conduct, *Der koyfmann fun Venedig* offers an account of ethnographic identity-formation that recalls features of Lorenzo's exchange with Jessica in act 5, scene 1 of Shakespeare's text, where Lorenzo outlines his vision for Jessica's Christian moral re-education. As I discussed in the previous chapter, that exchange draws on early modern discussions of Genesis 31 where the biblical Rachel steals her father's idols as well as Renaissance conduct manuals that address women's moral education. Several such guides identify Rachel as a test-case for moral reform, suggesting that the wayward Rachel transgresses the limits of what Christian moral re-education can accomplish. Rachel's waywardness, like Jessica's in that scene, is linked to her insubordination as a daughter and also, potentially, as a wife.

Freid's emphasis runs parallel in some ways to Renaissance discussions in identifying a young woman's upbringing as an important factor determining her behaviour later on in key moments of moral decision-making such as selecting a marriage partner. Renaissance English exegetical commentaries and conduct manuals emphasise the indelible effects of the biblical Rachel's pagan upbringing under Laban as a way of explaining her theft of Laban's idols. Freid's novella turns with an equally keen interest to Shylock's parental responsibility to locate the reasons why Dinah steals from her father and absconds with a Christian man. *Der koyfmann fun Venedig* suggests that Dinah's absconsion can be attributed to her father's failure to properly nurture his daughter's ethical development or provide her with a foundational moral and cultural education. Furthermore, Freid outlines how Dinah's estrangement from her Jewish identity and her eventual desertion of both her father and her faith follows from Shylock's obsessive focus on financial gain.

> The very clever Shylock had fooled himself when it came to one crucial matter. God had given him a beautiful daughter, an orphan from his long-dead wife. Shylock had always been so busy trying to make a success of himself as a businessman, trying to earn more and more money, that he had no time to spend with his only child. And the beautiful Dinah became lonely and sad all alone in her father's house among the gold and silver. She eventually turned her attention to the free world outside her window, and became acquainted with the handsome young Christian, Lorenzo. She became involved in one of those tragic (from a parent's perspective) dramas that happens so often to our Jewish people in the diaspora.[18]

Dinah's loneliness and Shylock's inattention hastens Dinah's flight into the arms of a Christian man in *Der koyfmann fun Venedig*. As a consequence of her father's negligence, Dinah becomes unduly receptive to Lorenzo's anti-Semitic slander, which she is unable to counter with a more authentic sense of her own identity as a Jew.

In the biblical story of Dinah, the loss of a Jewish daughter occasions vengeful retribution. As I discussed in the previous chapter, that loss is frequently coded as a tragic abduction rather than a romantic seduction by biblical commentators and translators. In Freid's novella, Dinah's absconsion registers as tragic while also reflecting considerable ambivalence about the religious mindset and its tendency towards destructive extremes. *Der koyfmann fun Venedig* describes Shylock's vengeance as a kind of single-mindedness that contributes towards his character's moral myopia. After realising that he has been robbed, Shylock vows: 'I'll use Antonio's flesh to feed the fish. And with that, I'll only have begun to slake my revenge . . . Antonio has humiliated me, and I want revenge. Revenge without end.'[19] Shylock 'licks his lips' in anticipation of exacting his pound of flesh when he hears that Antonio's last ship has sunk.[20] His pursuit of vengeance soon overtakes his desire to locate Dinah: 'Shylock had become so consumed with revenge, that he had even forgotten about his daughter.'[21]

Shylock's vindictive fury is punctuated by religious language that he uses to stake his claim to the pound of flesh. After Shylock has Antonio thrown in debtor's prison to await trial, Bassanio, arrives and attempts to pay off the debt by offering Shylock six times the original principal. Shylock refuses to consider the offer. 'I've already told you, and have sworn by everything that is holy to exact precisely what is written in the bond.'[22] Shylock's adherence to the letter of the bond is expressed through the swearing of religious oaths, which connects religious partisanship with a counter-rational intransigence that comes to define his character for the remainder of the story. Antonio, who remains consistently, generously self-sacrificial throughout the novella, 'finally understood that there was no reasoning with Shylock.'[23] Justified or not, Shylock clearly moves beyond the claims of reason in *Der koyfmann fun Venedig*, with the implication that he overlooks even the loss of his daughter in the course of seeking vengeance, just as he has overlooked her moral education in pursuit of financial gain.

The equation of religious partisanship with vengeance, and sociability with a secular viewpoint is not unusual if we contextualise Freid's adaptation within the tradition of

German Enlightenment Shakespeare adaptations, as Dror Abend-David suggests in *Scorned My Nation*.[24] Eighteenth- and nineteenth-century Continental European adaptations of Shakespeare tended to valorise so-called universal values such as friendship and love over and above religious affiliations, and often presented villainous, misanthropic Shylocks rather than misunderstood victims of persecution. In keeping with this tradition, Freid's adaptation constructs Shylock's vengeance as a form of villainy; conversely, it celebrates Portia and Bassanio's romantic union as well as Antonio and Bassanio's friendship in a way that deemphasises the inherent anti-Semitism of Shakespeare's text. Christian characters' religious identities are also somewhat neutralised in Freid's adaptation. There is very little explicit emphasis on Christian religious convictions or practices, making it possible to view Portia, Bassanio, and Antonio as the virtuous heroes of this story rather than as Jew-hating Christians. In *Der koyfmann fun Venedig* the most admirable characters resemble secular humanists, while those who claim partisan religious identities are either purveyors of racial hatred (Lorenzo), or dangerously unconcerned with the fate of their communities (Dinah), or excessively focused on self-enrichment at the expense of their ethical duties (Shylock).

One of the ways that Freid's novella articulates these moral priorities is by contrasting Shylock's moral shortcomings with the bond between Antonio and Bassanio, which is valorised as an ideal of beneficent fraternity. In an early episode where Bassanio asks Antonio to stake his credit for the loan, Antonio brushes aside questions about Bassanio's financial solvency and offers to help him by any means necessary. That scene strikes a notable contrast with the one that immediately follows in which Shylock is introduced as a 'rich Jew' about whom 'people used to say, he became rich through usury.'[25] His lust for financial gain becomes a distinguishing feature marking Shylock's difference from the

Venetian Christians, and the novella consistently reiterates that financial gain constitutes a morally impoverished path to happiness. Bassanio's choice of the lead casket to win Portia's hand in marriage, in contrast with Morocco and Aragon who choose the gold and silver, reflects this theme of affective bonds triumphing over fiscal concerns. The bond of love between Portia and Bassanio is underscored throughout their courtship, and Portia's wealth is cast as a fortunate by-product rather than an underlying motive for Bassanio's affection. This celebration of affective bonds and fraternity strikes a deliberate contrast with the scene where Shylock discovers his missing daughter and cries, 'Oh, my daughter, my gold, Dinah! She ran away with a *goy* [i.e. a non-Jew], and also with my fortune! Two sacks of gold; my ducats and my seal ring my only daughter stole from me! Oh, God in Heaven, give me back my child, my gold and silver!'[26] Shakespeare's play gives these invidious words to Solanio, who uses them to disparage and ridicule Shylock; Freid's novella locates them instead in Shylock's own response to the loss of his property.

In *Der koyfmann fun Venedig*, Freid's own narrative account of Jewishness emphasises the feeling of being bound up with the fate, language, and history of the Jewish people. Focused on accruing wealth, Shylock fails to display a Jewish ethos that lives up to the standard outlined in Freid's narration, nor does he provide the right kind of moral formation for his daughter.[27] Instead, Shylock becomes a figure for extremism. The more temperate, moderate and enduring virtues are located in the play's comic elements and its Christian characters – the romance between Bassanio and Portia, and Bassanio's friendship with Antonio. Ultimately, Freid's narrative presents Portia's triumph over Shylock as a morally satisfying conclusion to the story. *Der koyfmann fun Venedig*'s comic resolution sees reasoned intelligence triumph over emotional extremes through Portia's courtroom defeat of Shylock and the restoration of matrimonial harmony between Bassanio and Portia.

Der koyfmann fun Venedig is also decidedly celebratory of Portia's role in saving Antonio from certain death. Portia's swift decision to depart from Belmont and disguise herself as Balthazar to participate in the trial becomes the pivotal factor in the play's happy ending. The text's final lines call attention to Antonio's appreciation of Portia's keen intelligence and her agency in rescuing him. 'Antonio, with tears in his eyes, once again, recognized his good fortune, and that of Bassanio to have found his way to Belmont and married the clever Portia.'[28] In the end, Portia becomes a parallel Dinah-figure alongside Shylock's daughter; like the biblical Dinah, Portia engages with a multicultural world outside her home. Her facility at manoeuvring within that world marks her as the novella's comic heroine, while Shylock's daughter Dinah becomes its tragic victim. Portia is a kind of activist, but her activism serves the goal of marital felicity and, ultimately, a return to domestic life within the confines of insular Belmont. Conversely, Dinah's is a cautionary tale of a young woman insufficiently grounded in moral and religious values, and therefore vulnerable to corrupting influences that include anti-Semitic programming. Her foray into the wider world sees her eloping with a vicious predator. In this novella, daughters are rendered either tragic or comic because of the foundational moral educations provided by fathers – in Portia's case, via a posthumous love-test; and in Dinah's, no foundation at all due to Shylock's neglect.

For all of its simplifications and condensations, Meir Freid's novella offers a remarkably rich rendering of young women that is by turns both comic and tragic. Those turns hinge not only on the central bond plot, but also more crucially on the agency of its two female characters. These young women's ability to engage productively with their circumstances is importantly linked to accounts of their formative education and the attentive guidance provided by their fathers, which helps mould them as moral agents. Although emphatic about the importance of educating young women, Freid's adaptation also reinforces an essentially traditional, patriarchal view of women's roles by citing paternal guidance as the critical factor in women's moral development, and asserting that a woman's proper place ultimately lies in the domestic world under the protection of a father or husband. And yet, *Der koyfmann fun Venedig* also asserts the productive, even salvific value of women who break free of their domestic roles, if only briefly, to help establish moral and legal equilibrium in the world outside their homes and communities.

This keen interest in women who move beyond their insular households and the purview of their fathers – the narrative and thematic threads of the biblical Dinah's and Rachel's stories – becomes an increasingly common feature of Jewish writing in the century after Freid publishes his novella. When Freid's *koyfmann fun Venedig* laments the 'tragic drama that happens so often to our Jewish people in the diaspora', he gives voice to a pervasive preoccupation among contemporary writers with the assimilation and loss of Jewish daughters that endures well beyond Freid's own time and geographic context.

The most celebrated and iconic of these fictionalised accounts in Yiddish comes from the 'Tevye' stories of Sholem Aleichem. Born Sholem Rabinovitch in 1859 in Periyeslav, a part of the Kiev province of what was then the Russian Empire, Sholem Aleichem is a direct contemporary of Meir Freid's, though their paths diverge when Freid remains in Warsaw through the First World War and eventually emigrates to Israel in 1932; Sholem Aleichem leaves Russia for New York in 1906. The same year that Sholem Aleichem departs for New York, his story 'Chava' from the 'Tevye der Milkhiker' or *Tevye the Dairyman* series is published, and it becomes the most acclaimed, beloved and widely read of the collection. Set in a Russian-Ukranian *shtetl*, these stories focus on Tevye and his seven eligible young daughters, each of whom marries in ways that contravene her father's plans. 'Chava' centres on Tevye's cherished daughter Chava who runs away from home to marry a Christian man. The story follows the same basic plot trajectory as *The Merchant of Venice*'s Jessica plot, featuring a daughter who leaves her paternal home to marry a non-Jewish man. Both fathers share a remarkable tendency to cite Scripture. Shylock cites and explicates the parable of the parti-coloured lambs as he negotiates the bond with Antonio; Tevye's citation of Scripture represents a consistent through-line in the 'Tevye' stories, and represents an endemic character trait that follows him even in adapted versions of the story such as the English-language musical *Fiddler on the Roof*.

Tevye is renowned for his propensity to cite biblical passages and rabbinic commentary; he is always ready with a passage from the Torah or the Talmud to address whatever predicament life throws his way. Tevye appeals to biblical verses even as Sholem Aleichem's stories reveal the inadequacy of those traditional scripts to deal with the demands of the modern world and Tevye's increasingly modern daughters. In the scene just prior to Chava's disappearance, Chava has an argument with Tevye that unearths a rift between traditional biblical scripts and what Chava takes to be the ethical demands of the present historical moment.

> 'You mustn't forget "*Whence thou camest and whither thou goest*" – Who you are and who he is.'[29]
> 'God created all men equal,' Chava said.
>   'Yes, yes,' I said, 'God created Adam in his own image. But we mustn't forget that each man must seek his own kind, as it is written, "*From each according to his means . . .*"'

'Marvelous!' she cried. 'Unbelievable! You have a quotation for everything. Maybe you also have a quotation that explains why men have divided themselves up into Jews and Gentiles, into lords and slaves, noblemen and beggars?'[30]

Chava's questions are ones that Tevye himself begins to ponder, despite his continued insistence that a traditional outlook remains the best approach to answering present-day moral quandaries. Towards the end of the story, Chava's questions about the inherent validity of class-based distinctions and religious differences begin to seep into Tevye's own internal monologue, where they present themselves as 'peculiar thoughts'.[31] Those 'peculiar thoughts' persist in the form of questions that gnaw at him. Tevye reflects, 'And in order to chase away these painful thoughts I began to chant the words of the evening prayer: "*Blessed are they who dwell in Thy house, and they shall continue to praise Thee* . . ." But what good was this chanting when inside of me a different tune was playing? *Chava*, it went. *Cha-va*.'[32] Scripture begins to appear as less and less of a certain authoritative guide to the uncharted waters of modern Jewish family life in 'Chava'. Instead, Tevye's scriptural citation becomes the site of discontinuity between Tevye's traditional world-view and those more modern modes – the 'different tune' – he has been forced to hear at close range in the wake of his daughter's departure. Rather than offering comfort and certainty, scriptural citation instead becomes a prompt for Tevye's unrequited doubt and searching inquiry into the loss of cultural continuity and certainty.[33]

Early on in the story, Tevye implores Chava to remember 'who you are and who he [your non-Jewish love-interest] is,' and what he means by this is a version of 'Don't forget your *Yiddishkayt*' – the very thing that Freid in *Der koyfmann fun Venedig* insists is lacking in Dinah and which crucially determines her elopement with a Christian man. Within Sholem Aleichem's story, Chava's absconsion does not serve as a marker of her moral waywardness in an absolute sense, but rather of her divergence from her father's moral universe and her readiness to enjoin herself to a different world-view and commit to it through decisive action. The impact of that divergence on Tevye is registered with tremendous intensity in 'Chava'. At the story's conclusion, Tevye passes his daughter on the road and refuses to stop for her, whipping his horse hard as he heads home without acknowledging Chava's presence, despite the horse's clear recognition of her. Tevye is unable to silence his thoughts, which reflect a longing to reunite with his daughter and understand her motivations and the life she leads in his absence.

> All the rest of the way, as I drove, I thought I could hear her running after me, calling, 'Listen, father, listen to me.' A thought crossed my mind, 'Tevye, you are taking too much upon yourself. Will it hurt you if you stop and listen to her? Maybe she has something to say that is worth hearing. Maybe – who can tell – she is regretting what she has done and wants to come back to you. Maybe she is being badly treated and wants you to save her from a living hell.' Maybe and maybe and maybe . . . And I saw her as a little child once more and I was reminded of the passage: *'As a father has mercy on his children . . .'* To a father there is no such thing as a bad child. I blamed myself and I told myself, *'I do not deserve to be pitied* – I am not worthy of the earth I walk upon. What are you fuming and fretting for?' I asked myself. 'Stubborn mule, turn your wagon around and go back and talk to her, she is your own child.' And peculiar thoughts came into my mind. What is the meaning of Jew and non-Jew? Why did God create Jews and non-Jews? And since God did create Jews and non-Jews why should they be segregated from each other and hate each other, as though one were created by God and the other were not?[34]

Where 'Chava' takes up the absconding daughter plot featured in Shakespeare's *The Merchant of Venice*, it also supplements Shakespeare's storyline with this extended inner monologue that gives voice to a bereaved Jewish father's suffering and self-doubt. Where Shakespeare's play qualifies Shylock's grief through mocking send-ups of his loss by his Christian persecutors, Rabinovitch's story has no such 'comic' deflation and instead movingly narrates the loss of a beloved daughter to a world her father cannot understand, and to which he can never belong.

Rabinovitch eventually adapts 'Chava' into dramatic form and produces a version of it for the stage in the 1910s. In 1919 he adapts it again, this time as a silent film called 'Chava' or 'Broken Barriers'.[35] Those adaptations then inspire a 1939 Yiddish film featuring sound called 'Tevye' that becomes the prototype for the musical Fiddler on the Roof. 'Tevye' concludes with Tevye saying kaddish, the prayer of mourning for the dead, once he learns of his daughter's marriage to a non-Jewish man.[36] This innovation develops an important element of Rabinovitch's Yiddish story in which Chava's actions express a series of commitments that her traditional father is unable to understand, appreciate, or bear.

Rabinovitch's story signals a rift in generational continuity that creates a rift in the single, cohesive world of the Jewish family, resulting in two distinct worlds: the traditional one belonging to a father and the very different moral and ideological context adopted by his daughter. This turn represents one that the actor-director-writer Maurice Schwartz's adaptation of *The Merchant of Venice* exploits to great effect in the 1940s, not long after Schwartz stars as Tevye in Rabinovitch's 1939 film adaptation of 'Chava'. During his early years onstage, Schwartz is featured in a number of productions of *The Merchant of Venice* in Manhattan's Lower East Side. In 1930 he plays three scenes from *Merchant* in English on the Vaudeville Circuit, a prestigious performance venue where acclaimed actors like Sarah Bernhardt and Ethel Barrymore performed one-act plays. The 1930 English vaudeville programme featured Schwartz at the Franklin Theater in the Bronx and then moved to the Kenmore Theater in Brooklyn before concluding at the Palace Theater in Manhattan. Two and a half decades later, when Schwartz was widely celebrated as one the finest Yiddish actors on the New York stage, he took on a very different dramatic adaptation of the role of Shylock that he himself scripted from Ari Ibn Zahav's Hebrew novel *Shylock, ha-Yehudi mi'Venezia*[37] and renamed 'Shayloks Tochter'.[38]

Shayloks tochter opened on 29 September 1947 at the Yiddish Art Theater and became a critically acclaimed hit among Yiddish-speaking audiences as well as English-language journalists who reviewed the show. Bookended by the conclusion of the Second World War in 1945 and the creation of the State of Israel in 1948, Schwartz's play echoes the traumas of the Holocaust and the plight of Jewish refugee survivors as well as the fierce spiritual longing for a Jewish homeland that characterised the post-war Zionism. *Shayloks tochter* introduces several innovations to the plot and characters of Shakespeare's play, most notable among them the foregrounding of Jessica's plot. Courted by the non-Jewish Lorenzo and arranged to be married to the devoted Torah scholar Samuel Morro, Jessica awakens over the course of the play to a sense of moral solidarity with her fellow Jews after initially absconding from the ghetto to marry her fun-loving Christian paramour.

In Schwartz's hands, the rebellious Jessica becomes a figure for a particular social phenomenon with which Schwartz's live theatrical audience was intimately familiar: social activism. In the late 1940s, Schwartz's Lower East Side Jewish audience was comprised of Yiddish-speaking Jews, many of whom had immigrated to America in the decades prior to the Second World War and had participated in labour disputes, strikes, and trade union organising activities in the 1910s, 1920s, and

1930s. That activist history contextualises Jessica's spiritually energised activism, which gathers its force in the play through her concern with the material conditions of daily life and a desire to improve her own material fortunes and, eventually, those of her fellow Jews.

Shayloks tochter is set on the eve of Passover in the year 1559 in the Venetian Jewish Ghetto, and Jessica longs to escape the miserable poverty and gloom of the ghetto. She is courted by the fun-loving but money-obsessed Lorenzo, who sees in her the possibility of financial remuneration because of her rich father, and also admires her as a beautiful love-object he longs to possess. Lorenzo promises Jessica a life of ease, worldly luxury, status – the life of a Christian aristocrat replete with all of its comforts and privileges. For Jessica's father, the Venetian ghetto is a permanent home, one that he insists his daughter must regard as an immutable reality and to whose discomforts she must learn to acquiesce. He cautions: 'Shylock's daughter must find her happiness between the narrow walls of the Ghetto, even as her mother, peace unto her memory, has found hers.'[39] Shylock's allusion to his dead wife Leah whose life expired within the ghetto walls foreshadows a grim future for Jessica, one that Jessica longs to avoid and which she can foreseeably evade by accepting Lorenzo's romantic overtures. Lorenzo promises her a life of ease and splendour in Christian Venice, pronouncing 'I must save you from the Inferno in which you live . . . Jessica, the world is beautiful, the world is free. A blossom must needs have sunshine. A blossom cannot flourish in the Ghetto.'[40]

Where Lorenzo holds out the possibility of escaping the Jewish ghetto's misery, Shylock's provision for happiness maps out a stoic retreat from impoverished conditions in favour of a highly developed inner spiritual life fulfilled through the study of Torah. This same philosophy is also dramatised in the play through the figure of Samuel Morro, the Jewish refugee and Torah scholar whom Shylock intends Jessica to marry, and who arrives at Shylock's doorstep with only 'the books of his teacher, the *gaon*, Rabbi Samuel Aqualti'.[41] Shylock praises the values and mindset of the refugee Morro to Jessica, insisting that the life of the mind and spirit are far more significant than the material distractions of Christian Venice. 'Now, my daughter, you will at last get to know the treasures of our Holy Tongue. Read the Scriptures with her, Samuel. *(To Jessica.)* Knowing these, my child, you will forget the carnivals and the gilded gondolas . . .'[42]

Shylock sees little value in working to improve the conditions of ghetto life; instead, he imagines spiritual fulfilment and happiness through the study of Torah, which he figures as a retreat from the material world. The Passover setting of Schwartz's play that identifies the biblical story of Exodus as an important inter-text, however, suggests that something more than inward retreat is required to improve the fortunes of Jews under the oppressive Inquisition. The Passover story, a narrative of liberation featuring Moses leading the Hebrews out of slavery, forecasts *Shayloks tochter*'s concern with strategies of active resistance in the face of oppressive conditions.

Within the play, this is staged through a debate among residents of the Jewish ghetto about how best to organise aid efforts to help those unfortunate Jews imprisoned and suffering in Rome under the Inquisition. Tubal declares that funds have been amassed to help the Jewish prisoners, 'But who will be the messenger to go to Rome?' he asks.[43] A rabbi describes this mission in terms that explicitly recall the Exodus narrative: 'The great *mitzvah* of "Redeeming the Imprisoned" . . . *Avadim Hayinu* – slaves we were unto Pharaoh in Egypt, and even now we are slaves unto Paolo the Fourth.'[44] However, the rabbi lacks a practical plan. He instead prescribes keeping faith in God and a commitment to Torah study. Shylock reiterates the rabbi's perspective by emphasising that the current situation for Jews under the Inquisition will only be resolved by patiently waiting for the messiah. 'Only Messiah, the son of David, can save us from the Inquisition flames and the ghettos.'[45] Samuel Morro echoes this line of reasoning, locating salvation in the end times after the arrival of the messiah. 'Then shall we sing "*Az Yashir*" – the song of Moses and the Israelites – in the streets of Jerusalem. We shall live to see the Third Temple rebuilt in glory. And the nations of the world will rejoice in the spiritual light that will reach them from Jerusalem.'[46]

While Morro's comments reflect a profoundly Zionist hope that was soon to be actualised through the creation of the state of Israel in 1948, his insights also recommend a spiritual resolution to a series of immediate practical sufferings that identify hope, faith, and belief in the future rather than practical action in the present as optimal strategies. Shylock and Samuel Morro both express spiritual longings for a better future, and their comments reflect a conspicuous lack of practical planning to resolve and rehabilitate the material conditions of their lives in the here and now. In the context of war-torn Europe and the Holocaust, this tellingly reflects the horrific actuality of Jewish persecution under the Nazis, where there often was no practical course of action available to pursue.[47] However, the treatment of Jewish suffering in this play also positions audiences to see the type of spiritual patience advocated by Shylock and Samuel Morro in contrast to the far more activist approach subsequently adopted by Shylock's daughter, Jessica. Within the play it is Jessica who volunteers to leave the ghetto, travel to Rome, and surreptitiously visit the Jewish prisoners in order to better determine how to save them.

Jessica's willingness to act is bound up with her profound dissatisfaction with her traditional domestic role as the fiancée of a Jewish man much like her father, who insists that the best response to present-day problems is a cloistered life of study, scholarship, and retreat from the world. In Shakespeare's play it is Shylock who urges Jessica to 'lock up my doors ... clamber you not up to the casements.' In *Shayloks tochter* it is Morro, the man Jessica is betrothed to marry, who says to Shylock, 'Shut the window, Master Shylock. The air is cool, and you breathe heavily. Better that we study the teaching of the great Hillel.'[48]

It is Portia and Bassanio who fill the gaping absence left by Shylock and Samuel Morro's future-directed plan by furnishing a practical course of action for Jessica to follow: conversion to Christianity.[49] Conversion requires that Jessica turn her back on her people, an option that she finds enormously troubling. Further exacerbating the painfulness of Jessica's choice, Schwartz's play confers pointedly anti-Semitic attitudes onto Antonio, supplying him with a version of the line that Shakespeare gives to Shylock, 'I hate him for he is a Christian,' which becomes in *Shayloks tochter*, 'my hatred for them [the Jews] is in my blood, a heritage of many generations.'[50] Conversion becomes a prospect invested not only with the hope of escape from ghetto poverty; it becomes in *Shayloks tochter* a course of action heavily invested in the hatred of Jews.

Schwartz's play weighs the malignant anti-Semitism of Antonio and life in Christian Venice against a highly desirable present-centred existence oriented around pleasures and comforts that Jessica desperately lacks in the Venetian ghetto. Portia and Antonio reside in a marble palace surrounded by objects of beauty. Their life is comprised of lively celebrations, beautiful clothing, and dancing. Their attention is focused on sensual enjoyment and material splendour. 'Our home is a temple for those who love life,' Portia pronounces.[51] For Jessica, such scenes point up her own dissatisfactions with the wretched conditions in the Jewish ghetto while also suggesting at a clear and existentially transformative course of action in the present to remedy those sufferings. However vexed the prospect of conversion, it does offer Jessica a clear way out of her grim life, one that Portia declares will serve as a beacon for other potential converts.

Despite the compromises entailed by conversion to Christianity, Portia and Antonio supply Jessica with a way for her to create an identity for herself as a woman of action rather than a passive spectator to her own suffering. The play's dissatisfaction with passivity, reflected particularly strongly in Jessica who aims to improve first the material conditions of her own life and eventually the lives of Jewish prisoners, speaks poignantly to the lived experiences of Schwartz's Jewish theatregoing public, many of whom had engaged in labour activism in the early decades of the twentieth century. Women were particularly significant contributors to such activism; the first decades of the twentieth century saw the proportion of women in organised labour unions double. During the Great Shirtwaist Strike of 1909, Jewish women activists Clara Lemlich, Pauline Newman, Rose Schneiderman and Fania Cohn played instrumental and highly visible roles in organising and implementing that strike, which endeavoured to improve the terrible working conditions for employees of the needle trade in New York factories.[52] Such strikes persisted throughout the 1920s and 1930s in major metropolitan centres in America and Canada, particularly in cities that housed needle trade factories that employed a large number of Jewish immigrants.[53]

As *Shayloks tochter* progresses, Jessica commits to improving the welfare of her fellow Jews, all the while remaining deeply ambivalent about the pacifist approach expounded by her father and Samuel Morro. The comfortable life promised through conversion and marriage to Lorenzo fails to eclipse Jessica's concern over the fate of her people, and her desire for personal material comforts gives way to her commitment to what she describes as 'faring forth on a sacred mission to save refugees from prison'.[54] In Part Two of the play, Jessica develops a strong moral identity as an activist who moves from pining for luxuries to social justice work. The shift from self-serving materialist to social activism occurs when Jessica contracts an influenza-like illness after spending a day at the beach with Lorenzo at the end of Part One of the play. Through the experience of physical suffering occasioned by a pleasure-centred diversion harshly condemned by her father, Jessica experiences a spiritual awakening that renders her acutely sensible of the suffering of other Jews. After recovering from her near-death sickness, she confesses to her father, 'I understand you now more than I did before my illness, how your face is lined with wrinkles, Ghetto-wrinkles ... mother's death ... the sorrows of the Jews ... the pain I cause you.'[55] Through the experience of loss, privation, and physical suffering, Jessica becomes attuned to her fellow Jews' pain and cultivates a sense of solidarity with the Jewish people, one that quickly acquires the zeal of a spiritual mission leading her outside the ghetto walls. It is a zeal whose basic humanitarian impetus bears a strong likeness to contemporary Marxism, which flourished among Jews involved in labour activism in the early twentieth century.

Shortly after waking from her illness-induced fever, Jessica establishes her intentions to leave for Rome. Lorenzo has arranged for her to meet him there; Jessica proposes the trip to her father as a rescue mission to save Jewish Inquisition prisoners. It remains unclear at the very end of Part One of the play which of these two threads Jessica will grab hold of as she prepares to leave the Jewish ghetto: elopement with Lorenzo or Jewish resistance work. What does become increasingly clear is that Jessica remains subject to competing pressures from both Christian and Jewish communities. Shylock attempts to perpetuate a traditional way of life through her by insistently planning her marriage to Samuel Morro; Portia and Antonio are keen to have her convert and marry in a public ceremony intended to signal a preferred way of life to other Jewish women.

In positioning Jessica as the object of competing claims by Christians and Jews, Schwartz's play seizes on key aspects of the biblical story of Dinah's abduction in Genesis 34. In that episode, a young, unmarried Jewish woman occupies a pivotal role within a patriarchal economy, where she functions as an extension of her family's reputation and honour. She also serves as a potential boon to her non-Jewish neighbours, who leverage her captivity in order to negotiate inter-marriage and trade agreements with her family. Both the biblical Dinah and Schwartz's Jessica are valued as important sources of future profit by their non-Jewish 'families' – in Dinah's case the groundwork is laid via a lucrative trade agreement struck by the Shechemites and the Israelites; for Jessica it is established by Portia and Antonio who prize Jessica as a highly visible and potentially influential *converso*. During the second half of the play, Jessica effectively becomes a captive in Portia's home, pressured and coerced into conversion and marriage. Her heavily compromised situation is made clear in her exchange with Portia in which she resists her imminent entry into Christian Venetian life.

> PORTIA: After the ceremony, we shall all fare to the Ghetto. Let the Jewish virgins of the narrow Ghetto-lanes see how Venice exalts a Jewish daughter.
> JESSICA: No! No! *(Attempts to go. Portia prevents her. Bells toll. Enter Lorenzo in wedding costume, a bouquet of flower in his hand)*[56]

By having Jessica engage in a coerced conversion, *Shayloks tochter* picks up on the captivity narrative that underwrites Dinah's abduction and develops it by endowing Jessica with a voice of resistance. The biblical Dinah's response and, indeed, her voice is never heard at any point throughout Genesis 34, despite the chapter's obsessive return to her story. In *Shayloks tochter* Jessica expresses genuine dissatisfaction with her new Christian family after her conversion and marriage. Portia claims that she and Antonio have rescued Jessica from a 'crude, squalid, formless' faith and that 'you [Jessica] are now one of us. The entire world is now free and open to you.'[57] Jessica refutes Portia's claim that she has 'improved' her, insisting instead that 'the world was created for all human beings. But you Christians have appropriated the world for your own uses.'[58] Jessica's response notably reflects the same egalitarian concerns as Chava's speech to her father in Sholem Aleichem's story, and offers a parallel critique of social reification and the religious traditionalism that sustains it. It also offers a disparaging assessment of those ways in which Portia – and, by implication, also Shylock – have appropriated and instrumentalised her. If Schwartz's play represents an example of a Jewish writer who 'writes back' to Shakespeare's text, his response is equally deriding of both Christian and Jewish communities' capacity for the manipulation and silencing of young women.

Dinah's story furnishes a template for the literary trope of the absconding Jewish daughter that is developed by subsequent generations of modern Jewish writers. Over the course of the twentieth century, that trope begins to include women's responses and their subjective experiences of estrangement from their Jewish families, and not just those of their male relatives. Unlike the biblical story of Dinah whose young protagonist never utters a single line (in sharp contrast to her brothers, father, and captors), Shakespeare's Jessica begins to develop a voice of her own within Jewish writing that takes up the trope of the absconding Jewish daughter, even as her motivations remain somewhat obscure.

Jessica's final lines in *Shayloks tochter* have her asking to return to her Jewish home in order to quell Shylock's murderous pursuit of the pound of flesh. 'If I should return to him, he would recall his suit,' she pleads to Antonio and Portia.[59] Her plan reflects her desire to end the strife between Christians and Jews as well as a clear willingness to sacrifice to obtain that peace; however, her strategy also resonates with a great deal of ambivalence about Jessica's own subjective desires. Does Jessica truly want to return home to her father, the ghetto, and Samuel Morro? Does her rejection of her new Christian family necessarily mean that she could be fulfilled living a traditionally Jewish life in the confinement of the Jewish quarter? Jessica's absence from the concluding scenes of the play only amplify these unanswered questions about the possibility of her finding happiness and belonging within the established parameters of any religious community, Christian or Jewish.

The conclusion of the biblical Dinah's story spells out a clear resistance to a foreigner's claim on a young Jewish woman. Dinah's Israelite brothers brutally recover their sister and bring her back into the tribal fold. The chapter's final verse spells out the logic of that re-appropriation by insisting that Dinah had always been deeply imbricated in her family's fortunes and reputation, despite her brief foray outside the confines of her father's home. In response to Jacob's condemnation of their violent behaviour, Dinah's brothers Simeon and Levi exclaim: 'Should our sister be treated like a whore?'[60] In *Shayloks tochter*, Antonio, Portia, and Lorenzo, like the biblical Shechemites, cannot maintain their hold on their Jewish prize. But neither does Shylock successfully or fully reclaim Jessica. Jessica's fate is ultimately marked not by a cloistered re-absorption back into her community, but by exile and homelessness. The final lines of the play narrate her drowning death in the canal mere moments after Shylock gives up his brutal pursuit of the pound of Antonio's flesh.[61] It is Samuel Morro who utters the play's penultimate lines, 'Rejoice! Our Jessica has returned to us! Forbidden to come back to her people, she drowned herself by the Ghetto-shore!'[62] His joyous tone suggests that he sees this repossession as a genuine victory. Audiences would have a far more difficult time seeing past the fact that the body these men repossess is that of a lifeless corpse. Shylock's line, which concludes the play, echoes Morro's joyous declaration of victory. 'I praise thee, God, for thy loving-kindness. *Baruch dayan eme.*'[63]

The play's conclusion, which sees Jessica effectively exiled from both Jewish and Christian communities and crushed by the weight of those communities' pressures, reads as a harsh condemnation of religious partisanship akin to the one proffered by Meir Freid's *Der koyfmann fun Venedig*. However, *Shayloks tochter* also affords a glimpse of a young woman's response to religious traditionalism that does not forsake a Jewish moral outlook, but rather seeks to refashion it. The play accomplishes this type of responsive reshaping of religious orthodoxy, which both takes up and reformats traditional scripts, by having Jessica appeal to a biblical story midway through the play as she remakes herself as an activist. Before leaving for Rome, Jessica aligns herself with the biblical Esther, pronouncing that 'Queen Esther risked her life for her people, so will I.'[64] Through the play's staging of her public marriage to a non-Jewish man – a ceremony about which she has tremendous ambivalence even as she participates in it – the play establishes telling parallels with Esther's story, notably her strategic marriage to a non-Jewish man and her courageous self-endangerment in the interests of saving her people. Jessica's plotline in Schwartz's play adheres closely to these narrative precedents from the *Megillath Esther*.

Rather than offering a flatly tragic account of the pressures of religious membership that mourns the death of traditional Jewish values, *Shayloks tochter* stages a young woman's response to tradition that calls directly on the Esther narrative and attempts to reclaim its relevance in the wake of present-day dissatisfaction with authoritative moral prescriptions.

In responding to traditional Jewish scripts with a revised view of their subjective significance, Jessica evokes what Cynthia Scheinberg's work on female Victorian poets has discussed as a genuine and serious theological-poetic contribution to the scriptural tradition – what we might term women's midrash.

Scheinberg argues against the conviction commonly found in Marxist-influenced scholarship that maintains that women's socio-political progress necessarily involved a movement away from the theological domain into more secular areas that allowed them to escape traditional patriarchal constraints. Instead, Scheinberg brilliantly demonstrates that the theological-poetic tradition was in fact not categorically oppressive to women's voices or their meaningful spiritual-literary self-expression. She argues that the vatic tradition constituted an expressive medium within which both Christian and Jewish female Victorian poets such as Christina Rossetti and Grace Aguilar articulated poetically meaningful responses to biblical scripts very much on a par with the works of male English poets such as John Milton.[65] Scheinberg's argument opens up fascinating possibilities for understanding Jewish women's participation in increasingly secular activities such as labour activism in a twentieth-century North American context as still very much of a piece with the midrashic tradition, particularly when that activity took shape through the idiom of biblical stories and figures. When *Shayloks tochter*'s Jessica aligns her mission with the nation-saving actions of the biblical Esther, she attempts to refashion her identity as a Jewish heroine in a way that remains responsive to traditional figures even as she attempts to reimagine them within the circumstances of modern life. This movement from traditional biblical scripts to present-day circumstances reproduces the essential work associated with midrashic interpretation, which here is placed in the service of defining the role of the female activist who sacrifices on behalf of her people.

Produced in the wake of the Holocaust only one year shy of the official creation of the Jewish State of Israel, Schwartz's play presents the medieval persecution of Jews under the Inquisition as a clear forerunner to the persecution and annihilation of Jews under Hitler. By all accounts it is Schwartz's moving performance that draws audiences and critics to praise the play and make it a hit in New York and then in Los Angeles when it is mounted there in 1950. However, it is ultimately Jessica's story that drives this adaptation and makes *Shayloks tochter* a play deeply invested in a midrashic exposition of scriptural models, a process that lends emotional dimensionality and cultural resonance to her struggle in the play.

Jessica articulates her own cultural mission through the story of Esther; however, her suitors appeal to other biblical figures in attempting to describe her. Lorenzo sees Jessica as a Madonna; Samuel Morro figures her as 'like the shepherdess of King Solomon'.[66] By drawing on a broad index of biblical characters, the play calls attention not only to these stories' dynamic range and their potential to lend ethical force to present-day scenarios, but also the difficulty of accounting for Jessica's elusive subjectivity. While Jessica understands her own moral agency through the figure of an activist woman, she is perceived very differently by her suitors via biblical women who model salvific beneficence (the Virgin Mary) and physical beauty that elicits male poetic desire (King Solomon's shepherdess). The effort to map Jessica by ascribing biblical significance to her character is a project shared by several voices in the play, which speaks to the difficulty of accurately mapping her motivations and figuring her inner life, as well as the challenges of self-definition for Jessica in the face of those entrenched roles that women traditionally occupy in the eyes of men. The play's tragic ending reflects the failure of both of Jessica's suitors to understand her; instead, both men contribute to the mounting pressures to stabilise Jessica's identity according to models that she herself rejects. Jessica may be an Esther in her own mind, but she is other things to the men who love her. That incommensurability, figured through the shifting religious signifiers used to describe her, marks a profound disjunction between acceptable, established roles for 'good' Jewish and Christian women and Jessica's own sense of herself as a moral agent.

Jessica's departure from her father's household initiates a rift in the fabric of traditional Jewish values in *Shayloks tochter*, values that are aligned with the patriarchal authority of Shylock and Jessica's Jewish fiancé Samuel Morro. Like Sholem Aleichem's Tevye as well as the biblical Dinah's brothers, Shylock is unable to come to terms with the loss of his daughter or reconcile himself with the sources of her moral agency. Instead, he becomes increasingly bent on exacting vengeance as the play progresses, despite repeated warnings by the Venetian Jewish community that his actions defy Jewish legal and ethical imperatives. With Samuel Morro remaining loyally by his side, Shylock suffers excommunication by Venice's Jews due to his insistence on pursuing the pound of Antonio's flesh, a pursuit that is entirely precipitated by the loss of his only daughter. Shylock's willingness to defy the normative ethical standards set by his own community reflects the ardency of his desire to reclaim his daughter, even when doing so defies the very Jewish law that prohibits traffic in flesh. That desire to possess his daughter develops, over the course of the play, into the material pursuit of Antonio's flesh as retribution for his loss; symbolically, this shift evokes Shylock's overwhelming need to restore his daughter to the known framework of traditional ways of life and repossess her, just as Dinah's brothers do in Genesis 34.

Some of the most beloved and celebrated Jewish writing produced during the nineteenth and twentieth centuries features fathers who are unable to grasp the moral motivations of daughters who abandon traditional ways of life. Viewed from the perspective of bereaved fathers, the departure of young Jewish daughters becomes a site of bewildering loss and a prompt for scrupulous narrative self-examination in the face of encroaching modernity. This trope of the absconding daughter draws substantively on the narrative components of the biblical Dinah who 'goes out' from her home and exits the protective, insular world of her Jewish tribe. This trope becomes a site where twentieth-century writer Philip Roth famously examines the transformation of American Jewish identity in the modern diaspora, inquiring into what happens to American Jews in the period following the turbulent 1960s in the novel *American Pastoral*. Roth himself represents a particularly interesting example of Jewish writing because his early career was largely built upon his identity as a Jewish writer. However, Roth's work's relationship to Jewishness was also the subject of controversy, particularly in the early 1960s when his collection of stories *Goodbye, Columbus* was publicly disparaged by rabbis to their congregations as anti-Semitic. Roth himself notoriously prefers the designation 'American writer' to 'Jewish writer', even while his work has been widely cited as a chronicle of modern Jewish-American experience.[67]

Roth's fiction frequently portrays assimilated Jews who have little or no relationship to traditional forms of worship. His characters are notably devoid of devotion to Jewish theology – they do not attend synagogue, pray or read religious texts. The absence of these elements of Jewish practice is conspicuous enough that one scholar declared: 'In Philip Roth's fiction there is hardly any Jewish philosophy, Jewish tradition, mysticism, or religion, and there is no discussion of who is a Jew or what is a Jew . . . Roth's Jews are Jews without Judaism.'[68] Although these comments advance deliberately exaggerated and polarising statements about Roth's fiction, they nevertheless query in useful ways the changing ways that Jewishness has been encoded in modern North America. What sorts of practical moral commitments do, in fact, constitute Jewish identity in the modern world? Which are seen as unimportant and no longer worth perpetuating, less generative? These questions reside at the heart of a great deal of modern Jewish writing, including Yiddish adaptations of Shakespeare. The most renowned example of this kind of existential questioning is Jacob Gordin's 1892 *Yiddish King Lear*, a play whose narrative reinvention of Shakespeare's tragedy culminates in the recognition that the least ritualistically observant, most modern, and progressive of the protagonist's daughters in fact constitutes the most ethically Jewish of his children.[69]

Although Roth does not directly adapt Shakespeare's work in his writing,[70] his Pulitzer Prize-winning 1997 novel *American Pastoral* engages directly with one of the central tropes of Yiddish *Merchant* adaptations: the Jewish daughter who absconds from her father's household. That loss represents the main narrative thread of Roth's novel and is the key to its protagonist's psychological and existential unravelling. Even in the absence of overtly religious forms of Judaism, Roth's *American Pastoral* traces the clear outlines of the same story recounted by Sholem Aleichem in 'Chava' and developed in Schwartz's adapted reworking of *The Merchant of Venice*: the biblical story of Dinah, which is used to interrogate the transmission of a Jewish ethos across generational lines.

American Pastoral elegises the figure who stands as the novel's hero, Seymour Levov, a man who suffers the loss of his daughter Merry to a late 1960s radical activist movement.[71] Levov, a first-generation American and the son of Jewish immigrants, takes up the hopes and failings of his generation as the successor to his shoulder-to-the-grindstone immigrant Jewish father. *American Pastoral* advances the story of the American Jewish experience forward in time to examine the aftermath of gentrification and cultural assimilation that follows from the previous generation's more cautious, ambivalent experience of Americanisation.

Nicknamed 'the Swede' because of his blond, non-Jewish, athletic appearance, Seymour Levov represents a generation that positioned themselves as willing frontiersmen (or, according to Levov's own chosen imagery, a Johnny Appleseed), triumphantly, confidently, and good-naturedly navigating the very same waters of religious inter-marriage, cultural integration, and Americanisation that once scandalised their parents. The Swede is financially successful, married to an enviably beautiful non-Jewish former beauty queen, and settled in a patrician New Jersey country estate – he manages to look every inch the part of a great American hero when his teenaged daughter Merry plants a bomb that blows up the local post office, killing an innocent bystander in the process.

The Swede's life before Merry's bomb is shaped by a strong work ethic, one that he regards as quintessentially American but that is also a clear emulation of his immigrant father's approach to success. However, alongside that work ethic is the Swede's self-conscious movement away from the ethnic ghettoisation of his father's generation of Jews. The Swede wants to live out what he regards as the quintessential American dream: marrying a beautiful, non-Jewish woman and living in a picturesque New Jersey town surrounded by blue-blooded WASPish neighbours. As much as the practical ethos that the Swede brings to his professional life is informed by his immigrant father's belief in the virtues of hard work, the Swede's concept of Americanisation and success is also heavily invested in a departure from the types of practical habits espoused by his father when it comes to his own personal and family life, notably an openness to religious intermarriage and a more liberal, permissive parenting style.

Roth's novel interrogates the loss of generational continuity between parents and children and the effects that those ruptures have on modern Jewish identity – the very themes explored in the Yiddish-language fiction of Sholem Aleichem and in Schwartz's Yiddish adaptation of *The Merchant of Venice*. In *American Pastoral* that loss of continuity is explored in relation to the Swede and his father Lou Levov, but also more elaborately and articulately through Merry. Merry Levov stands at the centre of the Swede's aggrieved attempt to understand and process the historical changes of the late 1960s – its social radicalism, its activism and violence, and its rejection of the traditional moral scripts that authorised his generation's success and hard work. The elegiac form of the novel takes up the very same mourning for lost daughters articulated in Sholem Aleichem's and Maurice Schwartz's works, but it positions that loss as a phenomenon that returns with a vengeance even after a generation of cultural assimilation, material wealth, and domestic stability.

> It was beyond understanding . . . not only how Merry could have been a fugitive wanted for murder, but how he and Dawn could have been the source of it all. How could their innocent foibles add up to this human being? Had none of this happened, had she stayed at home, finished high school, gone to college, there would have been problems, of course, big problems; she was precocious in her rebellion and there would have been problems even without a war in Vietnam. She might have wallowed a long while in the pleasures of resistance and the challenge of discovering how unrestrained she could be. But she would have been at home. At home you flip out a little and that's it. You do not have the pleasure of the *unadulterated* pleasure, you don't get to the point where you flip out so many times that finally you decide it's such a great, great kick, why not flip out a lot? At home there is no opportunity to douse yourself in this squalor. At home you can't live where the disorder is. At home you can't live where nothing is reined in.[72]

American Pastoral narratively illustrates what Sholem Aleichem's 'Chava' depicts through Tevye's tortured inner monologue: a father's failure to grasp his daughter's moral motivations. In *American Pastoral*, that incomprehension is re-emphasised through Merry herself, whose motivations and whereabouts remain perpetually elusive to her father, and whose character yokes a radically disjunctive array of traits and typologies. The novel renders this through Merry's violent ideological and physiological metamorphoses. Her appearance changes from that of a sprightly, agreeable child into a massively overweight six-foot teenager, shifting again later in the novel to an emaciated waif. Her socio-economic circumstances are equally wide-ranging; she moves from a childhood of suburban affluence into destitute poverty in a Newark slum. Her moral commitments undergo radical revision over the course of the novel as well, from star-struck young girl who puts on the airs of Audrey Hepburn to militant activism in her teenage years, culminating in the murder of multiple bystanders; to Jainism after her absconsion, when she is found by her father living in squalor and abiding by the compassionate principle of *ahimsa*.

Like *Shayloks tochter*'s Jessica, *American Pastoral*'s Merry is unable and unwilling to fit into neatly prescribed social or domestic roles, reflecting the novel's preoccupation with women's changing socio-political agency in the second half of the twentieth century. Merry's ungainly appearance and her rejection of the normative feminine aesthetic modelled by her mother signals Merry's inability and, ultimately, her unwillingness to conform to the predominant roles available to women. Through her unkempt appearance, Merry consciously rejects the aesthetic of conventional feminised beauty that determined her mother's early life as a beauty pageant contestant. Merry's speech impediment, a stutter that appears and disappears over the course of the novel, also figures a disruption to the kind of fluency that has determined her father's auspicious, charmed existence. Merry's stutter effectively figures women's struggle to achieve a political voice and political agency in this period.[73]

Where the biblical Dinah is a woman who 'goes out' from her home to explore the diasporic world outside her familial home, Merry Levov goes out with the intent of destructively transforming that world, and along with it, her father's worldview. Her brand of activism is violent and utterly incomprehensible to her father. The Swede's loss of his daughter is represented as a literally and figuratively explosive entry into moral chaos that destroys the idyllic pastoral of his American Dream, and devastates his ability to apprehend the world through a recognisable moral lens. Alongside Tevye's inner monologue at the conclusion of Sholem Aleichem's 'Chava', Roth's novel as a whole supplies a missing soliloquy for Shakespeare's Shylock, the Jewish father who mourns the departure of his daughter and, consequently, loses the possibility of seeing his own way of life perpetuated through his offspring.[74] *American Pastoral* rehearses the tragic recognition that such continuity has come to an end, replaced and blown violently apart by relentless historical change that is experienced by the paternal gatekeepers of traditional values as chaotic and apocalyptic. The 'American berserk' that replaces the Swede's American pastoral fantasy brings about the collapse of the cohesive moral framework that forecasts a gradual positivistic climb towards prosperity, success, and cultural assimilation for Jews. The commitment to action adopted by Merry, which the revolutionary movement conceives as a means of rehabilitating the world, requires the destruction of the particular brand of moral architecture that underwrites her father's moral agency, and without which he suffers a devastating loss of moral and characterological orientation.

The questioning of Jewish identity in the face of an imminent modernity that threatens to dismantle traditional modes of moral orientation represents an expansive trope within twentieth-century Jewish writing, one that continues to prompt fictional writing by Jews well into the twenty-first century.[75] However, even in the face of a profound and sceptical existential questioning of Judaism's future, Jewish writers returned to biblical scripts to narrate stories of self-doubt and self-redefinition. Throughout this chapter, I have argued that the midrashic re-reading of biblical narratives has enabled Jewish writers to engage in a relationship with formative texts from the past even as they question the nature of Jewish values, identity, and community in the present.[76] Whether that story is being narrated by Sholem Aleichem, or in a dramatic adaptation of Shakespeare's play in Yiddish, or in modern American Jewish fiction by Philip Roth, the trope of the absconding daughter mourned by her bereaved Jewish father has become part of a broader cultural discussion among Jewish writers about assimilation and the claims of the modern world that has also enabled Shakespeare's *The Merchant of Venice* to participate in culturally seminal conversations about the nature of Jewish identity in modern North America.

Notes

1. Joel Berkowitz, *Shakespeare on the American Yiddish Stage* (Iowa City: University of Iowa Press, 2002): 2. Also, see Anita Norich, *Writing in Tongues: Translating Yiddish in the Twentieth Century* (Seattle: University of Washington Press, 2013): 12–13 for a discussion of the evidentiary basis for this claim.
2. See Farrah Leman, '*Nisht keyn Desdemona, nisht keyn Djulieta*: Yiddish adaptations of *The Merchant of Venice* and the Early Modern Father-Daughter Bond', *Borrowers*

    and Lenders, 4: 2 (Spring/Summer 2010): 1–17 for a discussion of several Yiddish-language adaptations of *Merchant*, including Maurice Schwartz's. Lehman addresses the theme of filial duty in these adaptations, reading the modern adaptations as re-readings of Shakespeare's early modern play.

3. Berkowitz, *American Yiddish Stage*, 8.
4. For English overviews of *purimshpiln*, see Nahma Sandrow, *Vagabond Stars: A World History of Yiddish Literature* (New York: Harper & Row, 1977): 1–20 and Israel Zinberg, *A History of Jewish Literature*, 12 vols, trans. Bernard Martin (Cincinnati: Hebrew Union College/Ktav, 1975): 7: 301–44. In Yiddish: B. Gorin, *Di Geshikhte fun Yidishn Teater* (New York: Literarisher Farlag, 1923): 1: 19–63; J. Shatzky, 'An Akhashveyresh-Shpil Mit 100 Yor Tsurik', in J. Shatzky (ed.), *Arkhiv far geshikhte fun yiddishn teater und drame* (Vilna: YIVO, 1930): 159–74.
5. My account of the development of Yiddish theatre draws on Berkowitz, *American Yiddish Stage*.
6. Berkowitz, *American Yiddish Stage*, 12. See also Mark Tobin, *Tenement Songs* (Urbana: University of Illinois Press, 1982): 3.
7. The second half of the twentieth century also saw a number of Hebrew translations of *The Merchant of Venice*, several of which Dror Abend-David discusses in detail in *Scorned My Nation* (New York: Peter Lang, 2013). Hebrew translations begin to emerge following 1948 after Hebrew is transformed into a modern Israeli vernacular.
8. The 'historical avenger' motivation for translating Shakespeare into Hebrew and Yiddish appears as early as 1874 in the first translation of a full Shakespeare play into Hebrew in Vienna. *Itiel*, a translation of *Othello*, was written by Isaac Edward Salkinson, a Jewish-born writer who converted to Christianity. *Itiel* was edited and introduced by Peretz Smolenskin, an important *maskil* or figure in the Jewish Enlightenment (*Haskalah*), who wrote in his introduction that the Hebrew appropriation of the English Shakespearean text constituted a form of revenge for the Christian appropriation of the Hebrew Bible. Leonard Prager, 'Shakespeare in Yiddish', *Shakespeare Quarterly*, 19: 2 (Spring 1968): 149–58, especially 149.

9. The quote is from Ari Ibn-Zahav, author of the Hebrew novel *Shaylok Ha-Yehudi Mi-Venezia* [Hebrew, 1943] (Tel-Aviv: Javneh, 1947), which Maurice Schwartz subsequently adapted into the 1947 Yiddish play *Shayloks tochter*. Ibn Zahav's remarks preface the printed play-text of the English translation of Schwartz's adaptation, titled *Shylock and His Daughter: A Play Based on a Hebrew Novel by Ari Ibn Zahav*, dramatised by Maurice Schwartz, translated by Abraham Regelson (New York: Yiddish Art Theater, 1947). In a published essay, Ibn-Zahav wrote that his Shylock is 'not the imaginary character presented by the misguided genius Shakespeare but rather the true historical figure who seeks revenge but is unable to achieve it because he is a Jew.' Ibn-Zahav, 'Vos Hot Mich Gemacht Tsu Shraybn 'Shaylok und Zayn Tochter' ('My intentions in writing *Shaylok and his Daughter*'). Cited in Yael Chaver, 'Writing for the Jews, Writing for the Goyim: Twentieth-Century Jewish Adaptations of *The Merchant of Venice*', *Jewish Social Studies*, 17: 2 (Winter 2011): 28–47, especially 30.
10. Interestingly enough, these Jewish writers manage to emulate the attitudes held by many of Shakespeare's early modern contemporaries about the work that translation and translators manage to do in refining and perfecting the rough sketch of an author's original work. See, for example, Golding's comment in lines 378–9 of his preface to his 1567 translation of Ovid's *Metamorphoses* that refers to Ovid's poem as a 'scantling' or rough draft that Golding imagines himself refining and improving: 'let us further see / How Ovids scantlings with the whole true patterne doo agree.' *Ovid's Metamorphoses: The Arthur Golding Translation of 1567*, ed. John Frederick Nims (Philadelphia: Paul Dry Books, 2000).
11. It was on Nalevki street that the first shots were fired in the Warsaw Ghetto uprising.
12. See the *Lexicon of New Yiddish Literature* (Congress of Jewish Culture, New York: Martin Press, 1958): 7: 494 for the entry on Freid. The novel sells 25,000 copies during its first run, and is subsequently translated into Russian and Polish.

13. All translations of Freid's work from the original Yiddish are my own. Meir Jacob Freid, *Der koyfmann fun Venedig: Shaylok: Ertsehlung nokh Shekspirs komedie* [Yiddish] (Warsaw: Tzukerman's Folkbibliothek, 1897–8): 3.
14. Freid, *Der koyfmann fun Venedig*, 9.
15. Freid, *Der koyfmann fun Venedig*, 8.
16. Janet Adelman develops an argument for proto-racial discourse in *The Merchant of Venice* in 'Her Father's Blood: Race, Conversion, and Nation in *The Merchant of Venice*', *Representations*, 81: 1 (Winter 2003): 4–30; as well as chapter 3 of *Blood Relations: Christian and Jew in the Merchant of Venice* (Chicago: University of Chicago Press, 2008): 66-98. See also M. Lindsay Kaplan, 'Jessica's Mother: Medieval Constructions of Jewish Race and Gender in *The Merchant of Venice*', *Shakespeare Quarterly*, 58: 1 (Spring 2007): 1–30.
17. Freid, *Der koyfmann fun Venedig*, 9–10.
18. Freid, *Der koyfmann fun Venedig*, 8.
19. Freid, *Der koyfmann fun Venedig*, 16.
20. Freid, *Der koyfmann fun Venedig*, 17.
21. Freid, *Der koyfmann fun Venedig*, 19.
22. Freid, *Der koyfmann fun Venedig*, 20.
23. Freid, *Der koyfmann fun Venedig*, 20.
24. Abend-David, *Scorned My Nation*, 66–7.
25. Freid, *Der koyfmann fun Venedig*, 5.
26. Freid, *Der koyfmann fun Venedig*, 14.
27. The revaluation of what constitutes a Jewish ethos – rigid adherence to traditional scripts or creative reinterpretation of their spirit in light of new circumstances – is a recurrent theme within Yiddish theatrical adaptations of Shakespeare during this period. Jacob Gordin's *Yiddish King Lear*, trans. Ruth Gay [1892] (New Haven, CT: Yale University Press, 2007) explores this same trope through the characters of his Lear figure, Dovid Moyshele's three daughters, only one of whom acts in the spirit of true *Yiddishkayt*. In Gordin's play it is the youngest and least traditional daughter who emerges as the most authentically Jewish, not because she acts in accordance

with her traditional father's *halakhic* notions of Jewishness but because she displays the kindness and care that the play ultimately identifies as the more significant kind of Jewish ethos.

28. Freid, *Der koyfmann fun Venedig*, 30.
29. This citation is from Genesis 16 which details the story of Hagar, the mother of Ishmael and mistress of Abraham, which is itself a telling episode of racial and ethnological plurality.
30. Sholem Aleichem, 'Chava'. *Tevye's Daughters*, trans. Frances Butwin (New York: Crown Publishers, 1949): 96–7.
31. Aleichem, 'Chava', 107.
32. Aleichem, 'Chava', 107.
33. For a fascinating discussion of the relationship between Scriptural citation and Tevye's response to his daughter's marriage in 'Chava', see Michael Stern, 'Tevye's Art of Quotation', *Prooftexts*, 6: 1 (January 1986): 79–96. Stern aptly argues that 'in "Khave" the quotations were carefully chosen to highlight both the rift caused by Khave's rejection of her Jewish identity and Tevye's feelings of pain and anger' (88).
34. Sholem Aleichem, 'Chava', 106–7.
35. *Broken Barriers (Chava)*, dir. Charles E. Davenport, 1919.
36. *Tevye*, dir. Maurice Schwartz, 1939. Yiddish.
37. Ibn-Zahav's novel was first translated into Yiddish by Menachem Glen in 1947 and serialised in the New York Yiddish daily *Morgen Zhurnal*, where it appeared under the title 'Shaylok Und Zayn Tochter, A Roman fun Amol un Itst' (Shylock and His Daughter: A Novel from the Past and for Today) in the autumn and winter of 1947–8. Glen's translation was timed to coincide with Schwartz's performance of *Shayloks tochter*. Schwartz's original Yiddish play-script was lost until recently, and known only through its English translation by Regelson until its rediscovery in 2008. See Yael Chaver, 'Writing for the Jews', 29.
38. There is some ambiguity about the name of Schwartz's play. On Schwartz's typescript, the play is titled *Shayloks tochter* ('Shylock's Daughter'); however, on the playbill the play's name is changed to *Shaylok und zayn tochter* ('Shylock and His Daughter'). Although relatively minor, the changes do

assign Jessica a different relative importance. For the sake of clarity, I refer to the name in Schwartz's typescript, 'Shayloks tochter'.
39. Maurice Schwartz, *Shylock and His Daughter: A Play Based on a Hebrew Novel by Ari Ibn Zahav*, trans. Abraham Regelson (New York: Yiddish Art Theatre, 1947): 24.
40. Schwartz, *Shylock and His Daughter*, 33.
41. Schwartz, *Shylock and His Daughter*, 25.
42. Schwartz, *Shylock and His Daughter*, 26.
43. Schwartz, *Shylock and His Daughter*, 36.
44. Schwartz, *Shylock and His Daughter*, 37.
45. Schwartz, *Shylock and His Daughter*, 39.
46. Schwartz, *Shylock and His Daughter*, 39.
47. As Chaver points out, Ibn-Zahav's Hebrew novel explicitly analogises sixteenth-century Venice under the Inquisition and twentieth-century Europe under the Nazis. 'Ibn-Zahav linked Renaissance anti-semitism with his own time and considered the anti-Jewish edicts of sixteenth-century Pope Paul IV to have been uncannily similar to those of the Nazi regime.' Chaver, 'Writing for the Jews', 30.
48. Schwartz, *Shylock and His Daughter*, 48.
49. In Schwartz's adaptation Portia and Antonio are married, Antonio is the Bassanio figure and Bassanio is mentioned only in passing as a former rival for Portia's hand in marriage, along with Morocco.
50. Schwartz, *Shylock and His Daughter*, 41. Chaver discusses this episode as an example of Abraham Regelson's transformation of Schwartz's Yiddish script in Regelson's English-language translation of *Shayloks tochter*. In Schwartz's play-script, Antonio's speech draws significantly on the Gospels to articulate its anti-Semitic argument:

When I come across the Jew Shylock who lives off Christian usury, I feel toward him the same hatred and fury that our holy son felt when he used a whip to drive away the money-changers from the Temple courtyard. According to the laws of our faith, love and compassion must reside in our hearts. We must love our neighbors as ourselves. And I love my neighbors like my own brothers, but not the Jews!

Cited in Chaver, 'Writing for the Jews', 39.
51. Schwartz, *Shylock and His Daughter*, 43.
52. Select sources on the expansive topic of Jewish involvement in North American labour activism include Jodi Giesbrecht, 'Accommodating Resistance: Unionization, Gender, and Ethnicity in Winnipeg's Garment Industry, 1929–1945', *Urban History Review/Revue d'historie urbaine*, 39: 1 (2010): 5–19; Nan Enstad, *Ladies of Labor, Girls of Adventure: Working Women, Popular Culture, and Labor Politics at the Turn of the Twentieth Century* (New York: Columbia University Press, 1999); James R. Barrett, 'Americanization From the Bottom Up: Immigration and the Remaking of the Working Class in the United States, 1880–1930', *Journal of American History*, 79: 3 (December 1992): 996–1020; Ruth A. Frager, *Sweatshop Strife: Class, Ethnicity, and Gender in the Jewish Labour Movement of Toronto, 1900–1939* (Toronto: University of Toronto Press, 1992); Gerald Sorin, *The Prophetic Minority: American Jewish Immigrant Radicals, 1880–1920* (Bloomington: Indiana University Press, 1985); Moses Rischin, *The Promised City: New York's Jews, 1870–1914* (Cambridge, MA: Harvard University Press, 1962); Ruth Milkman (ed.), *Women, Work and Protest: A Century of US Women's Labor History* (Oxford: Routledge, 1985); Nancy Schrom Dye, *As Equals and as Sisters: Feminism, the Labor Movement, and the Women's Trade Union League of New York: The Jewish Woman in America* (Columbia: University of Missouri Press, 1980); Paula Hyman, 'Immigrant Women and Consumer Protest', *American Jewish History*, 70 (September 1980).
53. For a fascinating collection of first-person accounts from Jewish women and men who worked in the needle trade in Canada during the first half of the twentieth century, see Semah Berson (ed.), *I Have a Story to Tell You* (Waterloo, ON: Wilfrid Laurier University Press, 2010).

54. Schwartz, *Shylock and His Daughter*, 83.
55. Schwartz, *Shylock and His Daughter*, 63.
56. Schwartz, *Shylock and His Daughter*, 117.
57. Schwartz, *Shylock and His Daughter*, 124.
58. Schwartz, *Shylock and His Daughter*, 124.
59. Schwartz, *Shylock and His Daughter*, 126.
60. Genesis 34: 31.
61. He exclaims, 'I cannot shed blood! I am a Jew.' Schwartz, *Shylock and His Daughter*, 145.
62. Schwartz, *Shylock and His Daughter*, 145–6.
63. Schwartz, *Shylock and His Daughter*, 146.
64. Schwartz, *Shylock and His Daughter*, 64.
65. Cynthia Scheinberg, *Women's Poetry and Religion in Victorian England: Jewish Identity and Christian Culture* (Cambridge: Cambridge University Press, 2002).
66. Schwartz, *Shylock and His Daughter*, 56. In her comparative treatment of mid-century Jewish adaptations of *Merchant*, Chaver aptly notes that this particular speech does not appear in Schwartz's Yiddish play-script. It was added by Abraham Regelson in his English translation. Chaver, 'Writing for the Jews', 38.
67. Those controversies were particularly fiery during Roth's early career in the 1960s when rabbis and rabbinical scholars denounced his work as anti-Semitic. For an excellent summary of how those attitudes have changed, along with some ways they have not, as well as Roth's own perspective on his work's reception by Jews, see Judith Thurman, 'Philip Roth Is Good for the Jews', *New Yorker* (online), 12 May 2014, http://www.newyorker.com/books/page-turner/philip-roth-is-good-for-the-jews.
68. Aharon Appelfeld, 'The Artist as Jewish Writer', Asher Z. Milbauer and Donald G. Watson (eds), *Reading Philip Roth* (New York: St. Martin's Press, 1988): 13–16, especially 14.
69. Gordin, *Yiddish King Lear*.
70. Some of Roth's later work does overtly appeal to Shakespeare's *The Merchant of Venice*, for example his 1993 novel *Operation Shylock*.

71. It is important to note that the Swede's story is itself a narrative fictionalisation in *American Pastoral*, narrated by the character Nathan Zuckerman who tells the Swede's story after learning of his death.
72. Philip Roth, *American Pastoral* (New York: Vintage International/Random House Books, 1997): 238.
73. On this point, see Christopher Eagle, '"Angry Because She Stutters": Stuttering, Violence, and the Politics of Voice in *American Pastoral* and Sorry', *Philip Roth Studies*, 8: 1 (Spring 2012): 17–30.
74. The portrayal of Shylock as a bereaved father who mourns the loss of his daughter was perhaps most memorably formalised in the English-language tradition through Laurence Olivier's performance of the role in the 1973 *Merchant of Venice* produced for television, directed by John Sichel. Olivier performs the scene where he realises that Jessica has departed by reciting *kaddish*, the Jewish prayer for the dead.
75. Most recently, this crisis has been explored in Yiddish writing by Mikhail Krutikov, *Yiddish Fiction and the Crisis of Modernity, 1905–1914* (Stanford: Stanford University Press, 2001).
76. See Gillian Steinberg, 'Philip Roth's "Defender of the Faith": A Modern Midrash', *Philip Roth Studies*, 1: 1 (Spring 2005): 7–18 for a discussion of Roth as a modern midrashist whose early short story 'Defender of the Faith' elaborates on the significance of the Passover narrative.

CONCLUSION

The question that prompts this book – Is Shylock Jewish? – asserts that Jewishness represents a vital and sufficient category of inquiry into Shakespeare's 'Jewish play'. In prototypically Jewish form, the book answers that question with another question: What does it mean to be Jewish? Although I have not attempted to argue for a singular model of Jewish culture or identity in the preceding pages, I have outlined a series of hermeneutic strategies that identify particular modes of reading as recognisably Judaic, evoking a distinctive orientation to practical moral questions. By considering the question of what constitutes a Jewish reading of a shared set of biblical stories, I have discussed how midrashic reading strategies constitute a tradition that has remained both conventional and responsive over time. The tradition's responsiveness arises from instances such as the one that Shakespeare scripts into his play, in which Shylock endeavours to find new meaning in a familiar biblical parable.

Such efforts to locate new or alternative meanings are not always given a warm reception. *The Merchant of Venice* models a particularly painful example in which Antonio disparages Shylock's biblical gloss and impugns his fitness to proffer it, labelling him a 'devil' who 'cite[s] Scripture for his purpose'. Unfortunately, a great many critics within the last century have followed Antonio's lead, describing Shakespeare's fictional Jewish moneylender as a mere placeholder, or foil, within an overarching Christian play.

We should be deeply troubled by the exclusionary implications of Antonio's response as well as the scholarly reluctance to unpack it more critically. We should likewise resist the temptation to see the play exclusively through Antonio's eyes when Shylock makes his own point-of-view eminently readable to us as well. Seeing exclusively through Antonio's eyes closes the door on discussions of Shylock's and Jessica's moral agency and discourages seeing Jewishness as anything more than a series of anti-Semitic stereotypes. Aligning our vision with Antonio's pre-emptively excludes the fuller subjective, first-personal, and ethical dimensionality of Jewish identity and lived experience. As later chapters of this book have elaborated, *The Merchant of Venice* has a fascinating history of adaptation by Jewish writers who used Shakespeare's play to creatively respond to questions about the pressures facing modern Jewish communities in the diaspora, such questions continue to resonate deeply for Jews today. These kinds of writerly responses have contributed to the long afterlife of Shakespeare's *Merchant of Venice* in ways that merit recognition and sustained critical engagement.

Like the biblical inter-texts that are introduced into *Merchant*, Shakespeare's plays have continued to fuel our re-interpretive efforts over time. The long afterlife of Shakespeare's plays depends upon such re-readings, and their relevancy is in no small part generated by interpreters who bring meaningful experiences to the process of encountering them. At the outset of this book, I suggested that we might more usefully designate this type of presentist approach, in which we bring our pressing concerns and experiences to bear on the text, as a form of ethical readership, in line with the Classical understanding of ethics as lifelong habit and practice that appeals to – and requires – the full range of a person's subjective resources. Such practices also reflect a focused commitment to ideals we deem objectively valuable. Aristotle's sense of what those ideals were are the ones that he associated with his father Nicomachus, and which he elaborates in *The Nicomachean Ethics*, including such virtues as temperance, moderation and courage. In our current historical moment, we Shakespeare scholars routinely profess a commitment to diversity and inclusiveness. That distinctly present-day ideal requires both a demographic shift in the composition of our scholarly community as well as a rethinking of the kinds of insights, experiences and intentions that we deem serviceable to the academic study of Shakespeare's writing. There is great ethical merit to reading Shakespeare by applying the fullest scope of our resources to plays like *The Merchant of Venice*. For Jewish readers, that has often meant taking seriously Shylock's intentional and emotional states, not with the aim of vindicating him, but with the goal of acknowledging in his character the contours of human moral agency.

This book began with a discussion of sixteenth-century English encounters with Hebrew and 'Hebrews' and a consideration of the historical circumstances that may have led Shakespeare, a sixteenth-century writer, to imaginatively fashion a Jew whose ethos was something more than a mere placeholder for stereotypes. When subsequent chapters turned to *The Merchant of Venice*, they located Shylock's and Jessica's sources of moral agency in their citation of biblical stories and their coordination of meaningful courses of action by refashioning biblical scripts. Shylock's and Jessica's insistent return to Hebrew biblical stories in *The Merchant of Venice* suggests that Shakespeare understood the Bible as an important medium for transmitting a nation's culture, history, and language. The proverbial designation of Jews as 'people of the book' would appear to confirm this sense of what it means to be Jewish, one that has on occasion been used to characterise Jews as rigid traditionalists. That designation of Jews as rigid or stubborn shares common ground with patristic accounts that once described Jews as hard-hearted literalists; however, the adaptation of Shakespeare's work by Yiddish writers, who creatively re-imagine its biblical inter-texts, showcases a dynamism at the heart of even modern encounters with biblical source materials that contravenes reductive characterisations.

In fact, Yiddish adaptations of Shakespeare speak to Jewish writers' willingness to engage with distinctly non-Jewish scripts and place them in dialogue with more familiar, orthodox ones in the interest of creating compelling new forms of popular art. Rabbinic literature scholar Michael Chernick has argued that an adaptive, integrative model has also long resided at the heart of the rabbinic tradition and its midrashic explication of written and oral law. Chernick's description for that kind of adaptive reading is 'turn it and turn it again', a phrase that he derives from *Pirkei Avot*, the compendium of rabbinic maxims and commonplace teachings from the Mishnaic period, whose English title, *Ethics of the Fathers*, cuts a striking parallel to Aristotle's *Nicomachean Ethics*. Biblical stories, Chernick suggests, were continually re-viewed and re-positioned to new vantage points by rabbinic scholars, who 'learned how to make use of the social, intellectual, and cultural developments emerging from their own surroundings as a prism through which to view their own tradition and culture'.[1] In dialogue with the concerns of their own eras, the rabbinic 'turning' of the texts of the Torah and Talmud meant that even the study of sacred Scripture was never insular or removed from the social and cultural life of the people. The key to the persistence of traditional scripts over time, in this account, is their responsiveness. However, it is also required that we see ourselves as active respondents in the dialogue. As Chernick insists, 'it is our "turn" now.'

Note

1. Michael Chernick, '"Turn It and Turn It Again": Culture and Talmud Interpretation', *Exemplaria: A Journal of Theory in Medieval and Renaissance Studies*, 12: 1 (Spring 2000): 63–103, especially 103.

INDEX

Abraham (Abram), 16, 91, 101, 115, 118–19, 127
Adam, 64–5, 71, 185, 212
Adelman, Janet, 29, 36–7
Ainsworth, Henry, 103
anti-Semitism, 5, 7–8, 36, 40–1, 210, 220, 246
  in Shakespeare's work, 208
Antonio, 7, 10, 30, 36, 42, 86, 91–3, 101, 103, 106, 109–11, 117, 128–9, 140–1, 144–5, 147–8, 245–6
  in Yiddish adaptations, 203, 207, 209, 220
  see also Der koyfmann fun Venedig; *Shayloks tochter*
Aristotle, 11, 124, 138n, 246–8
Attar, Chayyim ibn *see Or Hachayyim*

Babington, Gervase, 151, 176

Bassanio, 115, 124–5, 128–9, 140, 145, 181
  in Yiddish, 203, 208–10, 220
Batt, Barthēlemy *see* conduct manuals: William Lowth
Beaufort, Lady Margaret, 46
Bethlehem, 174, 185, 189
biblical exegesis, 10, 11; *see also* midrash
Bishop's Bible (1568), 161–2, 168
Boleyn, Ann, 50
Boleyn, James, 50

Calvin, John, 61–2, 82n, 106–7
Cambridge University, 45–7, 50, 54
Caro, Isaac, 108, 112
Catherine of Aragon, 49–53
Chilmeade, Edmund, 121; *see also* Modena, Leone

Christian Hebraism *see*
　　Hebraism, (Renaissance)
　　Christian
Christianity
　　and encounters with
　　　　Judaism, 28, 30, 32, 34,
　　　　41, 43, 66, 89, 115,
　　　　178–9
　　and interpretive approaches
　　　　to Genesis, 90–2, 102–4,
　　　　106–7, 109
　　and kinship with Jews, 37,
　　　　117, 133n
　　and tribal contest with Jews,
　　　　142, 144–50, 152, 178–9,
　　　　222–4
Ciserno, Franciso Jimenéz de,
　　44–5
classical antiquity, 17, 29, 32,
　　39–40, 55–62, 71, 145,
　　147
Clement VII, 51
conduct manuals (Renaissance),
　　181, 185–7
　　Thomas Bentley, *Monument
　　　　of Matrones*, 182–3, 185
　　William Lowth, *The
　　　　Christian Mans Closet*,
　　　　184
　　Thomas Paynell, *The
　　　　Ensamples of Virtue and
　　　　Vice, Gathered Out of
　　　　Holy Scripture*, 183–5
Coronel, Pablo, 45
Coryat, Thomas, 38–9

Der koyfmann fun Venedig,
　　198, 202, 209–10, 213,
　　226
　　Jessica/Dinah in, 203–8,
　　　　210–11, 213
　　Shylock in, 204, 206–10
Deuteronomy, 95, 133n
Dinah, 11, 142, 153–6,
　　159–71, 198, 225, 229
　　allusion to, by Yiddish
　　　　writers, 202, 210, 223,
　　　　225, 229, 231
　　in modern Jewish writing,
　　　　224, 229–31, 235–6
Douay-Rheims Bible, 162–4,
　　168–9

Elizabeth I, 30, 55, 59,
　　182–3
England (Renaissance), 30
　　Jews in, 26–7, 36, 39–40
　　languages in, 32, 39–40,
　　　　44–9, 62–6, 70
　　shift to Protestantism in, 28
Erasmus, Desiderus, 46
Esau, 37, 106–7, 118–20,
　　125–9, 140, 151–2
Esther, 199, 226, 228–9
Eve, 64, 183, 185
Exodus, 98, 218
Ezra, Abraham ibn, 100,
　　125–6, 166, 170, 188

Fisher, John, 46–7, 49–50, 54
Florio, John, 31

Index

Freid, Meir Jacob, 198, 202, 211, 213, 226; *see also Der koyfmann fun Venedig*

Galenic humoralism, 38, 104–5
Genesis, 9, 11, 16, 87, 90, 100–1, 110
   abduction of Dinah in, 142, 153–5, 159–70
   Jacob cycle in, 16, 86, 88–9, 95, 100–3, 105, 108, 110, 113, 116–20, 125–8, 148, 152, 187–9
   parable of the parti-coloured lambs in, 87, 90, 95–6, 102–3, 105, 109, 111, 113–15, 120, 148, 151, 188
   Rachel's theft of Laban's idols in, 142, 172–4, 176–7, 183–7
Genesis Rabbah, 112, 173
Geneva Bible (1560), 160–2, 164, 170
Golding, Arthur, 59–62, 82n, 238n
Gordin, Jacob, 231

Hannapes, Nicolas de *see* conduct manuals: Thomas Paynell
Haran, 87, 91, 112, 117, 173

Hebraism, (Renaissance)
   Christian, 18, 29, 31–5, 43–5, 47–54, 56, 64–70, 78n, 157
   Hebrew Bible, 10, 11, 16, 28, 30, 32, 41–2, 51, 55, 90, 150, 171, 247–8
   Masoretic text of, 164, 167
   Renaissance translations of, 33, 44
   Shylock's citation of, 90–7
   transliterated words or verses of, 100, 112, 125–6, 135n, 165–7
   Hebrew language, 17, 29–30, 32, 43, 247
   Renaissance English attitudes toward, 33–5, 39–42, 63, 66, 71, 75n
   on Renaissance portrait medals, 48–9
   study of, in Renaissance England, 31, 34, 45–7, 50–1, 53–5, 63–6, 69–71, 76–7n
   Hebrew Renaissance texts, 17, 29, 32, 44, 46, 56, 63–71
Henry VIII, 30, 47–55, 183
Holland, Philemon, 57–9
Huarte, Juan, 37
humanism, Renaissance, 31–2, 43–4, 53–4, 78n
Hutter, Elias, 67–70

Irving, Henry, 26–7, 72–3n

Isaac, 118–20, 125
Israel *see* Jacob

Jacob, 9, 11, 37, 86–7, 90–1, 95–7, 99–104, 106, 108–20, 125–8, 141, 148–52, 155–6, 173–6, 188
James I, 63, 83, 121
Jeremiah, 189
Jerome *see* Vulgate
Jessica
  absconsion of, 144, 146, 154, 158, 168–73, 185
  appearance of, 2
  and conversion, 142, 154, 170–4, 177–80, 186–7, 189, 220–4
  and the Hebrew Bible, 15, 198
  and Jewish paternity, 35–6, 142, 157, 175, 187
  and Leah's turquoise ring, 167–8, 173, 180
  as moral agent, 9, 11, 158–9, 169, 175, 227–9, 246–7
  as prize, 141–2, 144–7, 149–50, 152–3, 155, 169
  as rebellious, 158, 180, 186
  and sadness, 146, 170, 189
  and theft, 1, 101, 144–50, 153–5, 169
  on the Yiddish stage *see Der koyfmann fun Venedig*; *Shayloks tochter*

Jewish diaspora, 121–2, 188–90, 202, 211, 231, 235, 246
Jewish Historical Society of England, 28
Jewish identity
  Antonio on, 7
  and assimilation, 202, 230, 233, 235, 236
  and biblical stories, 9, 13, 87–8, 98, 121, 212–13, 226–9, 236, 245
  and Jewish 'blood', 36–7, 142, 156, 175, 186, 204
  and Jewish practices, 7, 128
  and language, 157, 204, 209, 247
  modern, 6, 15, 231, 232–3, 235–6, 246
  and moral agency, 9, 12, 87, 98, 171, 204, 245–7
  and moral education, 204–6, 209–11, 247
  and rabbinical exegesis, 88, 98, 171
  Renaissance, 1–2, 13, 15, 30, 177–9
  Victorian understanding of, 27
  and women, 156–7, 190, 201–2, 205–6, 210–11, 221–9, 234–5
  see also Yiddish: *Yiddishkayt*

Jews/Jewish nation
  and allegorical Jews, 93,
    184, 246–7
  conversion of, 39, 43
  money lending and, 122
  Renaissance English
    attitudes towards, 17, 26,
    30–1, 33–4, 40–1, 43, 71,
    149, 247
  as Renaissance tutors, 31,
    35, 41–5, 51–3
  resiliency of, 31, 37–9
  social activism among,
    216–17, 221–2, 227,
    233
  Victorian English attitudes
    towards, 17, 26–7, 37–8

Kaplan, Aryeh *see* Kaplan
  Living Torah
Kaplan Living Torah, 160,
  162
Kasher, Menahem, 99, 192n
King James Bible, 90–1, 125,
  159–60, 162

Laban, 37, 87, 91, 97, 100,
  102, 106, 108, 111–17,
  173–4, 184, 187–8
Launcelot Gobbo, 141, 150,
  158
Leah, 113, 167, 174, 182
  in Yiddish, 217
Levinus, Lemnius, 104–5
Livy *see* Holland, Philemon

Lorenzo, 144–7, 169, 177–80,
  184–7
  in Yiddish, 205–6, 208,
    216–17, 228–9
Lorenzo de Medici, 53, 55

Macklin, Charles, 4, 22n
Maimonides, 100, 114
Manetti, Giannozzo, 43–4,
  78n
Mary I, 183
Maxwell, James, 109
Merchant of Venice
  1879 production of, 26–7
  allegorical criticism of, 8,
    23n, 92, 245–6
  and biblical scholarship,
    11–12, 15, 89
  conversion and, 35–6
  materialist and New
    Historicist scholarship on,
    2–3, 9, 92–3, 132n
  and political thought, 14
  presentist approaches to,
    13–14, 88, 246–7
  translation of, into Yiddish,
    200–1
  and Victorian criticism, 16
  *see also Der koyfmann
    fun Venedig*; *individual
    characters*; *Shayloks
    tochter*
midrash, 10, 97–9, 112, 120,
  127, 198–9, 226–7, 245,
  248

Midrash Hagadol, 114
Modena, Leone, 120–2
More, Thomas, 183

Nahmanides, 106, 113, 126, 165–6
New Testament, 91
Nicholas V, 43

'Old' Jewish Publication Society Bible (1917), 159–60, 162
Or Hachayyim, 113–14, 165
Ovid *see* Golding, Arthur
Oxford University, 46, 50, 54

Paul IV, 122
Peretz, Y. L., 203
Petrarch, 43
Pirkei Avot, 248
polyglot bibles, 32, 44–5, 67
Pomis, David de, 122
Pope, Alexander, 4, 22n
Portia, 145–6, 158
  in Yiddish, 209–10, 220, 223–4
portrait medals, 47–9, 55, 79n
Protestant Reformation, 29–30, 32–4, 39, 43, 54, 162

Rabinovitch, Sholem *see* Sholem Aleichem

Rachel, 90, 113, 172–7, 182–9, 198, 205, 211
Ramah, 189
Ramban *see* Nahmanides
Raphael, Mark, 51–3
Rashi, 42, 99, 105, 127–8, 188
Rebecca, 118–19, 128
Reuchlin, Johannes, 45
Roth, Cecil, 1–5, 11, 22n
Roth, Philip, 201, 230
  and *American Pastoral*, 230–5

Sandys, Miles, 124
Sarah/Sara, 183, 185
Schwartz, Maurice, 198, 215–16, 224, 228; *see also Shayloks tochter*
Shakespeare, William
  attitude of, towards Jews, 3, 7, 17, 72, 200n, 247
  illustration of, 203
  religious identity of, 12
  and use of the Bible, 16
Shapiro, James, 3, 8, 26, 31, 72n
Shayloks tochter, 198, 216, 224, 226, 228, 231, 233–4
  Jessica in, 217–18, 220–2, 224–9
  Samuel Morro in, 216–20, 223, 225–6, 228–9

Shylock in, 217–19, 226,
    229
Shechem, 153–4, 159, 161,
    163–8, 170
Sholem Aleichem, 201, 211–12,
    215, 233
  and *Tevye der milkhiker/
    Tevye the Dairyman*,
    211–15, 229, 231,
    233–5
Shylock
  and citing of Scripture, 87,
    91, 95–7, 99, 101, 107–9,
    111, 114–16, 118–20,
    129, 141, 151–2, 188–9,
    245, 247
  and conversion, 148
  as devil, 92–3, 245–6
  Henry Irving as, 26–7
  as Jew, 30, 120, 177, 189–90,
    245–6
  as money lender, 9, 34, 143
  as moral agent, 8–9, 11, 89,
    94, 107–8, 120, 188–9,
    201, 245–7
  in recent scholarship, 3,
    92–4
  Cecil Roth on, 1–2, 4
  and vengeance, 153, 159,
    207, 229
  vernacular connotations
    of, 5
  and wealth, 110, 116–17,
    123, 169
  and Yiddish writers, 201

  *see also Der koyfmann fun
    Venedig*; *Shayloks tochter*
Smith, Emma, 3, 16–17, 27,
    31
Spinoza, Baruch, 15
Stow, John, 39–40
Sturtevant, Simon, 63–7,
    69–70, 82n, 83n, 84n

thrift, 9, 109–10, 148, 156,
    169–70
Toledo, Alfonso de, 45
Torah *see* Hebrew Bible
Tubal, 143, 173, 180
  in Yiddish, 218
Tyndale-Coverdale Bible,
    163–5

usance, 94, 121–4
usury, 8, 86, 92, 94, 109,
    121

Venice
  Jews and synagogues in, 2,
    38, 120
  in *Shayloks tochter*, 218,
    220
Virgin Mary, 228
Vulgate, 33, 43–6, 78, 162

Wakefield, Robert, 33–4, 41–3,
    45, 47, 50, 54, 77n
Willett, Andrew, 103, 176,
    188
Wilson, Thomas, 56–7

Wolf, Lucien, 28
Wright, Thomas, 104–5

Yiddish
  among North American Jews, 201–2
  fartaytsht und farbesert, 197–8
  goy, 209
  and linguistic nationalism, 199–201
  mameh loshn, 202
  seychl, 126
  and translations of *King Lear*, 197, 231
  Yiddishkayt, 204, 213
  see also Der Koyfmann fun Venedig; Shayloks tochter
Yiddish theatre, 199, 201, 215–16
  and *purimshpiln*, 198–9
Yitzhaki, Shlomo *see* Rashi

Zahav, Ari ibn, 216
Zamora, Alfonso de, 45

EU representative:
Easy Access System Europe
Mustamäe tee 50, 10621 Tallinn, Estonia
Gpsr.requests@easproject.com

www.ingramcontent.com/pod-product-compliance
Lightning Source LLC
Chambersburg PA
CBHW062124300426
44115CB00012BA/1806